Modern Introductions to Philosophy
General Editor: D. J. O'CONNOR

D.W. Hamlyn is Professor of Philosophy at Birkbeck College, University of London. He is the author of *The Psychology of Perception (1957), Sensation and Perception (1961), Aristotle's De Anima, Books II and III (1968)* and *Experience and the Growth of Understanding (1978).* He has contributed chapters to several other books and numerous articles to philosophical and classical journals. He has been editor of *Mind* since 1972.

THE THEORY OF KNOWLEDGE

D. W. Hamlyn

MACMILLAN

First published 1970
Reprinted 1972, 1973, 1974, 1976, 1977, 1980, 1982, 1983, 1985

Published by
Higher and Further Education Division
MACMILLAN PUBLISHERS LTD
Houndmills, Basingstoke, Hampshire RG21 2XS
and London
Companies and representatives
throughout the world

Printed in Hong Kong

ISBN 0-333-11548-1

TO EILEEN

Contents

Preface

The main substance of a large part of this book stems from lectures that I gave, and in some cases have continued to give, at Birkbeck College, University of London, over a period of several years. I have endeavored to keep the material up to date, but many generations of Birkbeck students will be familiar with the kind of thing that this book contains. The debt that I owe to these students is immense. Birkbeck students have always been ever-ready to comment upon and correct one's views, and I have derived a vast amount of profit from their interjections. It is more than appropriate that I should record my gratitude here.

I am also extremely grateful to the editor of the series, Professor D. J. O'Connor, for his encouragement in the writing of this book. He has read the complete typescript, and my thanks are due for his comments. I need hardly say that the responsibility for whatever faults the book contains is entirely mine, as is equally the responsibility for the views put forward.

My colleague, Dr. S. C. Brown, has also read the complete typescript and has made a number of very helpful comments. I am extremely grateful to him. I also owe much to other colleagues who from time to time have commented upon and criticized views that I have expressed on matters with which the book is concerned. I have received, in particular, extensive comments both from them and from other people on the material in Chapter 4.

I have to record yet again my thanks to Mrs. Susan Cunnew for her great help in typing the manuscript, and for much other assistance. I am grateful, too, to Miss Patricia Dymond for additional assistance of the same kind.

PART ONE

The Conditions
of Knowledge

CHAPTER 1

Why a Theory
of Knowledge?

(a) The questions asked

Questions about the status and extent of our knowledge of the world, of ourselves and other people, not to speak of particular branches of knowledge, like history and mathematics, have occupied the attention of philosophers for nearly as long as philosophy itself has been in existence. Such questions and the answers that may be given to them form part of that important branch of philosophy known as epistemology, or the theory of knowledge. To speak merely of a *theory* of knowledge gives little indication, however, of what is at issue. Cynics have sometimes said that when the term "theory" is used in philosophy it should be treated as a danger signal, a sign that something pretentious but not very informative is going to be presented to us. One meets in philosophy not only the theory of knowledge, but theories of truth, perception, memory, and so on—theories that are in a sense subtheories within the theory of knowledge itself, since whatever else they do they have at the least a connection with problems about the nature and extent of our knowledge. Still, it is not altogether clear that, as *theories*, they have much else in common; the use of the term "theory" in philosophy may suggest little more than that the philosopher who puts forward the theory is putting forward a point of view which, however much it may be argued for, does not admit of proof. It is vitally important, therefore, when discussing a philosophical theory to be quite clear what the issues are, what questions are being asked, what problems raised. For only insight into these can save a theory from being pretentious and uninformative. Why then a theory of knowledge, what are the philosophical problems about knowledge, and why should they be worth pursuing?

There are, first, problems about what knowledge is, what we understand by the term "knowledge." The answers that are given to these questions may also have implications for further problems concerning the scope of knowledge—what it is that in general deserves the title of knowledge. I say "in general" because the problems that confront the philosopher here are not the specific ones of whether any particular claims made by a scientist, a historian, or a specialist within any other discipline deserve the name of knowledge. The verdict on such claims can be arrived at only by those with the relevant specialist knowledge, or by those who have the techniques or knowledge of the methodology appropriate for the discovery of the truth in question. The same is true even of particular claims to knowledge made by the man in the street; for only those who have access to the relevant facts, who can make the relevant inferences, and so on, are competent to pass judgment on such claims. There is one important exception to this. A philosopher may, because of insight into what knowledge is and what in general can count as knowledge, declare that some particular claim *cannot* amount to knowledge, since nothing of this kind *could* amount to knowledge; the conditions that must be fulfilled if any claim is to count as a genuine claim to knowledge are in this case simply not fulfilled. This state of affairs may come about in a variety of ways. The person concerned may not have sufficient grounds for his claim, that claim may not in any case be true, or the terms in which the claim is expressed may not add up to a significant proposition. Hence any claim to knowledge presupposes, if it is to be a valid claim, the satisfaction of conditions concerning grounds, truth, meaning, and perhaps other things. To investigate these conditions is a philosophical task. To establish these general conditions is to elucidate the concept of knowledge, and this is a prime task of a philosopher concerned with the theory of knowledge.

So far then we have seen that some, perhaps the main, problems within the field of the theory of knowledge are those concerning the nature of knowledge and the general conditions that must be satisfied by any genuine claim to knowledge. These problems are general and do not demand for their solution special knowledge of the kind required within particular fields of knowledge. There may be problems peculiar to these special fields that are nevertheless philosophical in character, and I shall make a further brief reference to these matters in the third part of this book. In the main, however, my concern will be with the general issues, and the ones of the kind already mentioned will be the topic of the first part of the book. There are, however, other general issues that need to be mentioned, that will be the subject of the second and middle part of the book. These are issues arising from the fact that human beings have certain general capacities that are used in the acquisition of knowledge. They have senses, by means of which they acquire some knowledge of the world around them, and they have memory such that they retain at least some of the knowledge that they have acquired. This much would be admitted by most philosophers, although the ways in which perception and memory provide or constitute knowledge are disputed and require examination. Thus the kinds of questions that we have seen arise in connection with knowledge arise also in connection with perception, memory, and the like, i.e., what do these capacities amount to, and what count as instances of them? Some philosophers—those who have been labeled empiricists—have claimed that all knowledge is founded on perception in one way or another, and the stricter the conception of the ways in which knowledge is founded on experience or perception the more strictly may the philosopher in question be considered an empiricist. I have spoken of "experience *or* perception" since, first, the exact connection that exists between perception and the experiences that we have requires examination, and second, there may be knowledge of ourselves and of our own states of mind that may not be due to perception in any ordinary sense. There may also be other forms of knowledge we have as a result of capacities we possess as human beings. There is the knowledge we have of other people and their states of mind, a knowledge which is not perhaps obviously just a matter of perception. How do we know what another man is feeling? Perhaps what we see of him may be relevant in some way, but how? But the largest question is whether we can have knowledge that is not in any direct sense founded on experience at all. We have as human beings some power of thought; that is clear enough. Does this make possible the acquisition of forms of knowledge of any kind that are not available in any other way?

These questions are concerned with the scope of knowledge. In answering them we are not immediately interested in whether, for example, knowledge of scientific laws or mathematical theorems is possible. That is to say that we are not concerned with the question of whether any of the traditional disciplines are sources of knowledge, and if so, which. This would be an epistemological question of a kind, and one that would be appropriate to the philosophy of the discipline under consideration, but the questions that I have been surveying are in a sense more general and more fundamental. They raise the problem of whether whole ranges of forms of knowledge are possible, and if so, how. Without perception and memory, no knowledge of the world would be possible at all. There must be some way in which we can become aware of the feelings and thoughts of other people, for otherwise social life and communication would be impossible. But can we have knowledge beyond all this without reference in any obvious way to perception? Is knowledge that is a priori, independent of experience, possible, and if so, in what form or forms? These are important and fundamental questions that must be answered before consideration of the problems of particular disciplines.

The problems of the theory of knowledge with which we shall be concerned are therefore threefold: problems about the nature of knowledge in general and the conditions under which it is appropriate to speak of knowledge; problems about the scope of knowledge in the sense explained (with the correlative problem of whether knowledge is dependent entirely on sense perception); and problems about the epistemological issues that arise in special disciplines and fields of knowledge. I shall have very little to say about the third set of problems, since they raise issues for the philosophy of those special disciplines—the philosophy of science, mathematics, history, or religion, for example. Nevertheless it is important to realize that epistemological problems do not end when the general issues have been dealt with. On the other hand, it is equally important to realize that the theory of knowledge is not coextensive with the philosophy of science, and to suppose that it is so is to beg the question concerning the nature of knowledge itself. We must attempt to gain a firm understanding of the concept of knowledge in general before any examination of the specific forms that it may take.

In a certain sense, however, all the problems of the theory of knowledge, even the more general ones, arise against and by contrast with a quite different point of view. That is that knowledge is impossible, or at least that we can never be sure that we have attained it. This thesis, which may take a variety of forms, is known as philosophical skepticism; it raises fundamental doubts about the possibility of knowing anything at all. Skeptical tendencies have become apparent at many times in the history of philosophy for many different reasons. In ancient times the Greek Sophists raised skeptical considerations about the possibility of knowledge of nature because they wished to lay emphasis on the extent to which what was claimed as knowledge really depended on human conventions and individual human judgment.[1] Later the Greek Skeptics themselves, perhaps the only real example of a definite school of skeptics, cast doubt on all forms of knowledge, because they thought that only by abstaining from inquiry into the real nature of things and by going simply by appearances could human beings obtain freedom from anxiety and attain genuine tranquillity of mind.[2] Very much later still, Descartes adopted a systematic skepticism in order to see where the firm foundations of knowledge lay.[3] There are many other examples of a tendency to skepticism in the history of philosophy, though there are very few (if any) examples of wholesale skepticism since this is a position very difficult, if not impossible, to maintain consistently. But whether skepticism has ever existed properly or not, much of the discussion within the theory of knowledge must be set against the *possibility* of skepticism. For much of the traditional theory of knowledge has been concerned not simply with the nature and scope of knowledge but with a justification of claims to knowledge. If the general claim to knowledge

[1] This is especially true of Gorgias (who claimed that nothing exists, and second, that if it did we could not know of it, and third, that if we did know of it we could not communicate that knowledge to others) and Protagoras, whose thesis that man is the measure of all things amounts, at any rate on the interpretation of Plato in his *Theaetetus,* to an assertion of complete subjectivity.

[2] See, e.g., Sextus Empiricus, *Principles of Pyrrhonism* and Diogenes Laertius' life of Pyrrho in his *Lives of Eminent Philosophers.*

[3] See R. Descartes, *Discourse on Method* and *Meditations.*

has to be justified, this is so because there is at least the suggestion that knowledge is not possible. The tendency to suppose that it is not possible comes largely from the belief that knowledge implies certainty and that certainty is impossible.

There is thus a connection between the problem of the justification of claims to knowledge and the problem about the nature of knowledge, for as we have just seen in effect, skepticism may arise, and has most often arisen in the past, because of the supposal that knowledge involves certainty. It may then be argued that certainty of this kind is not attainable and hence that knowledge is not possible. Thus one foundation for skepticism is *a* conception (and, as I hope to show, an erroneous conception) of knowledge. Here as elsewhere in philosophy a correct account of a concept cannot show that skepticism is impossible, but it may show that grounds for skepticism must be sought elsewhere. A correct account of what knowledge is may thus prevent a skeptic from using the very nature of the concept of knowledge as a ground for skepticism about its application to anything. But since our skeptic is a hypothetical animal (he is for our purposes merely the exemplification of a hypothetical position that gives sense to the demand for justification of claims to knowledge), we cannot look to the ways in which skepticism has been expressed with every confidence that an answer to these will be the final refutation of the skeptical position. A skeptic could make his point or express his doubt in various ways. The philosopher who wishes to defend the possibility of knowledge must be prepared to meet the opposing arguments as they arise; and this is possible only with a firm grasp of what the nature and scope of knowledge is. Hence the theory of knowledge is, among other things, a set of defense-works against skepticism of the very possibility of knowledge.

Yet the theory of knowledge is primarily a theory about the nature of knowledge and about what makes it possible. Skepticism is a pertinent consideration only because the very question "What makes knowledge possible?," or more particularly the question "Is knowledge possible?" may suggest that perhaps it is *not* possible. This is a mark of the generality of the problems that confront the philosopher. At this level, an understanding of the concept of knowledge itself involves understanding why it is possible, and the attempt to acquire understanding of the concept must involve the attempt to see how the skeptic can be refuted or at least resisted. In what follows, a premium will be put on understanding what knowledge is, but it has to be admitted that a large part of the traditional approaches to epistemology consists in taking more or less for granted what knowledge is and asking instead how it can be given firm foundations. What I am suggesting is that this is in a sense putting the cart before the horse, and that if attention is given first to the concept of knowledge, the worries about firm foundations may perhaps seem unnecessary.

(b) Skepticism, knowledge, and the search for certainty

Traditionally, epistemology has involved what is sometimes referred to as the "search for certainty." Impressed by the possibility of doubt and by the supposal that if doubt be allowed its head this will undermine the foundations of knowledge, philosophers have sought to make those foundations unshakable. The architectural models involved here are not without significance. There is a tendency to think of the corpus of knowledge as a building that is rising upward and that those who increase the stock of knowledge are building additional stories on to the existing fabric. If the foundations are not secure the whole building will eventually come crashing to the ground. It is doubtful whether this analogy does justice to the facts. The growth of knowledge is not really like the growth of a building if only because knowledge does not grow simply by way of addition. The growth of our knowledge involves much modification and indeed abandonment at some places of what we earlier held to be true; it also involves the connection and linking of pieces of knowledge that have earlier seemed distinct, and occasionally the reverse. More important for present purposes, however, is the idea of foundations. It is true, as I have already indicated, that certain conditions may have to be satisfied if a claim to knowledge is to be a genuine one, but this scarcely justifies the architectural image of a foundation. What philosophers have had in mind here is the idea that unless some pieces of supposed knowledge are sure, the rest of the fabric or corpus of knowledge will be suspect. It does not matter that it would scarcely occur to the experts to doubt that knowledge is attainable in their field (although it must be admitted that *some* mathematicians, for example, have been led to wonder whether anything within their discipline could rightly be called knowledge). There is still the suggestion that if certain particular things are not known, nothing else will deserve the title of knowledge. I emphasize the idea that certain particular things must be known, since the direction in which philosophers have looked for foundations of knowledge is not in any way a contingent or accidental matter. In other words, insofar as the search for certainty is a search for sure foundations for knowledge, it is of some importance *where* philosophers have looked for certainty. Not any proposition would do as an instance of a truth known with certainty; its relations to other truths are also of importance.

But why look for certainty at all? It has sometimes been supposed that nothing can be known at all unless it is certain. There is a seductiveness about this supposition; for it is surely part of the concept of knowledge that one cannot be said to know something unless what is claimed as known is in fact the case; one cannot be said to know p unless p is in fact true. Hence, if there is any room for doubt as to the truth of p, there is room for doubt about the claim to knowledge. The next move is to suggest that there is always room for doubt as to the truth of what is claimed as known. For except in rare cases, it is impossible to give an absolute proof of the truth of a given proposition. Hence what we may ordinarily think of as knowledge does not really deserve the title. This is a form of skeptical argument; but it in fact takes us farther than we need to go at present. All we need in order to be seduced by the supposition that we cannot know what is not certain is the first stage of the argument. This is the claim that if we know we cannot be wrong; hence if we are to know that p it must be impossible for us to be wrong about p, and only of what is certain is it impossible to be wrong. But the argument presented in this way is in fact invalid. To say that if we know we cannot be wrong is merely to express what is logically involved in the concept of knowledge, that knowledge is incompatible with the falsity of what is claimed as known. It is to say that we cannot both know and be wrong. Nothing follows from this about whether what we know must be such that it is *impossible* to be wrong about it. To put the matter in other words, it does not follow from the fact that if I know that p it is impossible for me to be wrong about p that if I know that p the proposition p must be such that it is impossible for me to be wrong about it. To suppose that it does follow is to make a mistake of modal logic; it is to mistake the role that "cannot" plays in "If I know, I cannot be wrong." In fact, the "cannot" merely expresses the incompatibility between knowledge and being wrong; it does not say that the only appropriate objects of knowledge are things about which it is impossible to be wrong.

I have suggested already that the next move of the skeptic is to stress the point that it *is* possible to be wrong about most things that we ordinarily claim to know; and so he casts doubt on most of what we normally think of as knowledge. (I say "most things" because it has often been held that where proof is possible, where the objects of knowledge claims are propositions that are necessarily true, there certainty is possible; hence mathematics, for example, has often, though not always, been excepted from the general strictures on the possibility of knowledge.) Plato, to give one example, at one stage of his life cast doubt on the position that perception in any way provides knowledge; knowledge must be reserved for objects of a higher kind—the Forms. Thus in Book V of the *Republic* Glaucon is made to respond to Socrates' suggestion that knowledge and belief are not the same by saying "How could any intelligent man identify the infallible with the not infallible?"[4] The implication is clear: Knowledge and infallibility go together, and anything that is not infallible is not a suitable subject for knowledge, however much we may believe in its truth. Philosophers of this kind, however, have generally supposed that knowledge is to be found somewhere. Skepticism is in their case only limited; skepticism about perception is a mere preliminary to the identification of true knowledge, which is to be found elsewhere. Where this "elsewhere" is varies according to the predilection of the philosopher in question, and according to the direction in which his general argument takes him.

Other philosophers, however, have not been so prepared to condemn the mass of experience to mere supposition or opinion. Some of these have accepted the strict connection between knowledge and infallibility but have nevertheless tried to allow room for the things that we normally believe that we know, e.g., the truths of science, let alone the products of ordinary perception. Thus they have held that there must be some infallible objects of knowledge if we are to be said to know anything else. There must also be some kind of rational connection between the infallible or indubitable truths

4 Plato, *Republic*, 477e.

and the other more ordinary things that we believe we know. In effect this implies some kind of distinction between strong and weak senses of "know."[5] What we are said to know in the "strong" sense provides the foundations of knowledge in the way indicated earlier.

The search for indubitable and infallible truths is therefore a common feature of traditional epistemology. To some extent, however, there must be a connection between the place at which a philosopher looks for indubitable truth and the way in which he thinks that the rest of "knowledge" can be derived from these truths when found. Given that the primary task is to defend what we ordinarily claim to know about the world from the attacks of the skeptic, there may nevertheless be differences between philosophers in their conceptions of how this is to be carried out—how, that is to say, this supposed knowledge is to be seen as resting upon what is known beyond any doubt. In their views on this point philosophers have sometimes been influenced by the success or supposed success of certain specific disciplines, like mathematics and empirical science. If these disciplines can be successful in the attainment of truth within their domain, perhaps, it has sometimes been suggested, their methods may also be useful in philosophy in general. Thus philosophers of the rationalist persuasion, or at least the seventeenth-century ones, have tended to look to mathematics for their model, so treating the indubitable truths when arrived at as premises or axioms from which other truths can be derived deductively as theorems. Empiricists, on the other hand, have adopted a different model, treating the indubitable truths as data on which a body of theory is to be constructed. The fact that the problems and questions with which the philosopher is concerned here are of a different order of generality from those that are the concern of the mathematician or scientist makes it unlikely that the

[5] Cf. Ch. 4, sec. (d) for a further discussion of this notion.

methods of the more particular disciplines will be fruitful in philosophy as well. Why should it be supposed that the answer to the question "How is knowledge possible in general?" is to be arrived at in the same way as the answer to the questions "How is mathematical knowledge possible?" or "How is scientific knowledge possible?" Nevertheless, whatever doubts one may justifiably have about the methods employed in this connection, the whole program will seem even less plausible if there is no case to be made for the indubitables that are supposed to provide the axioms or data necessary for the application of the methods.

I shall go farther into these questions in the next chapter. It is sufficient to note here that the programs that I have considered briefly are part of a general search for certainty, a certainty that is thought desirable on the grounds that unless something is certain nothing can even be probable. In other words, unless these programs or ones like them can succeed, we shall be condemned to wholesale skepticism. It would not be enough to appeal to the fact that we do believe that we know some things for certain; it has to be shown that there is this certainty and that it is of the kind relevant for the task of basing the rest of the corpus of knowledge on its foundation. I have already cast doubt on the analogies presupposed here, I have cast doubt on the demand for certainty if knowledge is to be possible, and I shall in the next chapter cast doubt on the methods used and on the results supposed to be reached. One more thing requires discussion now. I have spoken of the supposed dangers of wholesale skepticism. It may be wondered, however, whether wholesale skepticism is itself possible. Is wholesale skepticism even a consistent position? Is skepticism possible at all unless freedom from skepticism is also possible? There have been suggestions in recent times that it is not, and that in consequence skepticism is not so much of a danger as is commonly supposed.

(c) Is philosophical skepticism possible?

The question that I ask here is whether skepticism is a possible position at all when it becomes wholesale and universal. It is of course possible to be skeptical about particular claims to knowledge or even about whole provinces or fields of so-called knowledge, e.g., about astrology. Indeed, skepticism is right and proper over many claims to knowledge, for there will be reasons for doubt in the fields in question, and thus reasons for refusing to admit the claims to knowledge. Could there be similar reasons for doubt whether knowledge is possible at all? If not, the skeptic may be disarmed; for if he can have no reasons for his wholesale doubt, such doubts become empty and otiose. In such a situation we need pay no further attention to him, especially if there are prima facie reasons in favor of the position that we do have knowledge, sometimes, at any rate. I shall return to this point in Chapter 2, but it may be noted now that to say that wholesale skepticism is empty and otiose is not to say that it is an impossible position in itself; it is merely to say that there are no grounds for its acceptance. The suggestions, already noted, that skepticism is an impossible position if wholesale, must have a different and firmer basis if they are to be valid.

There are two arguments that have been used recently that attempt to provide such a basis. There is in a way a certain affinity between these two arguments. They are, respectively, the argument from polar concepts, and the paradigm-case argument; they both depend on considerations about meaning. The first argument turns on the fact that certain terms or concepts come in pairs such that a given member of any pair is somehow essentially contrasted with the other; indeed, it gets its sense by way of this contrast. These pairs are polar in this way. It was pointed out by Norman Malcolm that real/unreal, knowledge/belief, and many other examples are polar in this sense.[6] The sense in question has been discussed critically by Colin Grant.[7] It is sufficient to say here that in claiming that a pair of concepts is polar, it is maintained not only that there is an exclusion between instances of the concepts but also that one of the concepts can be understood only if the other is understood also. (Whether knowledge and belief in general *are* polar is something that will be discussed in Chapter 4, but a polar contrast seems to be implied at least by the skeptic's position when he says that we do not know, but *only* believe or suppose that such and such are so.) A further point, which is not directly relevant perhaps to the present issue, is that it might be argued that one of the pair of polar concepts is in some way prior to the other, and it has been argued by J. L. Austin that in the case of "real" and "unreal" it is "unreal" that is really prior; as he puts it, it is "unreal" that wears the trousers.[8] This kind of point is relevant to the question where the onus of justification lies; it could thus be used to put the onus on the skeptic to prove his case rather than demanding that his opponents should prove theirs. But the central point of the argument from polar concepts is not this but the claim that if there are to be instances of one member of the polar pair there must be instances of the other. If there is to be mere supposition, there must also be knowledge; hence the skeptic cannot demolish knowledge in favor of mere supposition.

One of the best expositions of this argument is to be found in Gilbert Ryle's *Dilemmas*,[9] where Ryle uses it to argue against the supposition that all perception may be illusory or nonveridical. His argument in effect takes the form of a series of analogies to bring out the same

[6] N. Malcolm, "Moore and Ordinary Language" in *The Philosophy of G. E. Moore*, ed. P. Schilpp (Evanston, Illinois, 1942), pp. 343ff.

[7] C. K. Grant, "Polar Concepts and Metaphysical Arguments," *Proc. Arist. Soc.* (1955–56), pp. 83ff.

[8] J. L. Austin, *Sense and Sensibilia* (Oxford, 1962), pp. 70–71.

[9] G. Ryle, *Dilemmas* (Cambridge, 1954), p. 94.

point. He argues that there cannot be counterfeit coins unless there are genuine ones, and that ice could not be thin unless there were thick ice. Similarly, there could not be illusory perception if there were not veridical perception. Ryle's analogies are scarcely convincing in themselves. In the first place, "thick" and "thin" are relative notions. Of course, given knowledge of the range of thicknesses that ice can take, it is possible to say that a certain piece of ice is thick or thin by the standards of ice; and it may be argued that given this knowledge, and given that we wish to discriminate thicknesses of ice, we can infer that there must be pieces of ice of varying thicknesses that can be described as thick or thin. But the assumptions are necessary; for it might be that we had no interest in the varying thicknesses of ice, that we had no interest in speaking of "thick or thin by the standards of ice." In that case ice might be judged by other standards and thus might always be considered thin. There would then be no case whatever for saying that if ice is thin it must also be thick. It remains true, of course (and this is a point made by Grant), that the fact that we might not apply "thick" to ice has no implications for the question of whether it is possible to apply "thick" to other things. The point that does emerge is that if there is a thin X there need not be a thick X unless we mean "thin" or "thick" *by the standard of X's.* For example, are not razor blades always thin?

Ryle's other example is subject to similar objections. The supposition is that genuine coins must actually exist if there are to be counterfeit ones. But it seems conceivable that in a country where there were a large number of counterfeit coins the genuine ones might go out of circulation or be melted down, leaving only the counterfeit ones. Indeed, it is perhaps conceivable that there might not have been any genuine ones in the first place; the pattern for genuine coins might have been laid down but none minted, and from negligence or some other motive the authorities may never have taken steps to prevent circulation of the counterfeit

coins. These were manufactured by forgers, anxious perhaps to obtain foreign currency. So there seems to be no
necessity that genuine noncounterfeit coins should exist
if there are to be counterfeit ones. On the other hand,
the point about the pattern is important; in order to
speak of counterfeit coins at all it must be possible to
know what they are counterfeit of, what sort of thing
would count as a genuine coin if there were any. In
other words, it must be possible to know what it is for
something to be a genuine coin if it is to make sense to
speak of counterfeit coins. Not that one must actually
know this. One must of course know it if one is to be
justified in saying that any given coin is counterfeit;
but its making sense to speak of counterfeit coins and
our being justified in saying that any given coin is counterfeit are two quite different things. In sum, where two
concepts, *A* and *B*, are polar, in order for it to make sense
to speak of things being *A* it must make sense to speak
of things being *B*; hence, if there are things that are *A*,
it must make sense to speak of things being *B*; it must
be *possible* for things to be *B*, whether or not there *are*
any *B* things. Hence, if the skeptic casts doubt on our
ordinary claims to knowledge, saying that they are only
supposition, we can at least ask him what it is to know
something. He can quite properly *claim* that there are
no cases of knowledge, as long as he gives some sense
to the concept of knowledge. Without this his claim is
truly senseless, but nothing follows from this as to
whether there are any actual cases of knowledge.

The second argument, the paradigm-case argument,
might be invoked at this point. For this argument claims
that if a given concept is to be a genuine concept, if a
given term is to be meaningful, there must be instances
to which the concept and the term are applied as para-
digms. There may, therefore, be disputes about certain
supposed instances to which the term and concept are
applied, but if there were dispute about the paradigm-
cases of their application, they would be meaningless.
The paradigm-cases are those cases by reference to which

we explain the term in question. Put in this bald fashion, there seem to be obvious objections to the argument.
To say the least, it does not seem at all obvious in the
great majority of cases that we learn the meaning of
terms by reference to their applications in instances. It
has indeed been argued by J. W. N. Watkins[10] that
while we may learn the meanings of terms like "red" in
this way, we do not so learn the meaning of more complex expressions.[11] It is more than doubtful whether we
learn the meaning of *any* terms in this way. In its crud-
est form, the paradigm-case argument rests upon a rather
simple identification of meaning with use, in the sense
that it is supposed that a term has meaning only if it
has use, i.e., an application. There must, however, be
many terms that have meaning although there is nothing
answering to those terms. It may be argued that where
this is so, the meaning of the terms involved is to be
given by way of other terms that do have an application
to something, or at any rate this is so in the case of those
terms in which the question of their having application
arises at all. There is some truth in this, but it also remains true that it cannot be inferred simply from the
fact that a term supposedly has a meaning that anything
answers to it. We cannot in particular argue simply from
the fact that the term "knowledge" has meaning that
there must therefore *be* knowledge and that for this
reason skepticism about the general possibility of knowledge is incoherent.

On the other hand, a point already made has to be
mentioned at this stage in the argument—that if the
skeptic allows that the term "knowledge" has meaning,
he must also be prepared to say what he understands by
the term, what would count as knowledge. If, as is likely,

[10] By, e.g., J. W. N. Watkins, *Analysis*, 18 (1957), pp. 25ff.
V. also other articles in the same journal for 1958. See also
J. Passmore, *Philosophical Reasoning*, (London, 1961), Ch. 6.

[11] This point is connected with the whole question of whether
there is such a thing as ostensive definition, for which see the discussion in Ch. 2 and 3.

he also deviates from the normal conceptions of what counts as knowledge, the onus is upon him to justify that deviation. If a concept is to exist at all, as is in effect maintained by Ludwig Wittgenstein, there must be some general agreement about its understanding, and that includes the understanding of how it is to be applied.[12] There is thus the presumption that normal conceptions of what is to count as knowledge are correct, and that is why the onus is upon the deviationist to justify his case, and not vice versa. Therefore, insofar as the paradigm-cases referred to in the paradigm-case argument are indications of the normal use of the concept and are such that their acceptance forms part of any proper understanding of the concept, there remains some point to that argument. It cannot prove that there must exist, for example, actual cases of knowledge; but it can point to the normal conditions for our understanding of the concept—something that the skeptic appears at least to want to override. Thus the skeptic must either justify the case for a different understanding of the concept, or claim that there is no such concept, if he is to proceed with his campaign. If he does indeed claim that there is no such concept, then the argument from polar concepts may be reinvoked against him; for if knowledge and mere belief are polar concepts, then one of them cannot be rejected without the rejection of the other. That much is implied in that argument. The skeptic who wishes to continue in business must then challenge the claim that the concepts of knowledge and mere belief are polar.

I have in this discussion begun to chart some of the moves that a skeptic might make, and I shall return to the issues at the end of the next chapter. The fact that moves are possible at all indicates that there can be no short way with the skeptic; the arguments that may be directed against him depend largely on what he himself

[12] L. Wittgenstein, *Philosophical Investigations* (Oxford, 1953), I 242.

says. There is no one position that may be called "skepticism." One who says, "We never know anything" may be asked whether he knows this. To answer "Yes" to this question would be to land oneself in an obvious contradiction, which the Greek Skeptics recognized. To answer "No" robs the initial assertion of its point. Similar remarks apply to one who says that it makes no sense to speak of knowledge, and there is in this case the additional point that if he stands by his claim he cannot go on to say that we merely believe the things that we suppose ourselves to know; for in that case, by the polar principle, it makes no sense to speak of mere belief either. These kinds of skepticism are indeed incoherent. But perhaps the skeptic may act as the Greek Skeptics eventually did—he may merely question, and refuse to commit himself on any one issue. He may persist in asking whether knowledge is really possible. Is this an incoherent position? It might be said that it is not a position at all. It is certainly not a positive one, but negative positions are nonetheless positions, and the skeptic who insists on questioning any claim to knowledge that we make demands an answer of some kind. The attempts to provide an answer may serve to produce further clarification concerning the concept of knowledge itself— a task that I have said is perhaps the prime task for a theory of knowledge. But in this context the answers that must be given depend entirely on the questions. General skepticism seems possible in a theoretical sense as long as it remains negative, however difficult it may be to maintain in practice. The crucial question is whether the difficulties that beset it are more fundamental than this. I shall return to this point at the end of the next chapter.

CHAPTER 2

Traditional
Answers to Skepticism

(a) Rationalism

It has been made clear in the previous chapter that the skeptic's demands have been traditionally interpreted as satisfiable only as the result of a successful search for certainty. It has been thought necessary to discover truths that are indubitable and to show that the rest of what we suppose to be knowledge is based on or derived from these indubitable truths. Perhaps the most explicit instance of a belief in this procedure is the philosophy of Descartes,[1] and he provides also one of the most obvious attempts to deal with the problem along rationalist lines. Descartes employed the "method of doubt," a kind of systematic skepticism, aimed at withholding belief from anything of which, as he put it, we do not have "a clear and distinct idea." Descartes proposed, in other words, to hold in doubt for the time being anything that could not be seen in the light of reason to be certain and indubitable. This, however, was merely a preliminary to the establishment of the foundations of knowledge; the skepticism was not a genuine, thoroughgoing skepticism, since it was clearly

[1] See esp. R. Descartes, *Discourse on Method* and *Meditations*.

assumed that something would turn out to be indubitable, and that knowledge would be safeguarded. Descartes therefore thought of his method as a rational procedure aimed at discovering through the light of reason something that it is impossible to doubt, and from which by means of a chain of arguments we can arrive at sure beliefs in the objects of the senses. The purpose of this was not to show that we do in fact know this or that particular thing, but to show that we can and do have certain general kinds of knowledge, e.g., knowledge of a world independent of ourselves. Descartes' aim was thus to show that the general validity of science, mathematics, and what the senses tell us can be preserved against skeptical arguments; whether this or that particular claim to knowledge is in fact true must be left to the particular disciplines concerned, but the possibility of those disciplines themselves must first be guaranteed. The method is thus rationalist in the general sense that there is an underlying conception that reason can show that these things are so, that reason alone can prove that there are foundations for knowledge, and that even the senses require the guarantee that reason is supposed to provide.

In this general sense, as we shall see later, the empiricists of the same period shared a similar rationalist tendency, an anxiety to provide a rational justification of the claim for the possibility of knowledge. They equally demanded certainty, and thus in effect refused to give the title of knowledge to anything that was ultimately incapable of proof. Like the rationalists, they looked for certainty in truths that are certain because they are necessary—that is why it is feasible to speak of proof. They differed from the rationalists in their conception of the subsequent method to be employed in basing knowledge on these truths once discovered, and they differed on the question of where these truths were to be found—through reason or through the senses.[2] The question of the

[2] See my *Sensation and Perception* (New York and London, 1961), Ch. 4, for further considerations.

method to be adopted and of the source of the indubitable truths to which the method is somehow to be applied are not really independent of each other. Descartes and the other Rationalists of the seventeenth and eighteenth centuries had a more explicit conception of the way in which reason could operate than that given so far, and this makes them rationalists in a more specific sense than that indicated. Descartes was impressed by the results achieved in his day by mathematics in general and geometry in particular. If the axiomatic method employed in geometry—the method of deriving theorems by strict deductive means from intuitively obvious axioms in the light of carefully laid down definitions of terms—could be successful in geometry, why not elsewhere? If it were possible to arrive at certain indubitable truths that could act as the axioms of a deductive system, it might be possible to derive other truths from these. Since mathematics, too, is the supreme example of a rational discipline (it owes nothing to sense perception), the adoption of its methods fitted in with the general belief in the powers of reason. In fact, the philosopher who used the geometrical method most explicitly was Spinoza; Descartes expressed faith in it without using it in the same formal way as Spinoza. But Descartes' method of argument conformed to the general requirements of geometrical reasoning, and the presuppositions of the attempt to use any method of this kind to achieve the aims at present under consideration are certainly set out most clearly in Descartes.

I have already said that the truths at which both the rationalists and the empiricists aimed had to be certain because they were in some sense necessary; they were indubitable because there was supposedly some kind of necessity about them. It must not be merely a fact of psychology that we cannot doubt them; they must be beyond doubt in a more fundamental sense, beyond all possibility of doubt. This could be possible only if they were necessarily true. That is why it is feasible to speak of "proof" in this connection. Ordinary knowledge will have been proved to be possible if it can be shown to be based in one way or another on substantive, nontrivial truths about the world that are necessarily true and undeniable for that reason alone. If the way in which ordinary knowledge is based on these truths is in any sense deductive, if the propositions in which it is expressed can be derived deductively from them, then it will be even more appropriate to speak of necessity. However, not everything that is certainly true *is* necessary; it is certainly true that the paper on which these words are printed is white, but it is not in any way necessarily true that this is so. Of course, the truth that this paper is white is not in any case the kind of truth that could provide the foundations of knowledge; but even if it were, the fact that it is not necessarily true might seem to leave an opening for the skeptic. For he might argue that if it is not necessarily true it might conceivably be false, and it is thus open to possible doubt. I shall discuss later the question of whether the fact that something is conceivably false provides any real opening for the skeptic; whether, that is, it makes that thing in any real sense open to doubt. For present purposes it is enough to note that the traditional answers to skepticism have presupposed that the fact that something is conceivably false does leave such an opening for skepticism; that is why there has been the search for truths that cannot conceivably be doubted. In other words, if it is supposed that knowledge requires certainty, then it may also be supposed that the only way of preserving the possibility of knowledge from all attacks is to show that there are truths that cannot be doubted in any circumstances, those which are absolutely certain. This in turn will be the case only if those truths are necessary; for if they are necessarily so, there cannot be any circumstances in which they can be false, and they cannot be doubted *for that reason*. The questions are whether there are such truths, and whether in any case they can provide the basis for the rest of knowledge.

I shall not here go into the details of Descartes' argument. Basically Descartes' argument starts from the famous "Cogito ergo sum." The existence of oneself as a thinking thing is the necessary and indubitable truth from which the rest of the argument proceeds. Given the existence of oneself as a thinking thing, Descartes then points to the fact that among our thoughts are those of God and of the so-called external world of extended nonthinking things. He has to show that those thoughts are veridical in the sense that they actually correspond to something. Descartes invokes two distinct kinds of proof of the existence of God (the so-called ontological and cosmological proofs or arguments). Finally, he argues that given that God is not a deceiver, the ideas of external objects must themselves be veridical; they must in general correspond to something. Falsity and error are products of the will, not of the intellect. Hence, while it is possible to be mistaken in making certain judgments about the world apart from ourselves, those judgments would be wholly false only if God deceived us by giving us wrong ideas. Since God is not a deceiver, there must therefore be a firm basis for knowledge. It is possible to find fault with this argument at many places, and much, in any case, depends upon the apparatus that is generally presupposed in it—the story about ideas and their sources, for example.[3] It must therefore be taken that the argument is not strictly one of a valid deductive form; it would indeed be surprising if it were, since if the premises were necessarily true and the argument deductive and valid, the conclusions ought to be necessarily true also. But the conclusions purport to be matters of fact. As is pointed out by J. L. Watling,[4] a consistent rationalist ought to maintain that propositions about material objects (and the external world generally) are logically true, not just matters of contingent fact. What, however, about the premises of the argument?

The main premise is the "Cogito," though this has to be supplemented by other considerations as the argument

[3] See again my *Sensation and Perception*, Ch. 5.

[4] J. L. Watling, "Descartes," in *A Critical History of Western Philosophy*, ed. D. J. O'Connor (New York, 1964), p. 174.

proceeds, e.g., that among my thoughts is to be found
the thought of God, a being who possesses all attributes
in perfection, and who must exist for the two separate
reasons that (a) the thought could not come from any
other source than from such a being (cosmological argument) and (b) existence must be one of the attributes in
question (ontological argument). There have been many
interpretations of the "Cogito" itself. Descartes is rather
vague about the considerations that count in favor of its
necessity and indubitability, the official story being that
it is a proposition that we can see to be true by the natural
light of reason. (The difficulty is that it does not appear
from its form to *be* a proposition but an argument.) Yet
the fact that it is invoked at the end of the method of
doubt suggests that the process of doubting or refusal to
believe that the method involved must be relevant to its
acceptability. A further point is that Descartes explicitly
says that the proposition "I exist" by itself "whenever I
utter it or conceive it in my mind, is necessarily true."
It has been pointed out by several philosophers that this
is so in the sense that I cannot assert the contradictory of
"I exist" without absurdity, and the same applies to "I
think"; for the assertions in question would themselves be
evidence of the contradictory of what is asserted. One cannot assert these things without existing or thinking, so that
one's own existence and power of thought are presupposed in either their assertion or their denial. A. J. Ayer
puts it by saying "The sense in which I cannot doubt
the statement that I think is just that my doubting it entails its truth; and in the same sense I cannot doubt that
I exist."[5] But the fact that I cannot without absurdity
doubt that I exist does not mean that the proposition "I
exist" is in any way a necessary truth; indeed, it seems
manifestly a contingent matter that I exist. What *is*
necessary is that if I can engage in any form of thought,
including doubt, then I exist; for existence is a precondi-

[5] A. J. Ayer, *The Problem of Knowledge,* Penguin edition
(London, 1956), p. 46 (New York, 1956).

tion of doing any of these things. This is in one sense a trivial necessity, but it is a necessity all the same. It is not, however, sufficient for Descartes' purpose, since what he must show is that it is a necessary truth that I exist as a thinking thing.

What Descartes really wants to show is the indubitability of the proposition "I think"; then, given the point that the proposition "I exist" is necessarily true whenever I conceive it, the whole complex of propositions involved in "I think therefore I exist" will be indubitable. What has been admitted so far is the necessary inference involved in the transition from "I think" to "I exist." But this necessity is what might be called hypothetical only; the truth of the conclusion follows necessarily on the hypothesis that the antecedent is true. To get the absolute necessity that Descartes requires we need to show also that the antecedent is necessarily true. In effect this is to be achieved via the consideration that I can doubt all else, but there is one thing that I cannot doubt, namely that I doubt. Unfortunately, this is not true in the sense required. For if "doubt" here means suppose to be false, there does not seem to be any necessity in the proposition that I cannot suppose to be false the proposition that I am supposing other things to be false. It is necessary that, if I doubt, I cannot suppose it to be false that doubting exists. But this is once again a hypothetical necessity; it does not establish the absolute necessity of the proposition "I doubt" nor through it that of the proposition "I think." In other words, there is always involved at some step in the argument a proposition the truth of which is not necessary but is a simple matter of fact. And this remains contingent despite the fact that if I do doubt things I cannot be in doubt that I am doing so, since supposing something to be false implies our knowing that we are doing so. For this is a point that Descartes cannot rely upon without equivocation in the senses of "doubt" involved; and in any case it still rests upon the hypothesis "if I do doubt things." In sum, Descartes does not and cannot achieve the result that he requires of showing that his initial premise has the requisite character of a necessary truth; it is not therefore indubitable in the requisite sense either.

The same considerations, or ones like them, apply to Descartes' attempt to show that it is a necessary truth that God exists. The argument to this effect that he invokes first (a version of the cosmological argument or argument from the nature of the world) is that the idea of God that we have, the idea of a perfect and infinite being, could only come from a being of the same kind; it could not be produced by ourselves since we are imperfect and finite, and an idea of something possessing a given degree of reality could be produced only by a being of a higher or equal degree of reality. This argument depends to some extent on Descartes' own theory of the nature of ideas and of their causes. He assumes without much argument that the idea which we have of God (given that we have one) must be capable of corresponding to something, and he says that the idea itself is clear and distinct, from which he takes it to follow that it is true. Without going into the argument in all its details it must be apparent that there are a number of gaps or unjustified moves in it. Hence this particular argument cannot be taken to have achieved its purpose of showing that God's existence is necessary.

The other argument (a version of the ontological argument first put forward by St. Anselm) tries to show that God's existence is necessary in that it follows from the definition of God. God is defined as a being that possesses all attributes in perfection; existence must be one of those attributes and hence God must exist. The standard rejection of this argument is that provided later by Kant—that existence is not an attribute. This might be disputed, and although at least one of Anselm's arguments has been defended lately by Norman Malcolm,[6] the only tenable

---

[6] N. Malcolm, "Anselm's Ontological Arguments," *Phil. Rev.*, LXIX (1960), pp. 41ff.; reprinted in his *Knowledge and Certainty* (Englewood Cliffs, New Jersey), pp. 141ff.

position remains that it belongs to the concept of "God" that he must exist, i.e., nothing that is a "God" could cease to exist; a God is, as the Greeks put it, an ever-being God. It does not follow from this that there actually is a God, let alone that it is a necessary truth that there is. The only necessary truth is that if anything is a God it must exist; this is once again a merely hypothetical necessity, not an absolute one, as the assertion of the existence of God must be if this is to serve its purpose in Descartes' argument. Once again, Descartes' argument must be deemed a failure in its effort to produce premises of the kind required, let alone its attempt to derive from them by rigorous argument all that is required to meet the skeptic by providing firm foundations for knowledge.

I referred earlier to the point that a consistent rationalist ought to maintain that all truths whatever are necessary. Leibniz came explicitly to this conclusion. In his philosophy the form of the argument is less rigorous and overt than in either Descartes or Spinoza. In many ways Leibniz was an inconsistent rationalist; in his pluralism, his assertion that there were in the world many things or substances, as opposed to Spinoza's view that there is only one substance—God or nature—Leibniz relied to a great extent on common sense, not reason. It is undeniable that it was Spinoza who was the most rigorous and at the same time the most austere rationalist. But on this one point Leibniz was the most explicit—that all true propositions are necessarily true; in every true proposition, he said, the predicate is contained in the subject. Leibniz had a number of reasons for holding this position, the complexities of which cannot be entered into here. But his main point is the supremely rationalist one that what is true of a genuine substance must follow from the nature of that substance itself. Hence, while he was anxious to draw a distinction between truths of reason (logical truths) and truths of fact, he held in the end that truths of fact were no less necessary than truths of reason. Any proposition about a genuine substance was really to the effect that some property was included in the class of properties that make up that substance; for a substance just *is* a collection of properties. Leibniz realized that this blurred the distinction between logical and matter-of-fact truths and tried to save the day, as other philosophers such as Russell have done since, by an appeal to human ignorance. For God, he maintained, all true propositions are necessarily true; and so indeed they would be for us too but for the fact that we, unlike God, cannot know for sure which propositions are true. We can be sure only that if a proposition is true it is necessarily true; but as to whether it *is* true we have to appeal to the principle of sufficient reason, i.e., go by the probabilities and look for the reasons for saying one thing or the other. There is one vital snag about this position as far as concerns the theory of knowledge; that is that it offers the certainty that is to be set against skepticism as an ideal only. There is certainty to be attained in the sense that if something is true at all it must be true necessarily. God, who knows what is true, can provide the answer to the skeptic, but *we* can never be absolutely sure what is true; we can be sure only to the extent that we have reasons for our beliefs. For a determined skeptic this will not be enough. In other words, from the point of view of the theory of knowledge, Leibniz grasps the nettle that a rationalist must maintain that truths about the world are necessarily true, but he fails to provide the argument that could provide a justification for claims about what is in fact true.

It seems that a rationalist must fail in establishing his premises, or in providing a valid argument from his premises, or in linking his conclusions with what must be shown if the argument is to have any application to ordinary claims to knowledge. Most rationalists have failed in all these respects, but it was to the general credit of most of the rationalists of the seventeenth and eighteenth centuries that they tried to justify claims to know things about the world as we ordinarily take ourselves to know it. This has not been true of all forms of rationalism. F. H. Bradley, the nineteenth-century Idealist who was also a rationalist in tendency, maintained in effect that all propositions about the world are to some extent false; the world as we know it is appearance only and is subject to contradictions. Nevertheless, although in the end absolute truth is not attainable through judgment, there are some truths that are intellectually incorrigible.[7] These are truths about the Absolute, i.e., reality as a whole, which for Bradley amounts to experience as a whole. It is difficult to make this intelligible without going into the associated metaphysics, and I shall make no attempt to do so. All that requires to be noted here is that in effect Bradley was maintaining about reality as a whole what Leibniz maintained about each individual substance: that the only thing that can be true of it is what is necessarily true of it, what follows from its nature, what is logically true of it. This amounts to the point that the only incorrigible thing that can be said about reality is that it includes some part of the totality that it comprises. But in Bradley this intellectual incorrigibility has nothing to do with ordinary knowledge of the world; *that* is all illusion. Rationalism has thus become other-worldly; it now attempts to revise our conceptions of knowledge, not preserve them.

(b) Empiricism

To most modern philosophers brought up in the British tradition empiricism has none of the exotic and perhaps esoteric character of rationalism; it is much more down to earth, and perhaps has an obvious plausibility, if not truth, about it. Yet it is in a very real sense concerned with attaining the same goal as rationalism, as part of the general search for certainty. At the very beginning of his *Essay Concerning Human Understanding,* John Locke declares his purpose as being "to inquire into the original, certainty and extent of human knowledge, to-

[7] F. H. Bradley, *Appearance and Reality,* 2nd ed. (London, 1897), pp. 542ff.

gether with the grounds and degrees of belief, opinion and assent." And in the last book of the *Essay* he seeks to justify claims to knowledge in general. He claims, in a way that is reminiscent of Descartes, that we have intuitive knowledge of our own existence and demonstrative knowledge of that of God, but he does not, as Descartes does, use these supposed facts to justify claims to what he maintains is the third kind of knowledge: sensitive knowledge of "particular existences." Here he rests his case ultimately on the point that what he calls the simple ideas that we have of things are caused by those things and they cannot therefore in general be wrong. Complex ideas need not correspond to anything, since the human mind plays a part in compounding simple ideas into complex ones, and in this way error may creep in. But this consideration is not pertinent to simple ideas themselves; hence he concludes, though invalidly, that they must be veridical. The presupposition that lies behind all this of course is that error can arise only as a result of human judgment; but judgment must operate upon something that is "given," and what is "given" in this way cannot be wrong. This kind of reference to what is given in sense perception runs right through empiricist philosophies.[8]

The bulk of Locke's *Essay*, however, is given up to another but connected program, that of showing that all the ideas that we have, all the ideas or concepts in which knowledge is to be expressed, come ultimately from experience. They are derived either directly from sensation or from reflection upon what is given in sensation, or from the mind's activity in compounding ideas derived from sensation into complex rather than simple ideas. Much of eighteenth-century empiricism was given over to the question of the limits of human understanding, a problem that is essentially that of delimiting the kinds of ideas

[8] Cf. the notion of a sense *datum* that has played such a large part in twentieth-century empiricist discussions of perception. See further Ch. 6.

that we can have; and it sought to show that our under-standing of all ideas must somehow be based on expe-rience. This was sometimes portrayed as an attempt to answer skepticism. Berkeley, for example, claimed that his views prevented skepticism and gave "certainty to knowledge,"[9] in part because if all our ideas are derived from experience there is no room for speculation con-cerning what lies beyond the senses; for we could have no conception of such a thing. Hume reasons similarly in his *Treatise of Human Nature,* arguing that every idea (or at least every simple idea) is a copy of some im-pression either of the senses or of reflection, both of which he often speaks of as perceptions. Berkeley, how-ever, gives another reason for the view that his theory combats skepticism—that ideas given in perception are the objects of what he calls "immediate perception" as contrasted with mediate perception. Thus he claims that when we hear a coach passing in the street we hear the coach only mediately; what we immediately perceive are certain sensations of hearing. Immediate perception is certain because it is inference-free. Hume treats his sim-ple impressions in the same spirit. There is the assump-tion running right through these discussions that error and uncertainty are due to the mind's own operations; there is in perception something given that is not in any way a product of the mind's operations and must there-fore be free from error. This provides certainty.

What is central, therefore, to this form of empiricism is the idea that perception is at some point or other in-dubitable. It is free from the possibility of error, because error has no place in what is "given"; it is due to, say, the imagination or the frailty of human judgment. Be-cause certain truths are given in experience, they can-not be false; they are indubitable because they are in a sense necessarily true. This is, in a way, much more clearly so in modern versions of empiricism, because in these there has been more emphasis on the fact that ex-

[9] G. Berkeley, *Principles of Human Knowledge,* secs. 86ff.

perience is a source of knowledge expressible *in proposi-tions.* The eighteenth-century emphasis on ideas tends to obscure the point that the content of knowledge con-sists of *truths,* and truths are expressible in propositions. Hence the search for certainty is essentially a search for indubitable truths. This emerges more clearly in modern empiricism.

Empiricism in respect to knowledge of truths (as opposed to empiricism in respect to concepts or ideas) might be thought to be simply the thesis that all knowl-edge comes ultimately from experience. Few philoso-phers, however, have been inclined to maintain this thesis in this general form; for truths of mathematics and of logic do not seem to be known on the basis of experience, or at least not in any obvious and direct way. (J. S. Mill is one of the few exceptions to this rule, since he held that the truths of mathematics and of logic were just very highly confirmed and universal generalizations from experience.[10] On the other hand, it is commonly held that truths of mathematics and of logic do not state facts of a substantial kind about the world. Hence, em-piricism might be said to be the thesis that all knowledge of a substantial kind about the world is derived from ex-perience. Even so, much would need to be said about the sense of "derived" in question, and there has been much argument by philosophers within the empiricist tradition about how scientific statements of the kind represented by laws of nature can be said to be known from experi-ence. It has sometimes been said that it is better to state the issue not in terms of how truths are known but in terms of how they are verified. There is of course some connection between knowledge and verification. Since verification is the process of showing a proposition to be true, it seems to follow that if a given proposition can be verified it can be known to be true; it is not so obvious that the converse is the case, since there may be some

10 J. S. Mill, *System of Logic* (London, 1843, 8th ed., 1872), II, Chs. 5 and 6.

truths, e.g., about the feelings that one is having, that it makes no sense to speak of verifying, although they may be said to be known. At all events, in terms of verification, empiricism as so far presented would be the thesis that all propositions other than those about mathematics or logic are verifiable by reference to experience. (This is indeed a central thesis of the theory known as positivism; there is a close connection between empiricism and positivism.)

In order to provide a reply to the skeptic in furnishing a certain and indubitable basis for knowledge, one needs in addition the thesis that experience can provide a direct and certain verification of some propositions, and that the other propositions that form the body of accepted knowledge have these as their bases. Thus empiricism in its strongest version comes down to the thesis that the indubitable propositions that must form the bases of the defense of knowledge against the skeptic are to be found in experience. Other truths are built up from these in a variety of ways, but the details of the particular ways in which they are so built up is in general of less importance than the fact that the ways in question must provide a rational basis for an assessment of the truths in question in the light of the original basic propositions on which the others are founded. As I have already said, there has been much argument within the empiricist tradition about the ways in which scientific truths are to be verified; but the same applies to the verification of any propositions that go beyond direct reports of experience. Thus there is even a problem about the verification of propositions about so-called material objects, since these propositions are not propositions about experience alone; they go beyond direct reports of experience. This problem has generated a number of theories like that of phenomenalism, which will be discussed under the heading "perception" in Chapter 6.

The question that requires attention here is whether there are any propositions that constitute direct reports on experience and that are indubitably true. That there are such propositions has been a basic tenet of modern empiricism, although the question of how they are to be identified has been much disputed. They have been referred to as basic propositions, or sometimes (more usually by positivists such as Neurath and Carnap) as protocol propositions. (They have often been taken to correspond to sense data propositions, but since the term "sense datum" is a technical one belonging explicitly to the philosophy of perception, it will be discussed under the heading "sense data and appearances" in Chapter 6, and I shall not have recourse to it here; the notion of a *datum* is important, however, as it implies reference to what is "given" in experience and is not a construct on our part.) The question of what if anything counts as a basic proposition has gone through many vicissitudes in the writings of A. J. Ayer, who has been perhaps the leading British empiricist in modern times. His paper entitled "Basic Propositions"[11] is something of a last-ditch defense of the notion and provides an illuminating discussion of the issues.

Ayer begins by referring to the view that unless something is certain, nothing can be even probable. He ends by saying that doubt cannot be excluded completely, but there comes a point at which doubt becomes neurotic because interminable; and at this point "it ceases to be of any theoretical importance." In effect, doubt cannot be excluded completely because there is always the issue of whether language has been properly fitted to the world; there is always the possibility of at least a verbal mistake, like that involved in misusing a word or, more particularly, like the slip of the tongue involved in applying the wrong name to something. The possibility of this kind of mistake is inevitable because of what language is, because there must always be a gap between language and the world, which gap has to be crossed in applying language to the world. It might still be held that in making

[11] A. J. Ayer, "Basic Propositions," in *Philosophical Essays*, (London, 1954), pp. 105ff. (New York, 1954).

this kind of mistake one is not involved in substantial error. One really knows what is what; the mistake lies in the expression of knowledge only, and it is therefore for present purposes trivial. One important question is whether this is so, and we shall come back to it in due course.

After going into a number of issues that are preliminary to the main one, Ayer points to the view that statements that refer only to the content of present experience are such that we cannot possibly be mistaken about them. But how can this be so? Cannot one always misdescribe one's experience? Given that "I see what I see, feel what I feel, experience what I experience," it does not follow that I know what I am seeing, etc., since I may misdescribe what I am experiencing. In what does misdescription consist? Clearly it is more than misnaming. Ayer considers the possibility that "to describe anything is to relate it to something else, not necessarily to anything in the future, or to anything that other people experience, but at least to something that one has oneself experienced in the past."[12] In that case the relation in question may not obtain, and then there is misdescription. But Ayer rejects this suggestion on the grounds that it does not follow from the ascription of a given predicate to a thing that there are in fact any other members of the class of things in question. There is, in other words, nothing logically wrong with the idea that a description should be applicable to one thing only. Ayer is surely right in this, although there is always the presumption that the existence of other things of the same kind is possible. Ayer's own answer to the question of what description consists in is that I describe something "not by relating it to anything else, but by indicating that a certain word applies to it in virtue of a meaning rule of the language."[13] Meaning rules are those rules of a language that correlate signs in the language with actual situations, and

[12] Ibid., p. 116.
[13] Ibid., p. 119–20.

ultimately these rules will be learned ostensively. That is to say that in order to come to understand how language gets application to the world there must be *some* expressions whose application I learn not through their definition in terms of other expressions but through a simple correlation between them and their applications; the teaching of the rules for the use of these expressions will be ostensive in that it will be enough for someone to point to the thing in question while uttering the expression. This will not be true of all expressions, of course; to understand the majority of words I shall have to understand other things in order to understand what is being said by the use of the word. We have here a distinction parallel to the distinction between simple and complex ideas in earlier empiricism. With simple expressions, it is implied, their meaning is given purely ostensively, without reference to the meaning of any other expressions. We can understand "table," for example, only if we also understand "furniture," but we can understand "green" purely by reference to a color chart.

Given all this, Ayer puts forward the view that basic propositions are those "whose truth or falsehood is conclusively established, in a given situation, by a meaning rule of the language."[14] This will not give absolute certainty, since we can always misapply the rules. Yet in the ordinary way, of course, there always comes a point at which it is no longer plausible to suppose that such errors of procedure have occurred. Hence if what Ayer says is true, the possibility of there being propositions that are basic on the account given by him will provide all the certainty that is possible; to continue to doubt is neurotic. The big question is whether what Ayer says is true. It is to be noted that if it *were* true there would be the possibility of there being propositions about the world whose truth or falsity is determined purely by their meaning. This is a curious feature in itself. One account of so-called analytic truths (those that are logically

14 Ibid., p. 123.

true)[15] is that they are true solely in virtue of the meanings of the terms involved, and this would suggest that Ayer's basic propositions are in a sense analytic or logically true (shades of Leibniz!); yet they purport to be the most basic form of empirical proposition. A possible objection to this would be that when it is said that analytic propositions are true in virtue of the meanings of the terms involved, a different sense of "meaning" is involved than that employed in speaking of "meaning rules." In the latter case the meaning is the application or reference of the term in question, while in the former case it is the connotation of the terms that is in question, something that is explicable by means of definitions involving other words, not ostensively. I do not think that this objection will do. Ayer does not suppose that meaning rules involve an out-of-the-ordinary sense of "meaning." It is noticeable that Ayer's meaning rules are very close to *naming* rules. He has already rejected the suggestion that misdescribing is misnaming; but it does look as if misapplying a meaning rule and misdescribing something in consequence is very little more than using the wrong word in reference to something in the way in which one would use the wrong word if one called someone by the wrong name. But in fact words like "green" are not used like the word "Green" when the latter is a man's name. There is something very wrong with the whole idea of ostensive definition and with the notion of a meaning rule as Ayer uses it.

These last points are implicit in Wittgenstein's discussion at the outset of his *Philosophical Investigations*. Indeed, Wittgenstein's purpose there is to refute the idea that the meaning of a word is its reference—a view that he had previously held himself. He uses the notion of a language game for this purpose (a notion that will be discussed further in Chapter 3); this involves attention to specific and sometimes isolated uses of language apart from the complex structure that language as a whole

[15] See further Ch. 9, sec. (b).

forms. A situation, for example, may be envisaged in which one man says to another "Slab" or "Beam" or "Block," whereupon the other brings the object in question. Taken by itself this language game is such that we cannot understand "Slab," for example, as we might understand "slab" in the context of propositions describing or referring to slabs. What this brings out in turn is how much our understanding of individual expressions presupposes a wider web of understanding of what is going on, and in particular how what is going on is related to the forms of life that the people involved instance. If one reflects farther along these lines it will become evident that one could not come to understand the expression "green," for example, through someone's pointing to a green expanse while saying the word, unless much else were understood first. One would need to know that the other person was talking, not just uttering noises, that he was describing something, not doing the variety of other things that he might be doing with language, that he was describing the color of the expanse, not its area, shape, and so on.[16] It follows from all this that the notion of a meaning rule in Ayer's sense is far too simple-minded a notion, and that no expression gets its meaning simply in that way. It follows too that there can be no proposition whose truth or falsity is determined purely by meaning rules of this kind.

Ayer's purpose has been to attribute a kind of necessity to basic propositions, from which their certainty would follow. Thus his program has something in common with the rationalist programs to which it is in some ways quite opposed. For the same reasons as those for which the rationalist programs failed this must fail also. Ayer's argument is important in that it makes explicit the urge to make error in the case of basic propositions impossible. It is to be noted that he is prepared to leave

[16] See also P. Geach, *Mental Acts* (New York and London, 1957), secs. 10 and 11 for similar considerations about color concepts.

for further investigation the question of whether language is such that there *are* basic propositions of this kind; he also leaves room for error of a kind, in that it is always possible to misapply the rules, but the implication is that this kind of mistake is unimportant. This is where the likeness between Ayer's meaning rules and rules for the use of proper names becomes apparent. To misapply a proper name normally has no serious consequences other than social ones; for in doing this one will not have given any wrong information except about the name (though it has to be admitted that many erroneous suggestions may be implied in the wrong use of a name). But in the use of a descriptive expression like "green," information, right or wrong, is always given. Even if Ayer is right in saying that it is not part of the implication of a descriptive expression that there are other things to which the expression may be applied apart from the one to which it is currently being applied, the use of the expression nevertheless classifies the thing to which it is applied *in a certain respect;* misuse of the expression is therefore never really trivial, and it cannot be said that the only mistakes possible in connection with so-called basic propositions are verbal and trivial ones. Mistakes of this kind are always substantial even if they may not always be socially important. In fact it has always been difficult for defenders of basic propositions to provide examples that conform convincingly to the criteria that they lay down.

There is something else that approximates to indubitability that has sometimes been taken to be enough here. This is incorrigibility. There are certainly propositions that are incorrigible by others; they are not subject to checking on the part of other people. Propositions that report various kinds of private experience are of this kind—for example, propositions about the nature and location of one's bodily feelings, or indeed how things appear to one. Even here it is possible for others to become aware that we are not being sincere or that we are using words wrongly; but when factors of this kind are eliminated it remains true that we are the authority for pronouncements on these matters. It has sometimes been suggested (ostensibly following Wittgenstein's view put forward in the *Philosophical Investigations* that pain reports are to be construed as pain behavior) that these apparent statements about private experiences should not be regarded as reports of those experiences at all. There is an air of paradox about such suggestions. It is true that we should have no proper understanding of these propositions apart from the role that their utterances play in our life (the point which, in my view, Wittgenstein was concerned to make); but this does not make them any the less propositions that can be true or false. That, therefore, there are propositions that are incorrigible by others is clear enough; moreover, there is a sense in which they may be incorrigible by ourselves too. If something now appears to me F, but a little later it seems to me that I ought to say that it appears to me G, it does not follow that I was wrong in the first place in saying that it appeared to me F. If I correct the reports on some of my private experiences this is not because new evidence is available to me but because reflection on the situation makes it appropriate to decide that the experience is G rather than F. I might come to realize in this way that the feeling that I am having is a pain, not just an itch. But it remains true that what I felt was an itch.[17] Similarly, the only way in which I could come to correct the statement "That appears to me F" is by the realization that it is more proper to say that it appears to me G; but this does not make my original statement false. It did appear to me F at the time, and even if I might have used the wrong words to express how it appeared to me I could not be mistaken in any other way about how it appeared to me.

Such propositions, however, are of little use as providing the foundations of knowledge. In the first place, what they are about is essentially private, and it is impossible to build knowledge of what is public upon

[17] See further Ch. 8, sec. (b).

them; for the move from the private to the public would have to be justified at some stage. Second, they do not possess the right sort of qualifications for the job in that their incorrigibility does not amount to indubitability of the right kind. It is not, of course, nor could be, a necessary truth that something appears to me F, so that it is not indubitable for that reason; it is not in any way something that I could not intelligibly suppose to be false. It is that if something appears F to me there can be no question for me of its not doing so, and I am the authority for whether it does so or not. Someone else can doubt whether it does appear F to me, but he has ultimately to accept my authority. All this is part of the logic of "appears"; but it provides nothing in the way of indubitable truths on which knowledge in general can be based. In effect we have only the tautology "If something appears F to me it appears F to me."

Even if it were possible to discover basic propositions of the requisite kind, there would still be the question *how* the rest of knowledge is to be built up from them. Since the supposed basic propositions must, on empiricist principles, be propositions concerning objects of perception, this question is most suitably dealt with under the heading "perception," and I shall accordingly leave the matter until Chapter 6.

(c) Common sense and ordinary language

Attempts have been made by Thomas Reid in the eighteenth century and G. E. Moore in this century to base a theory of knowledge on an appeal to common sense. In both cases the philosophers in question were reacting against what they thought were absurd deviations from what common sense tells us on the part of rival philosophers and metaphysicians. Reid reacted against Hume, whose conclusions he thought were absurd although his argument was valid; the trouble had therefore to rest in the premises of his argument—the doctrine of impressions and ideas. Moore was reacting against the idealists. The ostensible difference between the two philosophers was that Reid was overtly concerned with the skepticism that he found in Hume; Moore claimed at any rate that he was never much concerned with skepticism, but rather with the analysis of what we mean when we say, for example, that we perceive material objects independent of ourselves. The refutation of idealism was the first stage in Moore's reaction against idealism toward realism. This having been carried out, it still remained for him a problem what we mean in speaking of knowledge of a material world. Moore's proof of an external world[18] was simply to hold up his hand and declare this as one example of something of whose existence he was certain. Similarly, his "Defence of Common Sense"[19] begins with a long list of things that he is certain he knows. What follows is an elaborate analysis of what is meant by such claims, which brings in all the paraphernalia of sense data, an apparatus that has been part and parcel of the traditional empiricist defenses against skepticism.

There is a certain disingenuity about these Moorean claims not to be influenced by skepticism.[20] There would be equal disingenuity in expecting a skeptic to be impressed by them. After all, the skeptic should be expected to know about common-sense beliefs; the crucial point is that he can produce arguments against them. Arguments can be met only with further and better arguments. The situation is as Wittgenstein put it in his

[18] G. E. Moore, "Proof of an External World," *Proceedings of the British Academy*, XXV (1939), reprinted in his *Philosophical Papers* (New York and London, 1959).

[19] G. E. Moore, "A Defence of Common Sense," *Contemporary British Philosophy*, 2nd Series (New York and London, 1925), reprinted in his *Philosophical Papers*.

[20] Cf. G. E. Moore, *Some Main Problems of Philosophy* (New York and London, 1953), Ch. 1.

Blue Book,[21] "There is no common sense answer to a philosophical problem. One can defend common sense against the attacks of philosophers only by solving their puzzles, i.e., by curing them of the temptation to attack common sense; not by restating the views of common sense." (It is possible to question the point about "curing" them, but the rest is sound enough.) Of course, the appeal to common sense is an excellent first move—though only a first move. It is good that philosophers should be reminded when their views go too far from ordinary beliefs. Nevertheless, it cannot be *assumed* that these deviations cannot be justified, even if the onus of justification is on the deviationist.

Similar things can be said about appeals to ordinary language.[22] There are many reasons for an appeal to how we ordinarily use words—to make clear, for example, that certain metaphysical uses of language are deviationist and require justification, or to bring out the characteristics and implications of the concepts that we use in a given context and that are expressed in certain usages of words—what Ryle has called "logical geography." Austin has argued[23] that ordinary language is the begin-all of philosophy though not the end-all. This is a move like the one I made above in connection with common sense. Ordinary language has evolved in the process of man's attempts to deal by means of language with a great variety and complexity of situations.

[21] L. Wittgenstein, *Blue and Brown Books* (Oxford, 1958), p. 58 (New York, 1958).

[22] Indeed, Norman Malcolm said, in his contribution to *The Philosophy of G. E. Moore,* ed. P. Schilpp (Evanston, Illinois, 1942), pp. 343ff., that the appeal to ordinary language, to what we should ordinarily say in a given situation, was what Moore was really concerned with, although he expressed his point misleadingly. This is not, I think, true, but it is a point worth noting all the same.

[23] J. L. Austin, "A Plea for Excuses," *Proc. Arist. Soc.* (1956–57), pp. 1ff., reprinted in his *Philosophical Papers,* ed. J. O. Urmson and G. J. Warnock (Oxford, 1961), pp. 123ff.

One would expect therefore that it would have become a tool particularly suited for the tasks with which it is concerned; the distinctions, etc., that are enshrined in it are likely to be significant. It embodies, as Austin puts it, "the inherited experience and acumen of many generations of men." To the extent that this says that the beliefs that ordinary language encapsulates are likely for evolutionary reasons to be correct, this says little different from what I said earlier about common sense. But Austin is mainly concerned with what ordinary usage indicates about the ways of thinking and concepts behind it; for it is thus a source of understanding of those concepts. In this it is the first word but not the last.

But even granted that ordinary language is to be presumed to have validity in general it may still be, as Wittgenstein says,[24] that ordinary language "holds our mind rigidly in one position, as it were, and in this position sometimes it feels cramped, having a desire for other positions as well." Such desires require diagnosis, and it cannot be assumed without this that there is nothing in them. There is no quick way with skepticism, and it is certainly no good saying in reply to it "We do not say that" or "We do not ordinarily believe that sort of thing." The skeptic may indeed know this but thinks that he has good reasons for departing from what is ordinarily accepted. If the onus is upon him to prove his case, he still has to be listened to.

(d) Dialectical argument and proof

It has been seen that it is impossible to meet the skeptic by producing indubitable truths that are beyond all possible doubt. In effect this amounts to the point that it is impossible to *prove* the existence of knowledge. This is what the philosophers presenting traditional answers to skepticism were looking for—something that would put

[24] L. Wittgenstein, *Blue and Brown Books*, p. 59.

the case against knowledge completely out of court. But in this they were looking for the wrong thing. Even if it could be shown that there are truths that are beyond even the logical possibility of doubt, this would not help to show that quite ordinary knowledge is possible, unless a link between the privileged truths and ordinary knowledge could be forged; and that there is good reason to doubt the possibility of such a link has been indicated by the discussion of rationalism and empiricism. Even so, the case for the belief that there are privileged truths of the kind in question has not been made. Indeed, to accept the possibility that it might be made is to play the skeptic's own game. It is to accept his suggestions about what is required for knowledge and therefore to proceed on his terms. This is indicated by the fact that the position that it is thought necessary to refute is often put by saying that claims to knowledge are shaky just because any supposed truth that is offered as a candidate for knowledge might conceivably be false.

In reply to this last suggestion it might be asked why it matters that a given proposition might conceivably be false. Surely more than that is required if knowledge is to be put in jeopardy. Is not some argument required that shows that there is reason to believe that the claim that knowledge exists is actually false? In other words, when someone shows skepticism about certain claims to knowledge, what is required is that the ball be put firmly in his court. He is the one who must produce justification for his position. Skepticism without grounds is empty, and empty suggestions need not be regarded seriously. To harp upon the fact that it is always logically possible that we might be wrong is empty in this sense; if we are to take it seriously we must be offered reasons why we should pay attention. This is not to say that a skeptic may not on occasion be able to offer such reasons, and in that case we have to listen to what he has to say and proceed accordingly. I have already said something about the extent to which universal skepticism is possible. A positive claim that it is possible is self-stultifying since it involves being definite about skepticism itself. But a skeptic does not have to be definite in this way. He may merely ask questions, and once again questions demand an answer as long as they are serious. But unless reasons are offered for any assessment, on either side, it is impossible to proceed with any hope of a result.

Thus if proof of the possibility of knowledge is neither necessary nor required, there is still room for argument of a kind that might be called "dialectical" in a sense laid down by Aristotle. That is to say that parties to the discussion must agree upon something if argument is to proceed; they must at least agree upon what is to count as a good reason. Given this, discussion can proceed. But the onus is upon the skeptic to prove his case, not upon the defender of knowledge. This is because the very existence of the concept of knowledge creates a presumption that knowledge exists—indeed, more than this. Wittgenstein said, as I noted earlier, that there must be agreement in judgments and not only in definitions if language is to be a means of communication. If we are to speak significantly of knowledge we must not only have agreement as to how knowledge is to be defined but some kind of agreement also on what is to be counted as knowledge. Questions about knowledge arise against this common understanding. This is not to say that parts of this common understanding may not turn out to be wrong; and the recognition of this may produce modifications in and even additions to our understanding. Thus the recognition that the concept of phlogiston had no application involved in its turn an improvement in men's understanding of physical matter. But the situation is different with a concept like "knowledge." To suppose that a concept of this kind had no application would imply such a vast and general ramification of modifications in our concepts that it is difficult to see how in such circumstances discussion could get under way. The possibility of knowledge is presupposed in the very possibility of argument, in the very possibility of having recourse to reasons. For what would it mean to say that X was a reason for Y unless it could be known whether the truth of X had any bearing on the truth of Y. Thus given the kind of concept that the concept of knowledge is, a willingness to enter upon discussion about its possibility presupposes or implies a willingness to accept that very possibility. If knowledge is not possible, how can discussion about its possibility have any hope of reaching a conclusion? How can it even take place? The parties involved might mouth words, but this would not be *discussion*. Thus the skeptic who doubts the possibility of knowledge in general is in the position of Aristotle's skeptic who doubts the principle of contradiction; he only has to be made to say something, and he is convicted out of his own mouth. He cannot both doubt the principle and enter upon discussion to support his case.[25] Nor can the skeptic who doubts knowledge in general. Merely to question the possibility of knowledge in general thus remains, as noted at the end of Chapter 1, a possible practice, but it becomes an empty form when, as we now see, it is impossible to back it with reasons. The existence of knowledge is thus a precondition of any rational discussion of its possibility. In this sense its existence cannot be rationally questioned.

It may still be possible for someone to doubt and raise questions about *particular* claims to knowledge or *particular kinds* of claims to knowledge. The doubt about claims to know anything about phlogiston was not only possible, it turned out to be right. But what about doubts about the claims of perception, memory, etc. to provide knowledge? Here again the implications of such doubts are extremely radical; they have vast ramifications. Because of the roles that perception, memory, etc. play in our life, because they are so essential to it and to the possibility of knowledge in general, skepticism about the epistemological roles of perception, memory, etc. needs to be justified. To remove the reasons for such doubts

[25] See Aristotle, *Metaphysics*, IV 4.

is the defense, indeed the only defense that is needed here. Such doubts may arise from misconceptions about what knowledge involves, or similar misconceptions about the nature of perception, memory, etc. That is why a conceptual investigation of these concepts is so important.

CHAPTER 3

Meaning
and Meaningfulness

(a) Knowledge and concepts

One way of excluding certain claims to knowledge from the corpus of knowledge proper is to say that what is expressed in such claims is meaningless. To say that we or someone else knows that X is F is to imply that there is such a thing as F for X to be; and similarly for claims to knowledge of other forms. Someone cannot be said to know that X is F if he has no idea of what it is for something to be F. Thus many kinds of knowledge (if not all of them) presuppose that the person who knows has certain relevant kinds of understanding, certain ideas or concepts, which form the basis of the knowledge and in terms of which the knowledge is to be formulated or expressed. Knowledge that something or other is the case is normally formulable in propositions. But this is not to say that the person who knows can himself formulate or produce propositions of this kind. His knowledge may be implicit only and unexpressed even to himself. It is perfectly intelligible to say of someone that he knows, for example, that his wife is unfaithful to him although he has not admitted this to himself, and would not express that knowledge to himself even in private. It is also intelligible to say of someone that he knows something implicitly rather than explicitly when he has at his disposal all the materials necessary for the solution of a problem, when he has been through them, has drawn all the necessary inferences, etc., but has just not bothered to formulate to himself the final solution, although he could easily do so if required. But we could not intelligibly say that he knew all this if he had no idea what would be meant by the solution. Thus knowledge presupposes a certain understanding; it presupposes that the person who knows has the relevant concepts or ideas, concepts that might conceivably be formulated in verbal terms so that the knowledge could be expressed in a proposition or propositions. To put the matter another way, one who knows that p must have at his disposal all the materials for knowledge that p, in that he must have the relevant concepts. To have a concept of F is to know what it is for something to be F. Thus knowledge of facts presupposes other forms of knowledge, those involved in having concepts; and whether or not a person has these prior forms of knowledge may itself emerge in what things of a factual kind he can be said to know, perhaps indeed in what propositions he will assent to.[1]

It is possible, however, for someone to think that he knows something but in fact not know it simply because he has no real understanding of what is involved. (This is just one of many ways in which the claim that someone knows something may fail.) This may indeed hold good of whole classes of people or perhaps of every one up to a certain point of historical time. It is a common enough philosophical criticism of certain claims to knowledge (e.g., knowledge about certain theological issues) that the claims cannot be valid because the terms in which they are expressed are unintelligible. In other

[1] Cf. P. Geach, *Mental Acts* (London, 1957), pp. 11ff. (New York, 1957), though I do not agree with his view that the possession of concepts must be restricted to language users.

words, people think that they understand something by certain words, but this is an illusion. This may be because words are used, like tools, for purposes for which they were never intended. But however it comes about, it is clearly possible for people to think that they have understanding where they have none. What is peculiar to certain philosophical criticisms of this kind is that they are directed not just to particular people or classes of people, but to whole sets of supposed concepts or ideas; they attack the very idea that there is any intelligibility in certain kinds of claim to knowledge. This is well exemplified in Hume's outburst in the *Enquiry Concerning Human Understanding*,[2] "If we take in our hand any volume; of divinity or school metaphysics, for instance; let us ask, *Does it contain any abstract reasoning concerning quantity or number?* No. *Does it contain any experimental reasoning concerning matter of fact and existence?* No. Commit it then to the flames: for it can contain nothing but sophistry and illusion." For it is not that such a book will contain merely false beliefs; it is that it will contain nothing that is really intelligible. Hume's declaration comes at the end of a work on the human *understanding*, the purpose of which was to set out the limits of that understanding, to make clear just what can be an object of that understanding and what cannot.

Hume's program is in this respect a typically eighteenth-century one; it is the culmination of the "new way of ideas" to show that all our ideas come in one way or another from experience, and that there could be no idea of which this was not true. Thus anything that purports to be an idea and which cannot be said to be derived from experience is not in fact a genuine idea, not a genuine object of the understanding. Thus the program sets out limits of intelligibility, and for that reason forbids us to suppose that certain supposed claims

[2] D. Hume, *Enquiry Concerning Human Understanding*, Sec. XII, Part III.

to knowledge can be claims to knowledge at all. For anything that is supposed to be knowledge must surely make sense. There is thus another aspect to empiricism apart from the supposal discussed in the last chapter, that experience can provide knowledge based on indubitable propositions, or that all claims to knowledge must in the end be based on such propositions. Empiricism typically involves also the thesis that all bona fide ideas must be derived from experience, or, in more general terms, that there are limits to what is intelligible, in that a condition of something being an intelligible notion is that it must be derived from or cashable in terms of experience in some way.

There are at least two sorts of objection to a thesis of this kind. The first accepts the terms of reference presupposed by the empiricist thesis but disputes the conclusions; the second disputes the terms of reference themselves. The first sort of objection is one to the effect that there are clearly some concepts that are not derivable from experience. Not all concepts or ideas are, as it is put, a posteriori; some are a priori, independent of experience. Philosophers who have not accepted the empiricist thesis in this respect have been quick to point to the concepts of logic and mathematics, as well as such concepts as those of space, time, and causality. There are at least two sorts of consideration that are relevant here, of which the second is the more fundamental. In the first place, some concepts, e.g., that of a triangle or straight line, do not seem to be derivable from experience because nothing in experience strictly conforms to the properties of a triangle or straight line (a point on which Plato relied in setting up his Theory of Forms). In this way the concepts in question are at best idealizations of what is to be met with in experience. Second, and more fundamentally, having the relevant sort of experience presupposes already having certain understandings. Thus it cannot be argued, as Locke supposed it could be, that the idea of time can be derived from experience. To say that we can notice one thing happening after another, that there is given in experience the notion of temporal succession,[3] invites the question of how we could have such an experience at all if we did not know what it was for something to follow another in time. To have the experience of one thing following another is not the same as having successive experiences; the things so experienced must be experienced within a framework of temporal relationships having certain logical properties (the relation of "following after" is transitive and asymmetrical; i.e., if A is after B and B is after C, A is after C, and moreover if A is after B, B cannot be after A). How could the knowledge that these relationships obtain be derived solely from experience? This is not to say, as has sometimes been supposed, that we must therefore have an innate idea of time that is applied to experience. Rather, as Kant said, we build up our idea of temporal relationships *through* experience, but not *from* experience. It may be true that we should have no idea of time if we were not aware of temporal succession, but this does not imply necessarily that we get that idea *from* the experience of temporal succession. The acquisition of the idea of time is a complicated affair, involving the recognition of one's own identity through time as well as that of some things around us; for one thing's following another can only be recognized against a continuing point of reference. Experience is necessary for this, but the idea of time is not a simple abstraction from the features of experience. The idea of triangularity involves a similar web of interrelationships with other ideas, and the particular interrelationships involved explain why nothing in experience strictly conforms to the properties of a triangle. It is for this reason that I said that my second point was the more fundamental.

The line of argument followed here could be generalized, and this takes us to the second objection to the

[3] Cf. A. J. Ayer, *The Problem of Knowledge,* Penguin edition (London, 1956), p. 152 (New York, 1956).

empiricist thesis, the one that disputes its very terms of reference. In what I have said so far there has been presupposed in the objections made to the empiricist thesis a distinction between ideas that might be derived from experience and those that cannot be so derived, a distinction between a posteriori ideas or concepts and a priori ones. This whole distinction is to be questioned. The issues are the same as those involved in the discussion of ostensive definition and meaning rules in the previous chapter. Just as a color expression cannot be explained simply by pointing to instances of the given color without some further understanding of what is going on—that the noise is a linguistic expression, that it is used to describe a color, not a shape, etc.—so the understanding of a color concept cannot be derived simply from having a number of experiences from which the idea of, say, redness is abstracted. Indeed, for an experience to be one *of* red it is necessary that the person concerned should already know what it is for something to be red—that is, to have the concept of red. We need experiences, of course, in order to come to know what it is for something to be red, since this knowledge includes not only knowing how red is related to other colors and things of this sort but also knowing what things count as red. But once again this does not mean that the concept of redness is simply derived or abstracted from red things or from experiences that we have in the presence of red things. If this is so, the whole distinction between a priori and a posteriori ideas becomes suspect; the distinctions where they exist are ones of degree, not of kind, depending on the degree to which experience is relevant to our understanding of the concept in question.

Given this, the empiricist claim to put bounds on the intelligibility of candidates for the status of idea or concept has to be rejected. This is not to say that there are no such bounds; there is, for example, the criterion of logical coherence; if any supposed concept is to be an intelligible and acceptable one, it must be logically coherent. Similarly, the ways in which certain concepts are given application may be unintelligible for one reason or another. Such considerations may give rise to a system of categories such that the conflation of a concept from one category with another taken from another category may give rise to nonsense of one kind or another.[4] To speak of categories of this kind is to make reference to a system of rough distinctions between classes of concepts with different logical characters or with different kinds of involvement with other concepts. Ryle has claimed, for example, that the concept of perception comes from a different category from that of activity for the reason, among others, that it is impossible to speak without nonsense of seeing something "slowly or rapidly, systematically or haphazardly."[5] Such linguistic nuances may provide clues to the different kinds of implications that the concepts in question may have, and these may sometimes be so great as to warrant the title of logical differences (e.g., as that between a class and its members). Except in cases such as the last, it is doubtful whether many categories are really firm; they provide at best a rough system of classifications of kinds of distinction, the blurring of which may give rise to different kinds of nonsense. Even so, the notion of "nonsense" itself is at best a relative one; even the most weird of linguistic expressions may be given a significant use in some context or other. It is in fact doubtful whether many, if any, philosophical issues turn on questions of meaning rather than truth. Once again, if a philosophical position about knowledge or about any other matter is to be ruled out of court, argument is

[4] Cf. G. Ryle, "Categories," *Proc. Arist. Soc.* (1937–38), pp. 181ff., reprinted in *Logic and Language,* ed. A. G. N. Flew (Oxford, 1953), II 65ff. (Garden City, New York, 1953).

[5] G. Ryle, *The Concept of Mind* (London, 1949), pp. 151–52 (New York, 1949). See also J. Passmore, *Philosophical Reasoning* (London, 1961), Ch. 7.

required for that conclusion; it cannot be dealt with at one fell swoop by appeal to some criterion of meaningfulness in terms of which the position in question can be eliminated because meaningless.

(b) Meaning and verification

Similar considerations apply to twentieth-century positivist attempts to eliminate certain philosophical positions by an appeal to the verifiability criterion of meaning, i.e., by appeal to the view that if a proposition or statement is to be meaningful it must be empirically verifiable unless it is logically necessary. Positivism has now gone so far out of fashion that it is perhaps difficult to understand why anyone should have ever supposed that it should be acceptable. Nevertheless, it cannot be denied that the verifiability theory of meaning has a certain seductiveness, and tough-minded, empirically-inclined philosophers always show a tendency toward it. It is seductive in that if someone says something such that there is no way of telling whether what he says is true or false, there is an inevitable temptation to ask what he has said. The answer must in fact depend on what it was intended should be said. It is only if the saying was a candidate for truth or falsity that it matters whether it is true or false; it is only if it is something that *can* be shown to be true or false that it matters whether there is a way of telling whether it is true or false. Even if it fails these tests, it does not follow that it fails the test of meaningfulness. The temptations of positivism arise from the easiness of sliding from one consideration to another, from truth to ways of telling the truth, and from this to meaningfulness. At the best, an emphasis on empirical verification is relevant to certain kinds of statement, not to statements in general.

The origins of modern logical positivism are in effect to be found in Wittgenstein's remark in the *Tractatus*

Logico-Philosophicus,[6] that to understand a proposition is to know what it is like for it to be true. But the philosophers who took this up—the philosophers of the so-called Vienna Circle, Schlick, Carnap, etc.—were already positivists who followed the tradition of Ernst Mach's approach to the philosophy of science. In that context it may be relevant to exclude certain statements from the language of science, on the grounds that they do no useful scientific work or that they are empty of scientific content. Even so, it is a further and larger step to the position that such statements are meaningless, and it is interesting that one of the more influential philosophers of science in this century—Karl Popper—did not take this step, preferring to take falsifiability (the converse of verifiability) as providing a line of demarcation between the scientific and nonscientific, not between the meaningful and meaningless. Indeed, a quick way of dealing with the positivist claims about meaningfulness is to say that we already have to understand what a proposition means before we can raise the question of its verification.

In addition, it could be said that questions of meaning are questions that arise with regard to *sentences* (or of course the words that go to make up sentences), not to propositions or statements.[7] Why, if a sentence is grammatically or syntactically unobjectionable and if the individual expressions can be given meaning, should one need a further principle concerned with the meaningfulness of any statement made by its means? There are cases, of course, where we understand the words that a man uses and see that they have meaning, but where we should say that we do not understand what

[6] L. Wittgenstein, *Tractatus Logico-Philosophicus,* new trans. by D. F. Pears and B. F. McGuinness (New York and London, 1961), 4.024. For the views of Karl Popper referred to later in this paragraph, see, e.g., his *Conjectures and Refutations* (London, 1963), esp. pp. 253ff. (New York, 1963).

[7] Cf. P. F. Strawson, "On Referring," *Mind,* N.S. (1950), pp. 320ff., reprinted in *Essays in Conceptual Analysis,* ed. A. G. N. Flew (London, 1956), pp. 21ff. (New York, 1956).

he means by what he says. We might even say that we do not understand him, or why he says *that*. There is a distinction to be made between *what a man means by what he says* and *what it is that what he says means*. Indeed, only if linguistic expressions have meaning can people mean things by them, however much it is also the case that unless people intended to communicate or express themselves, language would not exist.[8] Thus, although it may be possible to claim with some plausibility that in a context where verifiability is demanded (e.g., in certain areas of science), we should not understand what a man says if he says something unverifiable in principle, this should not be elevated into a general principle of meaningfulness. In those cases our failure to understand would be because of the fact that what he says is empty, it makes no difference to anything.[9] The objection to these cases would be that the assertions in question do not perform the function that is expected of them in this context. This is not in itself an objection on the score of meaninglessness.

In fact, the original positivist principles that the meaning of a statement is the method of its verification and that all nonlogical statements must be verifiable if they are to be meaningful, had to be progressively relaxed. In the first place, there are difficulties about what is to count as empirical verification, difficulties that are akin to, if not the same as, those involved in the notion of basic propositions discussed in the previous chapter. Second, there are difficulties in formulating the principle

[8] Compare and contrast H. P. Grice, "Meaning," *Phil. Rev.* LXVI (1957), pp. 377ff., reprinted in *Philosophical Logic,* ed. P. F. Strawson (London, 1967), pp. 39ff.

[9] Cf. the contraction, undetectable in principle, that was postulated as an immediate reaction to the Michelson-Morley experiment in pre-Einsteinian physics. The very fact that such a contraction was in principle undetectable led to Einstein's prima facie positivist move of restricting meaningful statements about simultaneity to those in which there is a method of measuring such simultaneity.

in such a way that it excludes what it was intended to exclude, e.g., metaphysics, but includes what it was intended to include, e.g., science. But these are in a sense technical difficulties, and are signs of the more fundamental difficulty that verifiability cannot be a criterion of meaningfulness in general. It might be argued, however, despite what has been said so far, that it is a criterion of the meaningfulness of empirical statements. The argument might go as follows. An understanding of words implies among other things an ability to apply them to things. If the words in question are empirical expressions, we shall need experience in order to apply them correctly (indeed, this is what constitutes an empirical expression like, for example, "red"). Hence it might be suggested that a necessary condition of our understanding empirical statements is that we should be able to verify them or at least know in general how they might be verified—and that this is a truism based on the meaning of "empirical."[10] It is *not*, however, a truism. There is in the argument as I have presented it a move from words to statements. To say that a word is an empirical expression is to say that we need experience in order to understand it fully, but to say that a statement is empirical is to say something different about the kinds of consideration that would show it to be true, i.e., the kinds of ways in which it might be verified. Hence verifiability by reference to experience might be a criterion of a statement's being an empirical statement,

[10] Thus R. W. Ashby (in his chapter on "Logical Positivism" in *A Critical History of Western Philosophy*, ed. D. J. O'Connor [New York, 1964], p. 496) says "Hence it seems to be at least a necessary condition for understanding a descriptive statement that one should be able to recognize the sensory experience that would verify it." Ashby speaks of a descriptive statement rather than an empirical one. The notion of a descriptive statement is clearly wider than that of an empirical one, but Ashby obviously means to restrict it to statements that describe empirical matters of fact. (Ashby's chapter also discusses the technical difficulties that beset the verification principle and gives references for further reading.)

but it is not a criterion of its having anything that might be called "empirical *meaningfulness.*"

What distinguishes one kind of statement from another (e.g., empirical statements from other kinds of statements) are, as indicated, the sorts of consideration that would show it to be true; these are what are termed its criteria of truth. To understand what type of statement a given statement is, we need to know its criteria of truth. It is important to note that we are concerned here with the *sorts* of consideration that show a statement to be true; that is what distinguishes truth conditions, the sorts of circumstances in which a statement is true, from what might be called verification conditions, the actual circumstances which would show it to be true. To know the truth conditions of a statement we have to see that statement in its context with all the implications of that context; we thus have to appreciate the form of discourse of which it is part. Fully to understand what is meant by a given statement we have to know all this, and that is why Wittgenstein's remark in his *Tractatus*—that if we are to understand a proposition we must know what is the case if it is true—is a quite proper one. But none of this is to say that to understand a proposition we must know how it might in fact be verified. It is at the most to understand the kind of thing that would be relevant by way of verification. There is thus a thin line between the notions of criteria of truth and verification, over which it is easy to step; but the line exists without doubt.

(c) *Meaning and use*

I have spoken in the previous section of "forms of discourse," and these have implications concerning the kinds of use to which people put language and linguistic expressions. The idea that meaning has something to do with use stems, in modern times, from the later Wittgenstein, and it brings with it in his philosophy other ideas, especially what he called "forms of life," with the suggestion that language should be thought of as something that is part of human behavior, that it is a human institution, and that meaning should be thought of in connection with what human beings mean by what they say. I have already indicated that what a word means cannot be simply identified with what someone means by it. Meaning in general presupposes the idea of people meaning things, although they can mean things by *words* only if words in general have meaning. It could be said that the meaning of a word is what is normally meant by it, and the use of "normally" here indicates how necessary the reference to a social context is to an understanding of the notion of meaning. At all events, if the meaning of a word cannot be identified with what anyone in particular means by it, meaning is a function of human practices and human institutions; hence the importance of Wittgenstein's reference to forms of life, and equally his invocation of the notion of language games.

Before considering this last notion, however, it is important to be clear about the different things that might be meant in speaking of the use of words. There is, first, what Ryle has called "usage,"[11] or what Austin has referred to as "what we should say when,"[12] the varying contexts or circumstances in which words can occur significantly. This sense of "use" is equivalent to "parlance" in the phrase "common parlance." There is, second, the role or function that words can have either within language as such or in connection with other human institutions; thus we may speak of certain expressions as having a referring use, and we can speak of the use of, say, the word "Amen" within religious ceremony or ritual. Finally,

[11] G. Ryle, "Ordinary Language," *Phil. Rev.* LXII (1953), pp. 167ff., and "Use, Usage and Meaning," *Proc. Arist. Soc.*, Suppl. Vol. (1961), pp. 223ff.

[12] J. L. Austin, "A Plea for Excuses," *Proc. Arist. Soc.* (1956–57), p. 7, reprinted in his *Philosophical Papers,* pp. 123ff.

there is that sense of "use" that is equivalent to purpose or point; we may speak of the use of words to bring about a certain result, or we may say that the point of certain words is to bring about these results. Austin has claimed that one snag in speaking of use is that it does not bring out the different kinds of use that words may have; he has laid weight also on the different kinds of "force" that locutions may have—the force a set of expressions may have as a locution (locutionary force), the force they may have when their utterance has a role as a certain kind of performance (illocutionary force; cf. the role of the utterance "promise," which itself constitutes promising and not merely saying of oneself that one is promising), and the force that the utterance of a set of expressions may have in bringing about certain results (perlocutionary force).[13]

Wittgenstein did not generally go into such refinements. In speaking of "use," as he frequently did, he had in mind most often function, purpose, or point. (Indeed, he sometimes uses those very words.) It is in these respects that his notion of language games becomes important. A language game is a specific (often restricted) activity carried on with language. The restricted forms of language game thus serve to isolate and highlight the different roles that linguistic expressions can play and the purposes for which they may be used. The first instance of such a game that Wittgenstein invokes in the *Philosophical Investigations* has been referred to in Chapter 2. It is that in which one man calls out "Slab" or "Beam" or "Block," and another man gets the relevant thing. If the game is taken by itself without reference to the rest of language, it would be wrong to say that the word "slab" is in this game the name of a kind of thing and that the speaker is ordering the other man to get something that has this name. Wittgenstein's purpose is to undermine the assumption that words have just one role—reference; and the con-

[13] J. L. Austin, *How to do Things with Words* (Cambridge, Massachusetts, and Oxford, 1962). Cf. J. Searle, *Speech Acts* (Cambridge, 1969).

struction of different language games serves to bring out the many different roles that language can have and the different purposes to which it can be put.[14] At the same time, however, it has to be asked what makes these games *language* games. Why, for example, do we not take the words used in the game just mentioned as mere noises that act like signals, on receipt of which the appropriate response follows, just as an animal may respond differentially to different noises as a result of training? What, in other words, makes a use of language a use of *language*? This is a very large question, into which I cannot go here, but it brings out the point that I have labored all along —that the use of language *presupposes* the idea that linguistic expressions have meaning, and that meaning cannot be fully elucidated by or reduced to use. Language involves an elaborate system of rules—rules of meaning, grammatical and syntactical rules, and so on. These rules must conform to criteria of objectivity; they must not be merely subjective or idiosyncratic. They must therefore be interpersonal and in a sense social. Language is a form of life, but it is first and foremost a form of social life, and an introduction into a particular way of using language is, among other things, an introduction into a set of social practices.

In some cases where we fail to understand a certain use of words it would be true to say that this is because we lack the relevant concepts or the relevant knowledge. In such cases we do not know what is meant when people say things, and to acquire such understanding the dictionary is not always of any use. The systematic connection between concepts, a connection the understanding of which we may not possess, makes this procedure fruitless. Dictionaries give the meaning of words, but they do not always make their use clear. Sometimes, however, it becomes clear that even more than this is required, and although this requirement becomes clear in certain cases, it

[14] Cf. L. Wittgenstein, *Philosophical Investigations* (Oxford, 1953), I 23.

is always there even if we in general take it for granted.
The something more is a knowledge of how it is proper
to proceed, of what social practice is involved. You could
not be said to understand scientific discourse if you
thought of it as some sort of magic incantation, nor could
you be said to understand religious discourse if you
thought of it as a form of scientific discourse. Finally
there is, in addition, the general necessity of understanding just what sort of practice the use of language is—a
point that I have already invoked in criticizing the notion of ostensive definition, and a point that was very much
Wittgenstein's concern.

(d) Concepts and criteria

Two sorts of considerations arise from the foregoing.
First, understanding the meaning of a word is a complex
affair, as is analogously having the relevant concept,
since one cannot be said to understand what "x" means
without also knowing what it is for something to be an x,
i.e., without having the concept of x. To give a full account of what is involved in understanding the meaning
of a word one would have to start with an account of
what it is to understand language, and end with the
kinds of application that the word has. It is a great mistake to suppose that the business can be done the other
way around. Second, the scope for misunderstanding and
for the generation of nonsense of one kind or another is
manifold. Wittgenstein spoke of the nonsense produced
when language goes on holiday, when we try to use
words out of their natural context or outside the language
game that is their natural home. This is misleading if it
be taken as an embargo on linguistic innovation, and it
would certainly be a mistake to suppose that all odd uses
of words lead to nonsense. Even so, the philosophers'
use of the word "nonsense" demands a caution; to speak
of a certain use of words as nonsense may merely be to
say that the words have been used without proper under-

standing of how they are being used or ought to be used. Nevertheless, it remains true that the places and ways in which such misunderstanding can take place are manifold. Just as there are countless different uses of language, so there are countless different ways in which misuse can take place. There is no one criterion of nonsense. Each case has to be treated on its own merits.

Nevertheless, there are conditions to which something has to conform if it is to count as a proper concept. To have the concept of x, to know what it is for something to be an x, we need to know not only the formal defining conditions for an x but also what counts as an x. That is to say that we must, in the appropriate circumstances, be able to recognize an instance falling under the concept, if there is one. Thus, if a putative concept is to be a proper one there must be not only formal defining conditions for it but also conditions for its applicability to instances. It is for this reason that Wittgenstein said that language depends not only on agreement in definitions but also on agreement in judgments.[15] There must be agreement because without it the conditions for the concept could not be objective; intersubjective agreement is a necessary though not sufficient condition of objectivity. The conditions for the concept to which I have referred constitute its criteria; they establish the sense of the concept in question, they establish what has to be known if it is to be known what it is for something to be an x. As such the criteria may be distinguished from other characteristics that xs may have but which in no way constitute part of what it is for something to be an x. Wittgenstein thus distinguishes in the *Blue Book*[16] between criteria and symptoms or signs. This notion of a criterion has been much misunderstood. It is sometimes supposed that a criterion for x is what provides direct noninductive

15 Ibid., I 242.

16 L. Wittgenstein, *Blue and Brown Books* (Oxford, 1958), pp. 24–25 (New York, 1958).

evidence for something being an x.[17] The difficulty with this can be shown by considering the most notorious case of a concept in connection with which Wittgenstein discusses criteria—that of pain.

The special difficulty with pain is that it is a subjective feeling; how then can the concept of pain be an objective one? This would be impossible if one were to come to an understanding of the concept of pain solely from one's own case; for in that situation there could be no intersubjective agreement about its application. Each of us would know about its application to our own case, but not to that of others. If there is to be the necessary intersubjective agreement there must be public criteria for the concept of pain; that is to say, there must be circumstances in which it would be agreed that there is pain. It is in connection with these circumstances that the concept of pain gets a sense. Indeed, they determine what pain is; for pain is not just any feeling, not even simply one that we find unpleasant. The circumstances in question are constituted by forms of behavior that are the natural expressions of pain. (Indeed, Wittgenstein invites us to consider the similarities between avowals of pain and expressions of pain.) When in normal circumstances there is such behavior, then there would be agreement that there is pain. It would not indeed be implausible to write the expression of pain into the definition of pain, so defining it as one that is expressed in certain sorts of ways, were it not for the fact that it is possible for people to suppress their groans, etc., and to disguise their feelings in a variety of ways, just as it is also pos-

[17] See S. Shoemaker, *Self-knowledge and Self-identity* (Ithaca, New York, 1963), p. 3; R. Albritton, "Wittgenstein's use of the term 'criterion,'" *J. Phil.* LVI (1959), pp. 845ff., reprinted in *Wittgenstein*, ed. G. Pitcher (New York and London, 1968), p. 231ff.; N. Malcolm, "Wittgenstein's Philosophical Investigations," *Phil. Rev.* LXIII (1954), pp. 530ff., reprinted in his *Knowledge and Certainty* (Englewood Cliffs, New Jersey, 1963), pp. 96ff. An excellent account of the matter is provided by Bruce Aune, *Knowledge, Mind and Nature* (New York, 1967), Ch. 5.

MEANING AND MEANINGFULNESS

sible for them to simulate pain. Thus it cannot be said that certain forms of behavior in any way constitute direct noninductive evidence of a person's feeling pain. On the contrary, that behavior may in some cases constitute at the best unreliable inductive evidence of a person's feeling pain (in circumstances where the person is known, say, to disguise his feelings as a general rule). There is no incompatibility between saying that the behavior is inductive evidence of this kind, something that is a mere sign of pain at the best, and saying that behavior of this sort is a criterion of pain. For the notion of a criterion has nothing to do with the grounds for applying the relevant concept in a particular case. It is concerned with the normal circumstances in which the concept gets application—circumstances that give sense to the concept itself and without which we could not properly be said to have the concept.

All concepts have criteria, not just those of subjective feelings.[18] To say that the criteria for the concept x are $y, z \ldots$, is in effect to invoke a connection between the concepts x, y, z, etc., since we can speak of the normal circumstances in which the concept x gets application only if we have the concepts $y, z \ldots$ in terms of which those circumstances are to be conceived. The circumstances have to be specified as normal because they reflect our understanding, in terms of their normal application, of the connections between the concepts involved; and these in turn are developed in relation to the world as we find it. (The "we" here is important; the development of concepts is normally an interpersonal, social matter.) Thus even in the apparently simple case of color concepts, we build up these concepts in their interrelationships, such that red is related to orange in a way that it is not to green, and within the general framework of the

[18] Or at any rate all concepts within a given category. Our understanding of the category itself comes via the concepts within the category. Thus there are no criteria for the category of conscious states, although there are criteria for forms that consciousness may take.

notion of color (which itself presupposes other concepts, since colors are features of extended objects, surfaces, or transparent substances). All this holds good in relation to the world as we perceive it, given normal eyesight and normal conditions of perception. Thus the understanding of one particular color concept already presupposes a complex web of understanding that is part and parcel of the view of the world that we have developed, against a background of public, interpersonal standards of judgment.

Talk of a view of the world in this connection may suggest that we might have had other views, that we might have developed a conceptual structure different from that which we have developed in fact. In a certain sense this is true; things might have seemed otherwise if we had been different creatures, if we had had, to use Kant's phrase, a different form of sensibility or, in Wittgenstein's terminology, had shared in a different form of life. But it is no use pretending that we could have any conception of what this might have been like; our form of life is, Wittgenstein says, the given, indeed the only thing that deserves that name.[19] It is not the case that the possibility of such differences in forms of life or sensibility implies a merely subjective view of the world. We can raise the question of what is objective or otherwise only within the conceptual scheme that we have, given our form of life, since to ask whether something is objective is to ask whether it is objective as a such-and-such. To have classified something as a such-and-such is already to have invoked and applied a set of concepts; we cannot get outside these concepts altogether to raise questions about objectivity independent of them. This is what is wrong with those forms of idealism that attempt to undermine the possibility of objectivity by emphasizing

[19] L. Wittgenstein, *Philosophical Investigations*, II, p. 226. Cf. my "Objectivity," in *Education and Rationality*, ed. R. Dearden, P. Hirst, and R. S. Peters (London, forthcoming), and P. G. Winch, "Wittgenstein's treatment of the will," *Ratio* X (1968), pp. 38ff., esp. pp. 49ff.

the fact that although the only conception of the world that we can contemplate is the one that we have come to have, we might always have come to a different one. The sense in which the last is true does not entail subjectivism or conventionalism, such that there are no standards of objectivity but all is subjective or a matter of human convention. Given the general view of the world that we as human beings have formed or inherited as part of our tradition, we can still ask what within it is objective. Indeed, even to talk of tradition may be misleading in that it suggests that we can make sense of speaking of other traditions. But although it does make sense to speak of rival traditions of thought upon particular issues—e.g., scientific conceptions of physical matter—it makes no similar sense in connection with our conception of the world as a whole—our conception of reality as such.

Any attempt to provide philosophical understanding of a way of thinking is thus an attempt to plot the relations between the concepts in terms of which a subject matter is conceived, and without which it makes no sense to speak of that subject matter at all. (That is to say that it makes no sense to think of getting at that subject matter in a way that is independent of concepts, and where the subject matter is reality in general it makes no sense to think of getting at it through any other concepts than those of the kind that we have.) Yet, as we have already seen, the relations between concepts that are presupposed in the understanding of a given subject matter are rarely of a kind that imply logical entailments. Such entailments exist in mathematics and the more formal disciplines, but not elsewhere to any extent. Yet we can still say, as I noted earlier, that if nobody expressed pain in the way that people do we would not have the concept of pain that we do have. Analogously, if colored objects did not look to people of normal eyesight and under normal conditions the way that they do look, we would not have the concepts of colors that we do have. And similarly for a whole host of other cases. Our concepts are developed in relation to norms, and these norms are not always conformed to. We may indeed suppose that what is normally so will be so generally. There are grounds for supposing there is a connection between what is normal and what is general, but to say that something is normally so does not *entail* that it is generally so. It is always possible in special cases for what is normal to become uncommon. If this happens often enough and long enough it may be that our conception of what is normal will change, but this does not impugn the separate status of the concept of the normal. Thus if we necessarily think of pains in connection with what they mean to people and what people do in response to them, we should not say that the failure of a person to respond in the normal way or of a pain to mean the normal thing to a given individual involves any contradiction. We should undoubtedly feel that the case requires some kind of explanation, or perhaps that it involves irrationality, or even in some cases something inhuman; but that by no means makes it impossible or inconceivable as a case. The complexity of the interrelationships between our concepts in their application to the world makes a sense of strain or lack of apparent fit at certain points inevitable; and the lack of fit is often to be explained by reference to other concepts, just as within science deviation from some given law of nature is often, if not universally, to be explained by reference to other laws (for here too the aim is to build up a system of concepts in terms of which a subject matter becomes intelligible). The notion of what is normal is of great importance here, and it receives what is perhaps its primary application in the connection between a concept and its criteria, as we have seen.

What I have been saying provides limits to the understanding of somewhat different kinds than those that were discussed in earlier sections. There is, first, the limit provided by the impossibility of getting outside our system of concepts altogether. Such nonsense as is produced by the attempt to transcend this limit is akin to that which Wittgenstein spoke of as resulting from bumping one's head against the limits of language;[20] and in these cases he recommended bringing back words to "the language game which is their original home." But of course it is unwise and premature in many cases to assume that these limits have been reached. There is virtue, as John Wisdom has suggested, in trying to say what cannot be said.[21] But that the limits are there is true enough. There is, second, the limit provided by the impossibility of sloughing off conceptual connections. Nonsense can be produced by the attempt to give application to a concept without reference to the other concepts that form its normal background. This is what Wittgenstein calls "the machine idling." In such cases the use of the concept is empty. In fact, both limits give rise to emptiness when they are ignored. For in the first case the concept is applied where its usual background is impossible, and in the second case it is applied where the background is simply missing. It is the absence of the background in each case that produces emptiness.

I have in this chapter attempted to indicate how literal nonsense can arise in many different ways. The understanding can fail in a variety of ways, and while one can provide some kind of diagnosis of these different failures, there is no simple or general way of doing so. There is in particular no one criterion of nonsense such that the limits within which knowledge is possible may easily and firmly be established. If the meaningfulness of any proposition in which knowledge is expressed is a condition of its expressing knowledge at all, there is no simple way of determining its meaningfulness in all cases, so that nonviable propositions can be straightforwardly excluded. Each case has to be taken on its merits, and as with skepticism on other grounds, every claim demands argument and has to be assessed accordingly.

[20] L. Wittgenstein, ibid., I, 119.

[21] John Wisdom, "Philosophical Perplexity," Proc. Arist. Soc. (1936–37), reprinted in his Philosophy and Psychoanalysis (Oxford, 1953), pp. 36–50.

(e) Appendix—Universals

In many works on the theory of knowledge there is a section on the problem of universals. I have not included a separate chapter on this issue. This is not because I think that there is no problem here, but because I think that the problems that do exist are either problems of logic and meaning or problems of metaphysics. Some might say that in speaking as I have done already about concepts I have assumed that the world has general features that are in some sense reflected in our thought; I have likewise assumed that there are general words that get application to the world in some way. This is true, and I think that if I have assumed these things it is because they are undeniable. The thesis that everything that exists is particular is a seductive one, perhaps largely because of the importance that particular things play in our lives. But if the world was not such that it had common and repeatable features, we would never be able to think of it as we do; we would never, for instance, be able to attribute to it predicates that are applicable and reapplicable to a number of different particulars. And it is only because this is possible that we can go on to think of abstract universals in their own right, using abstract nouns like "redness" for the purpose.[22] The crucial questions here are what is involved in this, what is the relative status of particulars and universals, what are the criteria for distinguishing them, and so on. These questions are in part questions of meaning, questions about the different ways in which different kinds of expressions get a meaning. To ask what makes it possible for words to have this kind of meaning at all is to ask questions about what happens at the frontiers of language or thought, questions about one general way of dealing in thought with

[22] See A. M. Quinton, "Properties and Classes," *Proc. Arist. Soc.* (1957–58), pp. 33ff.

the world. To say that what makes it possible to think generally about the world is that the world has features of a kind that make this thinking possible is to verge on a vacuousness or circularity that is inevitable at this point.[23] Questions about how thought gets a purchase on the world are not to be answered in the way that questions about how a specific kind of thinking gets a purchase are to be answered, and the supposal that they can so be answered leads to a reliance on metaphors that are likely to be extremely misleading. So it was with Plato's theory of forms to the extent that that theory was a theory of universals and to the extent that Plato spoke of particular things sharing in them. Plato's theory also reveals the other aspect that questions about universals can have. They can amount to questions about ontology, about what actually exists and in what way. Much of the perennial argument about universals, especially that which took place in the Middle Ages, has had this character. Granted that there are objects of our thought and that our thought is often or generally general in character, what is the exact status of those objects? Do they exist *in rerum natura* or only as what Brentano called intentional objects,[24] things which have existence for thought only; and if they do exist *in rerum natura*, do they do so in an independent way or only as features of more concrete objects? These are metaphysical or ontological questions, although they reflect questions about meaning. They have little connection, however, with the theory of knowledge as such.

[23] See D. Pears, "Universals," *Phil. Quart.* I (1951), pp. 218ff., reprinted in *Logic and Language*, ed. A. G. N. Flew (Oxford, 1953), II, pp. 51ff. (Garden City, New York, 1953).

[24] F. Brentano, *Psychologie vom empiricischen Standpunkte* (Leipzig, 1874; new edition, Hamburg, 1955). See also the extract in *Realism and the Background of Phenomenology*, ed. R. Chisholm (Glencoe, Illinois, 1960).

CHAPTER 4

Knowledge
and Belief

(a) Does knowledge involve belief?

What is it to know something? This question is obviously
a central one for the theory of knowledge, since until
it is answered it is impossible to rule out erroneous theories
based on misconceptions of what it is to know something.
The difficulty is to know exactly how it is to be answered.
A temptation to be resisted is that of breaking down or
reducing the notion of knowledge to something different.
This kind of temptation is common throughout philosophy, since if one is in fact able to reduce one notion to
another better understood, the way is wide open for a
proper understanding of the first notion. On the other
hand, it must not be supposed that where this procedure
cannot be carried out (and it is often the case that it cannot, owing to radical differences in the concepts), nothing can be done to further understanding. I emphasize
this point because it has commonly been supposed that an
analysis of the notion of knowledge must be carried out
by reference to such notions as belief or being sure.
There are objections to such analyses, but this does not
mean that we have to be content to say that knowledge

is an unanalyzable notion, about which there is nothing further to be said. There are other ways of becoming clear about a concept apart from analysis.

It is clear enough that knowledge cannot be identical with belief. In the first place, beliefs can be false, while if what someone supposedly knows turns out to be false, we are logically bound to withdraw the suggestion that the person concerned knows that thing. We may say that he does not know it, he only believes it—a form of speech that suggests, although it does not entail, a contrast between knowledge and belief rather than the inclusion of the one in the other. Thus one condition of being said to know something is that what one claims to know must be the case; if it is an object that one claims to know, this must exist, and if what one claims to know is formulable in a proposition, this must be true. On the other hand, true belief is not equivalent to knowledge; to be said to know p, it is not sufficient that one should believe p and that p should be true. This was clear to Plato, who in trying to define knowledge in his dialogue the *Theaetetus*[1] argues against the identification of knowledge and true belief on the simple ground that a jury may believe truly that a defendant is guilty, but not have sufficient evidence to claim knowledge to this effect. Something more is required for knowledge than true belief alone. Plato's example suggests that the something more is something in the way of a rationale for the belief. I say "rationale" rather than "evidence" since the former is a more general notion; not every case of belief is such that the rationale that might be given for it would be a matter of evidence. In some cases, as in mathematical examples, it would be a matter of proof instead; in other cases other considerations again arise. Plato considers in the *Theaetetus* what "rationale" (*logos*) might mean and asks whether any account of this can be offered such that when a man has a true belief in something together with a rationale he can be said to know that something. He comes in the

[1] Plato, *Theaetetus*, 200^{d}ff.

end to the view that any such account will, if it is to be sufficient, be circular. To speak of a rationale is to speak of what the person concerned knows as giving sufficient support to the claim to true belief. Thus it would appear that this line of analysis reinvokes knowledge at a crucial point in such a way as to make the analysis circular.

Plato ends his dialogue without resolving the problem overtly; but it is clear that since the view under criticism is the view expressed (like much else in this dialogue) in an earlier dialogue, the *Meno*, his solution of the problem, would have to come via a view of knowledge other than that presupposed in his earlier philosophy. In that earlier dialogue Plato takes the view that all knowledge is a matter of being acquainted with something through experience of it in this or some previous existence; when we experience something now we are reminded of what we previously knew but have forgotten. Knowledge is so far mere recollection; we know everything implicitly but have to be reminded of it for that knowledge to become explicit. Even so the state of mind produced by this recollection of previous knowledge is only belief until that belief is reinforced and made firm by "repeated and varied questioning." Then presumably the person concerned has the ability to provide the rationale for his belief, and for this reason can be said to have knowledge proper. Plato's rejection of this view in the *Theaetetus* entails a completely new account of what knowledge consists in; unfortunately he nowhere in the late dialogues tells us explicitly what this account must be. Nevertheless, the importance of Plato's comments is not limited to his own circumscribed views of knowledge; his argument has general implications. Attempts have been made to get around the sort of criticism involved by invoking a somewhat reduced condition in addition to true belief. It has been claimed, for example, that all that is necessary for knowledge in addition to true belief is that we should have the right to the belief, or that the belief should be justified. Unfortunately, such considerations are insufficient. We might have the right to believe *p* or be justified in believing the truth of *p* for reasons that are not relevant to the truth of *p* as such.[2] If a man has taken every possible step to discover the evidence for the truth of *p* and thinks as a consequence that *p* is true, then he may be said to be justified in believing that *p* is true even if the evidence that he has obtained is in fact utterly irrelevant to the truth of *p*. If in addition *p* happens after all to be true, although the evidence in question is quite irrelevant to its truth, the man will believe truly that *p* and be justified in his belief. He will not, however, know that *p*, because the rationale that he has for his belief is in fact irrelevant to it. Justified true belief is thus insufficient for knowledge.

It may not in fact even be necessary for knowledge, since there are cases in which we should be willing to speak of knowledge but in which the rationale is not at all apparent. These are cases in which the grounds for speaking of knowledge at all are simply that the person in question is consistently right. The case might be that of someone who like the boy in D. H. Lawrence's story "The Rocking-horse Winner" gets something right consistently without either he or ourselves knowing how. The boy in the story consistently got the winner of a horse race right simply by riding a rocking-horse. The case is of course fiction, and it might seem too incredible to be fact, but there are many more ordinary cases in which people consistently get something right without anyone being able to say how. In such cases we are likely to say "It is clear that he knows, although heaven knows how." It is clear that he knows, simply because he is always right; the consistency and generality of the result seem to rule out the suggestion that it might all be be-

[2] See, e.g., E. L. Gettier, *Analysis* 23 (1963), pp. 121ff., reprinted in *Knowledge and Belief*, ed. A. P. Griffiths (London, 1967), pp. 144ff.; Don Locke, *Perception and our Knowledge of the External World* (New York and London, 1967), Ch. 10; A. C. Danto, *Analytical Philosophy of Knowledge* (Cambridge, 1968), Ch. 5.

cause of chance or that the person is just guessing. However, the remark "heaven knows how" may suggest that we do think that the person has some kind of rationale for his beliefs about what happens to be true, even if neither he nor we can say what that rationale is. It is not at all clear that this would be a correct suggestion. People do know things by intuition, and the force of the word "intuition" is explicitly to rule out the possibility of a rationale. Intuitions may come more easily in some circumstances than in others; there may in some cases be causally necessary conditions for them. This is what was postulated in the case of the rocking-horse winner. If in these cases we have any inclination to say that the person who knows has justified true belief, we have to add that the only justification lies in the consistent truth of the belief; there is no independent justification, and hence these would not be cases of justified true belief in the sense originally proposed.

I shall return later to the question of exactly what account is to be given of knowledge. The question that now concerns us is whether any of the considerations so far adduced, or any other considerations that may be adduced, provide any reason for saying that knowledge does not involve belief at all. As far as concerns the considerations so far adduced, I think that the answer is "No." The fact that knowledge cannot without circularity be analyzed into true belief plus something else does not of itself show that when a man knows something he does not at the same time and for that very reason believe the same thing. If there are considerations that show the contrary, they must be additional to those so far considered. One thing must be noted at the start: Belief may fairly be described as a state of mind (in what sense will be considered in the next section), but knowledge cannot be so described. In an important sense, to say that someone knows something is not directly to ascribe to him a state of mind that he has on a specific occasion, or indeed on any occasion at all. It is certainly not necessary, if a person is to know that p, that he should on the occasion on which this is said of him be in a state of mind to be specified as knowing. I can say of someone that he knows the date of the Battle of Hastings, but in saying this I am not saying that anything is in the person's mind at the moment. Must he, however, have had the date of the Battle of Hastings before his mind on *some* occasion, and must it be possible for it to come before his mind in the future? I do not think that it must have been before his mind in the past, since he may know it without having learned it. What our grounds would be for ascribing knowledge in that case is another matter. Still, if a person knows that *p*, it seems that he must be capable in principle of producing *p* as a statement of fact on some occasion. I say "in principle" because there need be no suggestion that he should be capable of doing so in fact; circumstances may always prevent it. He may know that *p* but never throughout the course of his life show that he does. Once again, there would be difficulties over how we should ever know that he knows, but these do not prevent it being true that he knows. Hence, it is logically conceivable that a person should know that *p* but never have *p* before his mind at all. If this is so, and if belief is a state of mind, it may seem to follow that knowledge does not always involve belief. This, however, does not follow. The fact that belief is in some sense a state of mind does not entail that what is believed must be before the mind. There are such things as unconscious beliefs; similarly, a man may know something without being aware of this [a point to which I shall return in section (c)]. In sum, the fact that knowledge requires of the person only that he be capable in principle of producing the relevant information does not rule out the possibility of ascribing belief to him as well, since just the same may be said of belief.

When it is said, therefore, that knowledge cannot be considered as a state of mind, what is meant is that it cannot be *simply* so considered; indeed, so to consider it may be very misleading, since the truth of the belief held by the person who knows (or his getting the answer right) is just as important a condition of knowledge as any belief that he has. Something cannot be knowledge if it lacks truth, whatever else is necessary. Knowledge can be construed as a state of mind only if being able to produce the right answer, as the rocking-horse winner could, is a state of mind. Certainly no specific feelings of assurance or confidence are material to knowing; a person can get the right answer consistently without having any confidence in his ability to do so. It may be thought, however, that cases in which a person lacks confidence in his ability to produce an answer, for whatever reason, must be cases in which he does not believe that the answer is such-and-such. Thus, if a person can know that p despite a lack of confidence in its truth, if he even believes that he does not know that p, it may seem that he cannot also believe that p. Once again, I believe that this does not follow. The conclusion would be valid only if in order to believe that p one had to be sure about it or not be in doubt about it, and there seems no good reason for supposing this to be true. If a person refuses to acknowledge that he knows the answer to a question, he may know it nevertheless, and he may in fact believe that the answer is such-and-such without admitting to himself that he does so. This involves a kind of self-deception, and there are, no doubt, problems about how this is possible; but that it is possible is clear enough. What, however, about those cases in which we may wish to speak of knowledge, but where the person concerned seems to believe that the proposition known is false, where perhaps he refuses to believe that the proposition p (which is what we say he knows) is true at all?[3] I think that in these cases we have to say merely that he seems to believe that the proposition known is false; that is to

[3] Cf. A. P. Griffiths in Knowledge and Belief, ed. A. P. Griffiths (London, 1967), p. 10. It should be noted that there are cases of refusing to believe something, which are different from those discussed here—cases where the refusal is rationally based on evidence or grounds, and where the refusal may be one to accept pressures to ignore the evidence.

say, that we have to admit that he really believes that it is true, although he behaves to the contrary. The same applies to a person who refuses in this way to believe that p. The phenomenon is of the same kind as the self-deception already referred to; in both cases we have to say that the person concerned does believe or know something but that he somehow conceals from himself that he is doing so and behaves accordingly. I cannot go into an analysis of this phenomenon here, but it is real enough. I conclude therefore that these cases provide no warrant for saying that knowledge does not presuppose belief in the sense that when a man knows p he does not also believe p.

There is one further kind of argument that might be adduced for the contrary position. This is that there is a contrast between believing and knowing, in the sense that the very point of speaking of someone believing something is to mark a contrast between this and what we would be saying if we said that he knew it. To speak of belief therefore implies, even if it does not say, that the person concerned does not know. We may say, for example, that someone does not know that p, he only believes it, he only supposes it to be so, it is just an opinion on his part, or that he is merely under the impression that p. In so marking off belief from knowledge we may do so either on the grounds that the person is not in a proper position to know or that what he claims to know is false and therefore cannot constitute knowledge. It is of course true that claims to knowledge may fail for one reason or the other and that in such cases to speak of belief may not only be pertinent, it may also serve to point out the contrast and bring out the fact that the person concerned does not know. Idioms like "being under the impression that" or "merely supposing that" make this explicit. But even if the point of speaking of belief is often or generally to mark a contrast with knowledge, this does not mean that it is inappropriate to ask whether when a person knows that p he also believes that p. In speaking of knowledge we may be saying more than in speaking of belief, and this may be the basis of the contrast, since the something more may in many cases be all-important. It is to be noted that we do not so much say, "He does not know; he believes," as "He does not know; he only believes"; the "only" is important. I suggest therefore that the contrast is not one merely of opposition, so that if you know you do not believe and vice versa, but one that is more like that between, say, animals and men. We often oppose men to animals, and we may well say of someone that he is not a man but merely an animal; but this does not mean that it is inappropriate to say that men are animals. Similarly it is not inappropriate in all circumstances to say that when someone knows something he also believes it.

There seems to be no good reason, therefore, to suppose that knowledge does not involve belief. I shall return later to the importance that this has for an account of knowledge. Meanwhile, it is important to be clear about exactly what is involved in speaking of belief. It may be that in some sense we could not understand what belief is unless we already had some idea of what knowledge is. There would, in that case, be further objections to any attempt to provide any illuminating reduction of the concept of knowledge to that of belief, even with additional factors.

(b) What is belief?

I have already referred to belief as a state of mind. In the sense of "belief" so far considered, it is a state of mind concerned with propositions. This is clearly insufficient as a characterization of belief, since there are many things that one can do with propositions apart from believing them, even things that one can do mentally—e.g., question them, doubt them. Belief is a state of mind in which propositions are taken to be true. This cannot be taken as a definition of belief, since the words "taken to be" seem to be mere substitutes for "believed to be." But the connection with truth is important, and it has been suggested plausibly enough by A. P. Griffiths that belief is that state of mind that is appropriate to truth.[4] Our understanding of the concept of belief can come only through an understanding of the concept of truth. It is not that beliefs cannot be false; it is manifestly clear that they are so all too often. But belief is the appropriate state of mind to have toward what is true, and in this sense there is a conceptual link between belief and truth; without an appreciation of this link there is no hope of understanding belief itself. (Of course, one of the difficulties inherent in any discussion of belief is that some kind of understanding of it is presupposed in any discussion of it; one who did not know what it was to believe something could hardly enter upon a discussion of its nature, since the aim of the discussion is surely to arrive at true beliefs on this matter.) To come to know what it is to believe something involves coming to know what it is to affirm something as true. That is why it is plausible to offer an account of belief, as Geach does, which is analogical in that it rests upon the notion of affirming or saying, taking belief as a kind of mental or inner saying.[5] Once again there seems no hope of reducing belief to something else.

Attempts have been made to carry out such a reduction, and one particular form that this has taken is the attempt to analyze belief as a form of disposition. Thus Ryle[6] and others have taken belief statements as basically hypothetical in form; to say that X believes p is to say that if the circumstances were such-and-such X

[4] A. P. Griffiths, "On Belief," *Proc. Arist. Soc.* (1962–63), pp. 167ff., reprinted in *Knowledge and Belief,* ed. A. P. Griffiths, pp. 127ff.

[5] P. Geach, *Mental Acts* (London, 1957), pp. 75ff. (New York, 1957). Geach takes as the paradigmatic illustration of this thesis the biblical quotation "The fool hath said in his heart 'There is no God.' " Cf. also Bruce Aune, *Knowledge, Mind and Nature* (New York, 1967), Ch. 8.

[6] G. Ryle, *Concept of Mind* (New York and London, 1949), Ch. 5.

would do or say certain things. X is thus disposed to do
or say these things in these circumstances. But what
things and what circumstances? Clearly the things have
to be appropriate to the circumstances, but the problem
is to give a sufficiently general account of what would
be appropriate. What sort of things must a man do or
say in what circumstances if he is to believe that he is
inadequate in his job? Certain actions and certain things
said are likely enough in such a case, and we have a
good idea of the circumstances in which the actions and
remarks are probable, but it does not seem that any of
this is essential. It may be said that what follows from
this is that the relevant actions and things said form a
disjunctive set, which is open in that the best that we
can say is that if someone believes p he must do either
. . . or . . . or . . . , (taking saying as a form of doing,
for the sake of convenience), in circumstances of the
kind . . . or the kind . . . , or something of that sort.
The last phrase leaves the class open. There are two
insuperable objections to this supposal. First, the very
openness of the class presents the problem of knowing
what is to count as "something of that sort." Our ability
to go on here surely implies a knowledge of what is
relevant, and how can this be unless we know the
principle involved? In the present case, this would involve a prior knowledge of what belief is, since this
provides the principle of the series that enables us to go
on producing relevant factors. Second, it is conceivable
that a man should believe p without ever manifesting
it; he need never do or say anything that is relevant to
the belief in any circumstances whatever. He may simply
be very good at disguising or concealing his belief. To
say that he must at least be disposed to do or say certain things would in this case be an empty form. In
any case, a man may have the belief on a single occasion, and it may never cross his mind or ever become
relevant again. In these circumstances, to invoke the
notion of a disposition, or to say that he would . . . if
. . . , would be futile.

Of course, there must be expressions of belief if there are to be criteria for the concept of belief for the reasons given in Chapter 3 (d); otherwise we should have no grounds for saying that we have a proper concept of belief at all. We might therefore say that when a man believes *p* he must *normally* do such-and-such. But the relation between belief and behavior is not quite like the relation between pain and behavior; an avowal of belief is not quite like an avowal of pain. If this were not so we would have no grounds for distinguishing between them as different states of mind. The difficulty of saying what a man must normally do if he is to believe *p* is an indication of this fact; such difficulties do not arise in the case of feelings like that of pain. Thus, in the case of belief, although there must normally be expressions of belief (expressions that may be lacking for some reason in a given case), it is impossible to specify those normal expressions as we can the expressions of pain. For this reason belief cannot be defined in terms of its expressions in a way that is at all illuminating. It requires for its elucidation reference to its connection with other concepts like that of truth, as already mentioned.[7]

I spoke earlier of "the sense of 'belief' so far considered." I have so far been concerned solely with belief *that* such and such is the case. There are other constructions with the verb "to believe." We may speak of believing a person, and we may speak of believing in something—God, a theory, or a person, for example. The idea of believing a person presents no great difficulties, since to believe him is to believe what he says, and this clearly presupposes believing that something is the case. This is not to say that believing Smith when he says *p* is simply believing that *p*. Believing Smith is believing what

[7] Cf. A. P. Griffiths, ibid., and the conclusive arguments against reductive analyses of belief provided by R. Chisholm in "Sentences about believing," *Proc. Arist. Soc.* (1955–56), pp. 125ff., and *Perceiving* (Ithaca, New York, 1957).

Smith says, and if he says that p then of course we believe that p, but believing Smith is only believing that p insofar as p is what Smith says. Believing *in* Smith, on the other hand, may or may not involve believing what he says (it is possible to imagine circumstances in which we do not believe what someone says, but nevertheless for certain obscure reasons have a definite belief in him). "Belief in" seems often to involve some element of trust or confidence in whatever one believes in. There are some occasions in which we speak of "belief in" when it may seem that we are concerned simply with the existence of the thing in question. We may speak of believing in fairies or even of believing in God in this way. Nevertheless, I do not think that we are concerned simply with the existence of fairies or God when we speak of believing in them. Indeed, if we wish to emphasize that we are concerned simply with existence, we may make this explicit by speaking of belief in the existence of fairies, etc. (Where we speak of belief in a property or state of a thing we are speaking merely of belief that the thing has this property or is in this state, and similar considerations apply to existence.) It would perhaps be wrong to say that whenever we speak of belief in a person or being we always imply trust in that person or being. Someone who believes in the devil may have no trust in him or reason for trust in him. Nevertheless, some form of personal relationship or supposed personal relationship *is* implied. Similarly, believing in a theory implies some attitude toward the theory other than the belief that what the theory says is true; the attitude in question is normally one that could be expressed by saying that the person concerned would be prepared to bet on it. Yet whatever else they involve, all these states of mind entail some *belief that*. Part of a man's state of mind when he believes in something could be expressed by saying that he believes that something is the case, if it is only that the thing in question exists. Thus it seems that "belief that" is a necessary though not by any means a sufficient condition of other forms of belief. It is perhaps the basic form of belief; it corresponds to the basic sense of "believe."

I also spoke earlier of belief as a state of mind concerned with propositions. This may give rise to certain questions. In particular, what is the proposition with which the state of mind is concerned; is it an object of the state of mind, and in what way? The problem may seem greatest with respect to false beliefs, since in their case there is no fact corresponding to the belief; if we are to postulate something to be the object of a false belief, this is likely to offend against what Bertrand Russell called a "robust sense of reality." Such problems have seemed most pertinent to realist philosophers who have taken the most stringent attitudes toward the question of what actually exists. When we believe something falsely we believe *something*. What is this something? (There have been many worries about false belief. Plato, for example, raised issues about false belief in the *Theaetetus*, but these arise out of limited conceptions of what knowledge is and in consequence of what failures of knowledge are possible; if you either know something or do not know it, you cannot be mistaken about it if you know it, and you cannot be in the position to be mistaken about it if you do not know it.) The difficulties for the realist are well expressed in Russell's *Problems of Philosophy*,[8] where he puts the point that false belief cannot consist of a relation to some one thing, like a fact, since there is no such actually existing thing corresponding to a false belief, in the way that a fact corresponds to a true belief. Moore had previously introduced the notion of a "proposition" to perform specifically this role, taking his cue from Meinong; but he too came to doubt whether any such thing actually existed. Both philosophers had no doubt about the existence of the objects that the belief was about, e.g., Cassio in "Othello be-

[8] B. Russell, *The Problems of Philosophy* (London, 1912), Ch. 12. Cf. also G. E. Moore, *Some Main Problems of Philosophy* (New York and London, 1953), Chs. 14 and 15.

lieved that Desdemona loved Cassio." Russell took in consequence the view that belief consisted in a complex, many-termed relation between a person and these objects. Thus in "Othello believed that Desdemona loved Cassio," the belief consists in a many-termed relation between Othello, Desdemona, loving, and Cassio. The assumption in all this is that the terms of the belief all pick out actually existing things. Russell later came to see that there were objections to taking the verb "love" in this way. In *The Philosophy of Logical Atomism*[9] he pointed out the crucial role played by the word "that" in any statement of the form "X believes that p." The statement of the belief involves a subordinate clause such that what follows the "that" is of propositional form. It is thus impossible to take belief as any kind of relation between a person and a complex of entities, since to put the matter in this way would not bring out that what the person believes has to be expressed in propositional form. (On the other hand, the statement "X believes that p" is not a truth function of p; its truth or falsity is not dependent on or related to the truth or falsity of p, and it thus remained a problem exactly how p figured in the statement of the belief.)

There are thus objections to taking belief simply as a kind of relation between a person and an object or set of objects, or indeed a relation between a person and a fact. If the proposition that is believed is to be construed as an object of the belief, it can be only as what Brentano[10] called an "intentional object"—something that exists only as an object of consciousness and that need not have any physical existence or existence as fact. To be content with saying just this would not be illuminating, since it would appear to imply only that in belief we are aware of something, but not some

[9] B. Russell, "The Philosophy of Logical Atomism," Ch. 4 (*Monist*, 1918–19), reprinted in his *Logic and Knowledge,* ed. R. C. Marsh (London, 1956).

[10] F. Brentano, *Psychologie vom empiricischen Standpunkte* (Leipzig, 1874; new edition, Hamburg, 1955).

thing in the ordinary sense. There is, however, a more substantial point behind all this, one that is also implied by the fact that the statement of the belief involves a that-clause, such that what follows the "that" is of propositional form. Belief that *p* is possible only for one who is capable of having the thought that *p*; the content of the belief is that thought.[11] We have here a further conceptual connection between the concept of belief and another concept (i.e., that of thought), apart from that already mentioned (i.e., truth). We need both connections since we need to specify the kind of thought involved—that to which truth and falsity are applicable. In this way the problem of how it is possible to believe what is in fact false (to the extent that it is a problem at all) shifts to the problem of how it is possible to think what is not the case.[12] Insofar as thought can for these purposes be construed as inner sayings, the problem is then simply one of how it is possible to make false statements, as Plato saw in the *Sophist*.[13] Such a problem is to be dealt with by answering the dual question "What is a statement and how can it be true or false?," as Plato also saw. This issue will be taken up in the next chapter.

If the belief that *p* involves or presupposes the thought that *p*, anyone who believes that *p* must have the concepts that the thought itself implies. In other words, thinking that S is P involves having the concepts of S and P, and this in turn involves knowing in some sense what it is for something to be S and P. It would thus seem that the possibility of believing something

[11] Cf. Frege's point that in subordinate clauses of the kind involved in belief statements, the reference of the clause is what would be the sense of the proposition expressed in the clause if it were taken by itself, i.e., the thought that it expresses. See G. Frege, "On Sense and Reference" in *Translations*, by P. Geach and Max Black (Oxford, 1952), pp. 56ff.

[12] Cf. L. Wittgenstein, *Blue and Brown Books* (Oxford, 1958), p. 31 (New York, 1958).

[13] Plato, *Sophist*, 259dff.

already presupposes a certain form of knowledge. It is this that renders impossible a reductive but noncircular analysis of knowledge into belief plus something else. Knowledge cannot be said to *consist of* belief with or without other things, since an adequate account of belief itself must make reference to knowledge at some stage. None of this goes counter to the thesis that when someone knows that p he believes that p. All that has been maintained is that even in the cases where we wish to speak of belief that p but not knowledge that p, we still imply knowledge of something. This does not affect the question whether when we do speak of knowledge that p we may also speak of belief that p. It may, however, be argued that if we may so speak we are involved in an infinite regress, since knowledge that p implies belief that p, this implies knowledge of something else, which implies belief about that something else, and so on. But if this were a vicious regress it would apply equally to knowledge alone without invoking belief, since knowing that S is P implies knowing what it is for something to be S and P, i.e., knowing that S is such-and-such and that P is such-and-such, and this implies knowing that . . . , and so on. Hence the position that belief plays here cannot be crucial. But in fact there is no regress in a way that is at all material. When it is said that knowing that S and P implies knowing other things, it is meant that if a man knows that S is P he must know other things and that he cannot be said to know that S is P if he does not know these other things. But this does not mean that he has to know these other things *first*. It is not that he must first have the concepts before he can go on to acquire the knowledge that depends on them; on the contrary, the acquisition of the concepts may be part and parcel of the process of acquiring the knowledge. Similarly, there is no question of first having to acquire concepts, then beliefs, and then the knowledge that implies those beliefs. Hence there is no real regress.

The reductionist account of knowledge in terms of

belief is, however, saddled with a regress, since the whole point of a reductionist account is to get rid of the concept that is being reduced to other concepts. There is involved in this the idea of the priority of one concept to another in that one concept cannot properly be understood unless and until another is understood. What I have said about the conceptual connections between belief, thought, concepts, and knowledge shows that one cannot without a regress break down the concept of knowledge into a cluster of more basic components of which belief is a member. The concept of belief does not stand on its own feet in this respect; it does not and cannot make any claims to being basic. (Indeed, to suppose that it might do so is to embrace an erroneous theory about our understanding, which is of a piece with the empiricist view that was criticized in earlier chapters. It is to suppose that we are "given" certain basic concepts and that all others are built up from these.) If the demand is made that belief should be elucidated, this can be answered only by the attempt to locate the position that the concept of belief has in relation to concepts like those of truth and thought. Elaboration of this will inevitably imply reference to knowledge.

(c) What is knowledge?

I have been at pains to say what the relationship between the concepts of knowledge and belief is *not*. I must now say more about the concept of knowledge for its own sake. Whether or not knowledge involves belief, and whether or not belief is a state of mind, the distinction between knowledge and belief that should be our concern is not a distinction between states of mind, and is not to be elucidated by reference to features of states of mind. There are indeed grounds for a refusal to call knowledge a state of mind at all. Certainly it is not just a state of mind.

The crucial point is the fact that we should not normally allow that someone knew something if it was not true. I say "normally" because we might be prepared to waive this condition in special cases. Israel Scheffler,[14] for example, indicates that we might *say* that the Greeks knew that the mountain on which their gods lived was Olympus, although we know that there were no such gods and that they did not live on any mountain. This is, however, rather like a case of knowledge about something in fiction; we waive, before we start, all questions about the truth or falsity of the description in terms of which we express the subject of our knowledge claim. Such cases do not affect the general point. The fact that the truth of the proposition said to be known is a normal condition of the valid ascription of knowledge indicates beyond question that knowledge is not just a state of mind; the truth conditions of statements about knowledge must include reference to things other than states of mind. But what state of mind *is* involved? I have already argued against the suggestion that belief is *not* involved; I must now give a more positive account. First, however, it is necessary to eliminate further misunderstandings.

Ayer has attempted to give an account of knowledge in terms of the two notions of being sure and having the right to be sure.[15] The difficulty with the notion of having the right to be sure is that it is very close to the notion of justified true belief that was discussed in the first section of this chapter. Did the "rocking-horse winner" have the right to be sure about the winner of the horse race? Well, perhaps he did, but only because he seemed to have a method of forecasting winners accurately. What about people who know things by intuition? We may in the end say that they have the right to be

[14] I. Scheffler, *Conditions of Knowledge* (Glenview, Illinois, 1965), Ch. 2. He himself deals with the case by claiming that "knew" in this case is elliptical for "believed that they knew."

[15] A. J. Ayer, *The Problem of Knowledge* (New York and London, 1956), Ch. 1.

sure, but only because they are right about the things that they claim to know, and not for any other reason. However, it might seem that people who know things do in some sense have the right to be sure and that this is therefore a necessary condition of knowledge. It is not, however, sufficient; people may have the right to be sure of something if they believe it on the best of authority, yet what they think they know may turn out to be false and is not for that reason knowledge. Still, as far as concerns the necessary conditions of knowledge, the notion of having the right to be sure is on firmer ground than that of the justified true belief discussed in section (a), because the former notion is wider than the latter. There is a difference, of course, between being sure and feeling sure. To be sure of something it is not necessary to have feelings of any kind; all that is required is preparedness to stand by the truth of what is claimed. At the same time it does not seem necessary that even this should be the case with someone who knows something. The schoolboy who for one reason or another is too hesitant, too shy, or too frightened to give the right answer to a question may still know it. Hence, being sure is not by any means necessary to knowledge, even if in the majority of cases people who know things are also sure of them.

So far from being sure of what they know, it is even possible for people not to know that they know. The boy who is too hesitant to give the right answer to a question may nevertheless know the answer, although he does not know that he knows it. It has sometimes been held that if he knows he must know that he knows. Indeed, members of the philosophical school known as phenomenology have sometimes presented as something of a dogma the thesis that "knowing is knowing that one knows" (Jean-Paul Sartre refers to it as Alain's formula).[16] In a somewhat different way and for some-

[16] J.-P. Sartre, *Being and Nothingness,* trans. H. E. Barnes (London, 1957), pp. lii–liii, 53 (New York, 1956).

what different reasons, H. A. Prichard[17] said, "When we know something, we either do or can by reflecting directly know that we are knowing it." On the face of it, the claim that if we know something we must know that we do is clearly false. Certainly it is possible to discover that we knew something all along without realizing it; children may know things without knowing that they do, and a teacher may have to draw this to their attention. The temptation to accept Alain's formula arises from the assumption that knowledge is a "form of consciousness." There is good reason to say that a conscious activity is, by definition, one that one cannot carry on without being aware, and thus without knowing, that one is doing it. One cannot be aware of something without knowing that one is (consciousness is to that extent self-consciousness). But there are no grounds for supposing that knowledge is a conscious activity or state, nor for supposing that knowledge and awareness are the same. For this reason, too, knowledge cannot be explained in terms of being sure, since if we are sure about something it seems clear that we must know that we are, while this, as we have seen, is not true of knowledge.

It is not true of belief either. There is no objection to someone being said to believe something without knowing this. The idea of unconscious beliefs is unobjectionable. Someone may be quite unaware that he really believes something, and he may come to realize that he does so with some sense of shock; it may also be quite clear to others, from his behavior, that he believes something without his being at all aware of the fact that he does so. This is not to say that the belief *is* his disposition to behave in this way; but the behavior may be the grounds on which we ascribe the belief to him. He may be quite unaware that he has the disposition to behave

[17] H. A. Prichard, *Knowledge and Perception* (Oxford, 1950), pp. 85ff., reprinted in *Knowledge and Belief*, ed. A. P. Griffiths, pp. 60ff.

in a way relevant to the belief; he may be quite unaware that he has the relevant thoughts. Alternatively, if he is aware of having them he may not be aware of them as constituting the belief in question. Thus, even if being sure is ruled out as part of what it is to know something for the reasons that we have surveyed, the same considerations cannot similarly rule out belief.

We have seen that, in order to know that *p*, a man need not be sure that *p*, he need not know that he knows that *p*, he need not have *reasons* for belief that *p*. On the other hand, *p* must normally be true, and if this condition does not hold we cannot speak of knowledge. There seem also to be other considerations that rule out knowledge. A man need not have reasons for believing that *p* if he is to know that *p*; but if we discover that he is merely guessing, if we *know* this, we should refuse to allow that he knows *p*, however often he is right. Of course, if he is right sufficiently often we may refuse to admit the possibility that he is merely guessing. It is not implied by this that he must in that case have reasons for what he says; but there must be a reason why he says it. I do not think that with a case like that of the "rocking-horse winner" we should necessarily be forced in the end to say that he must have reasons or grounds for his predictions, although we may be forced to say that there must be reasons why, or causes of the fact that, he is constantly right; there must be reasons why he comes out with the right answer so consistently. To this extent a causal theory of knowledge is a viable one. But to say this is merely to say that if a man knows something he cannot be merely guessing or merely getting the right answer by chance; it is not to say that reasons or grounds are *always* irrelevant, or that such reasons and grounds can be reduced to causes without more ado. Another consideration that would rule out knowledge would be the discovery that the person who gives the answers does not really know what he is saying. It might have turned out in the case of the "rocking-horse winner" that the explanation was that stimulation produced by the rocking horse caused him to utter certain words that turned out to be the names of winners in horse races. As a matter of empirical fact, of course, the causal explanation invoked in that case would be a mysterious one, but this is not an objection of principle to it. A similar explanation might be given of oracles, though this again does not altogether deprive them of their mystery —to the extent that they are really oracular. But if we knew that this was the explanation, we should undoubtedly say that the "rocking-horse winner" or the oracle did not *know* what was implied by their words; they did not know what they were saying. They had no relevant thoughts. Thus whenever we know that the person of whom knowledge is claimed does not have any relevant thoughts we can surely rule out knowledge.[18]

I argued in the first section of this chapter that failure to believe that p would also rule out knowledge that p. I think that this conclusion is reinforced by the present considerations. If a person is consistently right in his answers to certain questions, we should still not ascribe knowledge to him, if we knew quite certainly that he did not at all believe that his answers were right. Of course, in such circumstances we might come instead to question whether he really did not believe these things; otherwise he might more plausibly be like the oracle where the priestess speaks with raving lips, i.e., without knowing what she is doing. But if he knew what he was saying, was not guessing, but did not in any way believe what he was saying, what on earth *was* he doing? If he positively disbelieved what he was saying he might be lying, and this, in conjunction with the fact that what he said was true, would rule out knowledge on his part. On the other hand, it does seem that knowledge requires some attitude on our part to what is true. The cases

[18] This is clearly relevant to the question of the conditions under which telepathy, if it exists, can be counted as knowledge.

where we speak of someone discovering that he must have known something all along do not show that he did not believe it all along, merely that he did not know that he did. Hence such cases do not show that there need be no attitude toward what is true for there to be knowledge. If belief is the state of mind appropriate to truth, as Griffiths maintains, its failure to be present with regard to a proposition that is true must equally rule out knowledge.

One might say, in sum, that someone knows that p if he is in the appropriate position to certify or give his authority to the truth of p. Someone will be in this position if one or more of a number of relevant considerations do not rule it out. The considerations mentioned thus furnish necessary conditions of knowledge. The formula that I have used presupposes the truth of the proposition said to be known. If a man does not believe that p he is not in the appropriate position to certify or give his authority to the truth of p; people may on occasion give their authority to the truth of things that they do not believe, but that does not mean that they are in the appropriate position to do so. These two conditions —truth and belief in it—are positive, but other necessary conditions of knowledge—or some of them, at any rate —are negative in form. The man who knows must *not* be guessing, he must *not* hit on the truth by chance, he must *not* rely on bad reasons if he relies on reasons at all. It is the fact that these conditions are negative that makes it impossible to give the sufficient conditions of knowledge except in a vague and general formula of the kind that I have invoked. Another way of formulating what is at stake would be to say that the man who knows has to be right and for the best of reasons. Not, as we have seen, that these reasons need to be *his* reasons, for in some cases the reason why he is right may be causal in form. But at all events, the reasons in question must rule out such things as guessing, chance hits, or incorrect procedures for arriving at the answer.

The formula that I have adopted, however, has a further merit, in that it brings in one of the features that Austin pointed out with regard to the first-person utterance of "I know." In his paper "Other Minds,"[19] Austin invoked the notion of "performatives." Utterances like "I promise" are performatives in that the saying of "I promise" is the performance of the promise itself; it actually *does* what it seems to say that the speaker is doing. Austin was eventually to incorporate the notion of a performative utterance into the general theory of locutionary, illocutionary, and perlocutionary forces, to which reference was made in Chapter 3. In the paper now under consideration Austin assimilated "I know" to "I promise." It is not true of course that "I know" is just like "I promise" in its performative aspect, and Austin recognized that fact. Nevertheless, Austin claimed, saying "I know" is not just reporting a fact about oneself; it is giving one's warrant to something, and a warrant that is somehow different in degree from that involved in saying merely "I believe." There is much in this, and in a sense it explains why it is pertinent to say that knowing is being in the appropriate position to certify or to give one's authority or warrant to the truth of what is said to be known. One might indeed put the matter by saying that second- and third-person uses of "know" are in a way parasitical on first-person uses, so that to say "He knows *p*" is to say that he is in the appropriate position to claim "I know *p*." This of course would not be illuminating without the further consideration about the force of saying "I know *p*"; but given that, it sets off the concept of knowledge against the background of certain human practices and institutions that are essential to it.

19 J. L. Austin, "Other Minds," *Proc. Arist. Soc.* Suppl. Vol. (1946), pp. 148ff., reprinted in his *Philosophical Papers*, ed. J. O. Urmson and G. J. Warnock (Oxford, 1961), pp. 44ff. (New York, 1961), and in *Logic and Language*, ed. A. G. N. Flew (Oxford, 1953), II, pp. 123ff. (Garden City, New York, 1953).

(d) Types of knowledge

In my discussion so far I have in general assumed that knowledge is knowledge of facts, and I have restricted my discussion to a range of facts that might be thought of as unproblematical. Such restrictions are of course unjustified in general, and it is necessary to consider further distinctions that can be made in this connection.

There is, first, the distinction between "knowing that" and "knowing how," of which much has been made by Ryle in the *Concept of Mind* and elsewhere.[20] "Knowledge that" might be said to be theoretical and "knowledge how" practical, and Ryle has argued forcibly that not all "knowledge how" presupposes "knowledge that." Indeed, he has argued that the counterthesis would entail an infinite regress, since every item of theoretical knowledge requires formulation and application, and this implies "knowledge how"; thus, in a way, "knowing how" is prior to "knowing that." It could be objected that the distinction need not be so sharp as is implied in this argument, and that there could be forms of knowledge that are both theoretical and practical at the same time. Whether or not this is so and whether or not it is correct to view one form of knowledge as having priority over the other, the general distinction is real enough. At the same time, a further distinction needs to be drawn between knowing how to do something and merely being able to do it. It is reasonable to argue that animals that are able to do things instinctively do not really know how to do those things, or that it would be misleading at least to say so. This is because "knowing how" normally implies some understanding and knowledge of the principles involved in the activity in ques-

[20] G. Ryle, *The Concept of Mind* (New York and London, 1949), Ch. 2. See also his "Knowing how and knowing that," *Proc. Arist. Soc.* (1945–46), pp. 1ff.

tion. In cases where there is no question of having such understanding, it seems wrong to speak of "knowing how." Thus I can flex my muscles in raising my arm, but it would seem strange to say that I know how to flex my muscles. The situation would be different where I have to learn to do things—like wiggling my ears. If I can do that it is because I have learned the knack; I know how to go about doing it because I have learned the procedure. Whether or not someone can *say* how he does such things, if he has learned to do them, he in some sense knows the principles involved. "Knowing how" is knowledge of a technique, the principles of which could be formulated in theory, whether or not they could be in practice. Techniques are normally acquired by learning and reveal themselves in a certain flexibility in the circumstances in which they are manifested. It remains true that a man cannot be said to know how to do something unless he can do it, except in the sense that he knows in theory how to do it although he cannot do it in practice; he knows the principles but cannot apply them. Moreover, we do not, as we have seen, speak of knowing how unless there is a good reason for the ability. To that extent "knowing how" and "knowing that" are parallel, and it is intelligible that we have the locution "knowing how."

Next, there is the distinction between "knowing that" and "knowledge of" a person or thing. There are perhaps greater refinements attached to knowledge of persons than to knowledge of things, since knowledge of persons normally involves personal relationships, without which it is feasible to say that it is an illusion that one knows the person concerned.[21] Knowledge of things requires no such conditions. Both with knowledge of persons and knowledge of things "knowledge of" is close to "acquaintance with." If I know someone I may equally be said to be acquainted with him, the implication being

[21] Cf. the feeling that one may have that one knows television personalities whom one has never met. I shall return to this point in Ch. 8, sec. (e).

that I know things about him, generally on the basis of having met him personally. In this sense knowledge by acquaintance is knowledge of someone or something on the basis of some confrontation, but it implies knowledge that certain things are so about the person or thing in question. Knowledge of something is knowledge of the thing under a certain description at the very least. Knowledge of the thing presupposes an identification of the thing; it thus presupposes knowledge that the object of knowledge is a such-and-such. "Knowledge of" is for this reason not independent of "knowledge that." This is so despite the fact that in some languages there are distinct words for marking off the difference between acquaintance with and knowledge of facts; e.g., the French *connaître* and *savoir*. The reference to a confrontation between subject and object, however, may suggest a distinct state of mind involved in that confrontation—a state of awareness. There is indeed such a state as an awareness of a thing, although it is something more special than simply having knowledge of the thing. Such a state of awareness is implied by the Greek term *gnosis*, and there was a tendency in Plato and Aristotle to think of such awareness—the direct intuition of an object—as the paradigm of knowledge. Even so, the content of any such awareness could be expressed only in terms of what the subject knows about the object, what relevant facts he knows; hence, once again, what a person knows when he has direct awareness of an object is "knowledge that."

These remarks are of some importance in the light of the tendency on the part of some philosophers to give a special sense to knowledge by acquaintance—one that makes it equivalent to the direct awareness that I have just mentioned. The most important instance of this (though the *idea* can be found in many other places) is the Russellian distinction between knowledge by acquaintance and knowledge by description.[22] Russell

[22] B. Russell, *The Problems of Philosophy* (London, 1912), Ch. 5.

distinguishes first between "knowledge that" and "knowledge of," and then within the latter between knowledge by acquaintance and knowledge by description. What I know by acquaintance is supposed to be what is directly present to me when I am aware of something. Such knowledge is supposed to be direct, immediate, certain, and incorrigible, and according to Russell all other knowledge, which is knowledge by description, must be founded upon it. The objects of such knowledge by acquaintance do not include physical objects, since error is possible with them and we can thus know them only by description. We have knowledge by acquaintance of sense data, memory data, the self, and universals. Without going into the details of this list, it must be apparent that Russell's reason for introducing this idea is the search for certainty that was mentioned in Chapter 2. It is thus part of the empiricist program of finding objects of experience of which there is no possibility of doubt. Yet this knowledge must be essentially contentless, since any attempt to say what one knows must be to go beyond the immediate experience and desert knowledge by acquaintance. In this sense, therefore, the concept of knowledge by acquaintance is both useless and misguided. There is no such thing as knowledge by acquaintance in this sense, since what one knows must always be identifiable under a description and thus implies knowledge by description. The incoherence of this special notion of knowledge by acquaintance, however, does not entail a similar incoherence in the ordinary notion of acquaintance with a thing or person.

The next idea that I wish to discuss is what Miss G. E. M. Anscombe calls knowledge without observation.[23] This notion is meant to cover in her discussion a number of things that are possibly quite different, and it is per-

[23] G. E. M. Anscombe, *Intention* (New York and Oxford, 1957), secs. 8ff. and 28ff. See also her paper "On sensations of position," in *Analysis* 22 (1962), pp. 55ff., and G. N. A. Vesey, "Knowledge without observation," in *Phil. Rev.* LXXII (1963), pp. 198ff.

haps doubtful whether the concept as she presents it in detail is a coherent concept with a single principle of unity. I shall not discuss all the details of her presentation. She illustrates it by reference to such things as knowledge of the place and disposition of one's limbs and knowledge of one's actions such as is involved in intention. The point is that such knowledge is not ordinarily arrived at *on the basis of* anything else that one knows; it is not based on observation. In particular it is not based on observation in the way that some of our knowledge of physical objects is based on what we discover of them in sense perception. When we know the disposition of our limbs, it may be that we have this knowledge because we have certain sensations, but our knowledge is not then *based on* those sensations. The sensations do not provide us with observational data from which we conclude that our limbs are in such-and-such a position. When we do something intentionally we know what we are doing because we intend to do just this and not because we come to a conclusion about what we are doing on the basis of what we observe about ourselves. When we intend something for the future we know what we shall do in the same way. In all these cases we *may* be wrong; our limbs *may* be otherwise disposed than we think, and our intentions *may* be unfulfilled. In that case we did not know after all; for, in keeping with what is true of knowledge in general, being wrong prevents it from being knowledge. This does not prevent our sometimes knowing the disposition of our limbs and what we are doing or going to do, although we have no reasons of an observational kind for saying what we say we know.

Of course, even if we had no reasons at all, this would not matter, as we saw in earlier sections, as long as there was a reason why we knew, as long as there was an explanation. In the case of our knowledge of the disposition of our limbs, there may be such an explanation— one of a causal kind in terms of the sensations that we are having and that are produced by the stimulation of nerve endings. In any case it is possible in some instances,

if not in all, to say that our reason for saying that our
limbs are in a certain position is that that is where we
feel them to be. But it should be noted that this does not
constitute knowledge on the basis of observation. Feeling
is knowing provided that what we feel is correct. In the
case of knowledge of one's intended actions, too, it is in
a way possible to speak of having reasons; our reason for
saying that we are doing such-and-such is that that is
what we intend. In exactly what way intention constitutes a reason for saying that we are doing something is a
complex question, but there is again no place in the
ordinary way for the idea that the knowledge in question is based on observation. The way that intention
comes in here gives this "practical knowledge," as it is
sometimes referred to, a particular importance as well as
providing special difficulties for a philosophical account
of it—difficulties into which it is impossible to enter here.
This kind of knowledge is sometimes referred to, e.g.,
by Stuart Hampshire, as nonpropositional.[24] I do not
think that this is the way to put it. Whether the knowledge can be formulated in propositions—and often there
is no reason why it should *not* be—is beside the point.
The important point is that this kind of knowledge is
not ordinarily founded on anything that we observe
about ourselves and that thereby constitutes its basis.

Another form of knowledge of the same kind might be
knowledge of our sensations and their location. There
is, however, a difference. It is sometimes said that judgments about our own sensations are incorrigible. It may
be better to say that in this connection the notions of
being right and wrong do not have a purchase in the
ordinary way. If we can be mistaken about what sensations we are having we are nevertheless the ultimate
authority on the matter, and if we come to the conclusion that what we felt was really different from what we
supposed, this is as much like a decision on our part as

[24] S. N. Hampshire, *Thought and Action* (New York and London, 1959), Ch. 2.

it is like a discovery.[25] In the case of the localization of our pains, it is part of the concept of pain that its location is where we feel it to be, no matter where its cause is objectively located. We may change our minds about where the location of the pain is. This may be because the pain now seems to us to have shifted its location, or it may be because we now decide that we were wrong in the first place; but in either case what we say goes. Wittgenstein said[26] that where there is no possibility of being wrong it is pointless to speak of knowledge. This is acceptable as long as it is a matter of whether it has *point* so to speak and not whether it makes *sense* so to speak; for it will make sense if it is given a sense. Whether or not we decide to say that we know where a pain is located will depend on whether a sense can be given to speaking in this way—and there is no doubt that some circumstances will provide that sense. What those circumstances are is a matter of empirical fact.[27] In sum, knowledge of our sensations and their locations is, like knowledge of the place of our limbs, and knowledge of what we do intentionally, noninferential, and in that sense nonobservational; but there are differences between them as regards the possibility of public verification of the knowledge claims. It should, however, be pointed out that these forms of knowledge constitute the *normal* ways in which we know these things; in abnormal circumstances nothing prevents our coming to knowledge of these things indirectly. I shall not argue this point here. It seems obvious enough in the case of knowledge of the

[25] See also Ch. 8, sec. (b).

[26] L. Wittgenstein, *Philosophical Investigations* (Oxford, 1953), II, p. 221.

[27] Cf. Wittgenstein's remark at the same place as that referred to above, that remarks to the effect that I know what I want, wish, believe, feel, etc. are "either philosopher's nonsense or alternatively *not* a judgment a priori." Comments on this position have often concentrated on the first of these alternatives, but there is also the second.

place of our limbs, and least obvious in the case of knowledge of our sensations and their locations. But if the point holds good, it may suggest that "knowledge without observation" does not constitute a category of knowledge all by itself. It is simply a form of direct, as opposed to indirect or inferential, knowledge. We may know about the disposition of our limbs *in* feeling them there, we may know about what we are doing *in* intending so to do, we may know about our sensations *in* having them, and not on the basis of inference from other data, whether or not we can have this other kind of knowledge in addition.

One final issue: Where there is no possibility of being wrong, for whatever reason, it may seem more in place to say that there is no doubt about the fact that we know than to say that perhaps we should not speak of knowledge at all. I have already mentioned some of the issues relevant to this point; it needs to be added that there is certainly a difference between knowledge claims where we *recognize* the possibility of being wrong and those where we recognize no such possibility. Norman Malcolm[28] goes so far in this connection as to distinguish between strong and weak senses of "know," but not in such a way that the strong sense is restricted to those propositions that are incorrigibly or necessarily true in the way typical of the search for certainty. Malcolm gives as an example of the strong sense of "know" that involved in the claim to know that there is an ink bottle before him. The point here is simply that sometimes when we say we know something we should be prepared to go on to admit that something might count as evidence that we were wrong. At other times a claim to knowledge might imply that "the person who makes the statement would look upon nothing whatever as evidence that *p* is false." I cannot say "I know *p*" and add in the same breath "but

[28] N. Malcolm, "Knowledge and belief," *Mind*, N.S., LXI (1952), p. 178ff., reprinted in his *Knowledge and Certainty* (Englewood Cliffs, New Jersey, 1963), pp. 58ff.

I may be wrong," but I can say "I know p" while envisaging the possibility "that what I say to be true should turn out to be not true." In other cases, such as those discussed by Malcolm, I may be unable to envisage any such possibility. We are not here confronted with different kinds of knowledge, perhaps not even with different senses of "know" as Malcolm claims; but it is certainly true that knowledge claims can be made against differing backgrounds of presuppositions. Not all claims to knowledge involve the consequence that we should stake everything on them. We do ordinarily distinguish between knowing and knowing for certain; which of these we say we do depends on us and not on the logical status of what we claim to know.

CHAPTER 5

Truth

(a) What are the problems about truth?

Knowledge involves the truth of what is said to be known; hence a complete account of knowledge must involve an account of truth. What then is truth? Unfortunately Pontius Pilate's question is not exactly clear in its import. In philosophy the question has tended to give rise to theories of truth, and the cynic might say that when full-blown theories arise by that name in philosophy it is time to look for misunderstandings. The classical theories of truth are the correspondence and coherence theories; and to these may be added the pragmatic theory as a more modern and less important accession to the list. It is of no avail, however, to try to assess the relative merits of these theories until some attempt has been made to decide what questions they are trying to answer.

It is important, first, to distinguish between truth and verification, and therefore between questions asking what it is for something to be true and questions asking how it may be verified as true, how we may come to know that it is true. Second, it is necessary to distinguish these latter questions from questions derived from the tradition of the search for certainty that ask under what conditions something may be known for certain as true. The question "What is truth?" is on the face of it a request for information either about what is said when something is asserted as true or about the conditions under which it may rightly be so asserted (as distinct from the conditions under which it may be known as such). Ayer has claimed that the question of the conditions under which something may be asserted as true is comparatively easy to deal with, and that the main and most interesting questions are really about verification.[1] Whether or not the latter is true there is still much to be said about truth and its conditions.

I have so far not committed myself to what it is that can be said to be true. In common parlance all sorts of things can be said to be true—from beliefs to persons—but for present purposes it is clear that the main things to which truth is to be attributed are beliefs and what beliefs are expressed in, i.e., statements. Indeed, an account of the conditions of truth can be given in terms of the conditions under which a statement can be said to be true, and the account adapted *mutatis mutandis* for beliefs. The same cannot be done for persons; truth in their case is a derivative sense of truth. On the other hand, truth and falsity should not be attributed at all to sentences, despite the views of some philosophers on the matter. A sentence as such is not a candidate for truth; it is a mere grammatical entity, and until it is decided what is to be done with it, it is not clear what is to be said of it other than things appropriate to grammar. Until a sentence is used to state something it is not a candidate for truth. Thus it is to statements that truth and falsity are attributable, or, as already indicated, to beliefs of which these statements may be the expression.

Given that a statement is true, the following questions, at least, can be raised. What do we mean when we say

[1] A. J. Ayer, "Truth," in his *The Concept of a Person* (London, 1963), pp. 162ff. (New York, 1963).

that it is true? Are we attributing a property to the statement when we say that it is true, and if so, what property? What are the necessary and sufficient conditions of its truth, i.e., it is true if and only if what? These questions and ones that may be raised concerning any statement whatever, and not just one particular statement, are all possible candidates for what is meant by the general question "What is truth?"

It is not altogether clear what is meant by asking whether truth is a possible property of statements. That it is not in any sense an observable property of what is said or written is evident enough. This would, first, make truth a property of sentences, a view that I have already rejected, and, second, it would have the consequence that it would be possible to tell whether what was said or written was true by a mere inspection of it or by a consideration of it in itself. It is not possible to tell even when a *statement* is true by considering it in itself.[2] It might, however, be the case that truth is a consequential property of statements. That is to say that it might be a property that statements possess in virtue of the fact that other things are true of them. In that case one of the tasks for the philosophy of truth would be to decide what these other things are that have to hold concerning a statement if it is to be true. In effect this comes down to asking for the necessary and sufficient conditions of truth—a statement is true if and only if what?

Not all philosophers would agree, however, that it is right to speak of truth being a property at all. There is here a certain parallel to be drawn with the course of twentieth-century ethics—a parallel with what has been said about words like "good." In that field, too, there have been arguments about whether good is a property, and if so whether it is an ordinary property of actions, one that has generally been called naturalistic in that it is

[2] This is obviously true of empirical statements, where we need recourse to evidence of their truth, and it is true, though less obviously, of a priori statements, as will be seen in effect in Ch. 9.

definable in terms of natural phenomena of one kind or another. G. E. Moore took the line of saying that it was a nonnatural property—a property of a quite different and special kind—and W. D. Ross asked the question that I have asked about truth, whether it was a consequential property that holds, if it does, in virtue of other things. A dissatisfaction with the idea of nonnatural properties led philosophers to say that good was not a property at all, and they therefore tried to explain the use of the word "good" in other ways than by saying that its use is to ascribe a property to anything. It was said by so-called "emotivists" that the use of "good" was to express emotions, and by "imperativists" that its use was to commend actions and so to influence people in the way that commands may do. Attempts have similarly been made to explain the use of "true" in other ways than by saying that its use is to ascribe a property of some kind to a statement; thus P. F. Strawson has said that its use is to confirm some statement already made or supposed to be made.[3] Neither the suggestion that the function of "good" is to commend nor the suggestion that the function of "true" is to confirm can escape the charge of circularity, since they both invite the question "As what?" Thus whatever is said about the function or use of the expressions concerned, there are still questions to be asked about the conditions under which the expressions have their proper use or function. (In fact, a better parallel would be that between "true" and "right," since something can be more or less good, whereas a statement is either true or false and cannot be more or less true, except in a loose sense; "right" and "true" are parallel to the extent that they both signal in their use the attainment of a standard. The crucial question in each case is the nature of the standard.) What

[3] P. F. Strawson, "Truth," *Analysis* 9 (1949), pp. 83ff., reprinted in *Philosophy and Analysis,* ed. M. MacDonald (Oxford, 1954), pp. 260ff. Other writings by him on this subject are in *Truth,* ed. G. Pitcher (Englewood Cliffs, New Jersey, 1964).

seems to follow from this is that it is a question of relative unimportance whether truth is a property of statements or not—although the reasons for saying that it is not a property in *any* sense of that word seem as dubious as those for the parallel view that goodness is not a property. The real issues are those surrounding the notion of objectivity—how the ascription of truth (and *mutatis mutandis* of goodness) can be objective and not a matter of subjective decision or attitude. I shall return to this issue in the last section of this chapter.

The issue that I have expressed in terms of the necessary and sufficient conditions of truth is sometimes put in terms of the notion of the criterion of truth. We are not concerned here with criteria of truth in quite the sense in which this idea was discussed in Chapter 3, section (b). There I was concerned with the criteria of truth for a given statement or kind of statement—the truth conditions that give it the kind of sense that it has —and I tried there to distinguish sharply between truth conditions and verification conditions. The same distinction needs to be made here where we are concerned with the notion of truth in general; we need, as I said earlier, to distinguish questions about truth from questions about verification. Hence if we look for criteria of truth in general we must not expect to be provided with something that will tell us when and whether a statement is true. It is the fault of the classical theories of truth that, to one extent or another, they seem to attempt to provide this. On the other hand, if we are concerned with criteria of truth in the sense of criteria for the concept of truth, as specified in Chapter 3, section (d), and look to the necessary and sufficient conditions of truth to provide this, we shall be in difficulty, as will appear later. For the only thing that can be provided in the way of necessary and sufficient conditions for the truth of any statement whatever is something uninformative as to the concept of truth—even something that involves circularity. This is the notion of correspondence with fact—a statement is true if and only if it corresponds with fact. The concepts of truth and fact are logically interconnected, but we get a purchase upon them through the notion of intersubjectivity, for this is the criterion of objectivity, a notion that includes those of both truth and fact. In other words, the criterion of objectivity and therefore of truth and fact is public agreement. Normally if people agree on something it is true. Not that this follows necessarily, any more than it follows necessarily from the fact that someone manifests expressions of pain, that he *is* in pain. But this is the normal pattern, and if people did not agree in judgments there would be no room for the notion of truth; if there were, for example, universal disagreement about every matter, it would be unintelligible to speak of truth, since the notion would not get a purchase.

It follows from this that questions about what is going on in ascribing truth, questions about the necessary and sufficient conditions of truth, and questions about the criteria for the concept of truth are all different, though in some ways connected, questions. The classical theories of truth in their traditional forms are inadequate answers to these questions in one way or another.

(b) Classical theories of truth

The correspondence, coherence, and pragmatic theories of truth purport to offer what are in some sense criteria of truth. (Here the strictures expressed in the previous section apply.) They claim respectively that the criteria of truth are correspondence with fact, coherence with other propositions of judgments, and success in practice, i.e., the leading to successful results, which may take the form of successful predictions or be of a more obviously practical kind. It is far from obvious that these theories *could* be taken as theories about what "truth" means. Let us take coherence, for example; it is scarcely a plausible suggestion that what it means to say that a statement is true is that it coheres with other statements. Apart from any other consideration, it seems difficult to give an account of coherence itself that does not already presuppose the notion of truth. (For example, when it is said that the statements of a theory cohere with each other, what is meant is that the truth of some of them has a bearing on and goes to confirm the truth of others.) This is less obvious with correspondence, perhaps, although one way of stating what is involved in correspondence with fact would be to say that the correspondence holds if something is true of a statement or proposition that is also true of what corresponds to it in the world. On the other hand, certain versions of the pragmatic theory seem to presuppose the notion of truth in a rather flagrant way. What could be meant by "leading to successful predictions" other than leading to ones that are true? On grounds such as this, it has been maintained[4] that the so-called classical criteria of truth are really grounds on which we may appraise different kinds of statement as true—coherence being more suited, for example, to mathematical statements, and correspondence to empirical statements. Even if this last suggestion were plausible (and there are grave difficulties in working it out—for correspondence, at least), it would turn the classical theories into theories about verification rather than truth, and that has certainly not been the direct intention of their proponents; nor has it been the intention of their proponents to restrict the scope of their theories to certain kinds of statement only.

All this suggests that we should look for further reasons why the theories were put forward, for further intentions on the part of the proponents. This can be done only by looking to the background of ideas from which the theories sprang. What is important about most of the expositions of the classical theories of truth is that they are part and parcel of the classical theory of knowledge, the search for certainty. This is less true of the prag-

[4] By, e.g., A. R. White, "Truth as appraisal," *Mind*, N.S., LXVI (1957), pp. 318ff.

matic theory, which is concerned with something less than absolute certainty and advocates a content with what works in practice; but this theory arose by way of reaction against the classical theories of knowledge and is thus imbued with the same spirit. William James, the originator of the theory, took over the central idea from C. S. Peirce, but altered it in the process. Peirce had put forward practical usefulness as a criterion of meaningfulness, with the plausible suggestion that a scientific term can be considered meaningful only if its use has practical consequences.[5] James applied this idea (perhaps confusedly) to truth in the attempt to supply a down-to-earth substitute for certainty within the theory of knowledge.[6] But merely to reject the search for certainty by putting something less in its place without diagnosis of the reasons for the demand for certainty in the first place is to some extent an abrogation of the philosopher's responsibility. The pragmatic theory cannot therefore be put on the same level as the other two theories—the correspondence and coherence theories. I shall not discuss it further. (It would not be unfair to say that it is founded on a muddle.) The other two theories have arisen repeatedly in slightly differing forms throughout the history of epistemology. Correspondence has an association with the empiricist tradition, coherence with the rationalist. From the point of view of each tradition, the alternative has seemed unintelligible.

The issues may be put more or less crudely in the following way. For the empiricist the paradigm of knowledge is direct perception of the world and is thus expressed in sense data statements, statements about the immediate deliverances of the senses. It is thus to be expected that for him the paradigm of evident truth is to

[5] See, e.g., the papers by C. S. Peirce included in *The Philosophy of Peirce*, ed. J. Buchler (London, 1940), Chs. 3, 7, 17–19.

[6] William James, *Pragmatism* (New York, 1907); *The Meaning of Truth* (New York, 1909).

be found in the same place. Truth will be seen to be evident if it is seen that the true statement in question corresponds directly to what it reports. Other statements that are built up from sense data statements will be connected with the world with which they are ultimately concerned more indirectly. But if the basic statements can be shown to be true because they correspond directly with the world, and if an account can be given of how other statements are built up from the basic ones, it should be possible in principle to show how nonbasic statements correspond with the world also. Thus Locke could say, quite generally, "Truth seems to me, in the proper import of the word, to signify but the joining or separating of the signs, as the things signified by them do agree or disagree one with another."[7] This statement involves a theory about the nature of statements ("the joining or separating of the signs"), a theory about meaning ("signs" and "things") and a theory about facts or the world ("things . . . agree or disagree one with another"). Ultimately words mean or denote things, and they are put together in propositions, if these are to be true, in ways corresponding to the ways in which things belong together. There are difficulties about all these aspects of the theory, and the difficulties have been fastened on by opponents and critics of the theory. Do words get a meaning in this simple-minded way? Are statements or propositions simply conjunctions or disjunctions of signs of this kind? What are the "things" in question, and how do they go together in such a way that one can speak of their agreement or disagreement being similar to the agreement or disagreement of signs?[8]

The most systematic attempt to work out answers to these questions is to be found in Wittgenstein's *Tracta-*

[7] John Locke, *Essay Concerning Human Understanding*, IV, 5.

[8] On the face of it, since words can be related only in spatial or temporal ways, the things that can be mapped by the words can be related only in those ways too, or at any rate only in ways that have the same degree of complexity.

tus Logico-Philosophicus,[9] with its view that elementary propositions, which form the basis of all other propositions, are mere concatenations of names, the structures of which correspond in some way, if they do not actually mirror, the structures of objects in the state of affairs in the world that make the propositions true. Wittgenstein said that he got this idea of propositions from a court case in which actual objects were made to do duty for the things the case was about. Thus his view was that in elementary propositions words do duty for things, and it is the fact that the words are arranged in the way that they are that enables a proposition to represent or picture a fact. Its truth thus depends on its being a correct picture in this sense. Wittgenstein had little interest in the traditional concerns of epistemology, which I asserted earlier were intrinsic to this kind of theory of truth (though Russell, who adopted a similar, but perhaps less radical and less sophisticated view, did have such interests); he was more influenced by questions about meaning and about the relations between language, thought, and the world. One of his concerns was to explain how one could arrive at definiteness in the sense of propositions as demanded by Frege for the foundations of mathematics. On the other hand, it is not clear why truth should be linked *in this way* with meaning, unless the aim is to provide by the link a way of telling for certain whether a given statement is true. Like Locke's, Wittgenstein's theory of truth depends on theories about the nature of statements, meaning, and the nature of the world. It rightly associates meaning with truth conditions, but it in effect presumes that the only way to definiteness of meaning is to look for it in those cases where the fulfillment or otherwise of truth conditions is obvious. (It is worth noting how close this is to a verificationist theory of meaning. It should also be

[9] L. Wittgenstein, *Tractatus Logico-Philosophicus,* new trans. by D. F. Pears and B. F. McGuinness (New York and London, 1961), esp. 4.03ff., 4.06ff.

noted that Wittgenstein came eventually to reject the whole theory.)

I have in all this only hinted at the difficulties involved in answering the questions that I made explicit about the correspondence theory earlier. It will at all events be evident that the questions can be answered in a way consistent with the theory only via a full-blown metaphysical theory of the kind put forward in Wittgenstein's *Tractatus*—one that raises as many questions as it answers. The difficulties intrinsic to a correspondence theory of this kind are those of providing an account of propositions, facts, and the correspondence between them such that investigating whether a proposition corresponds to the facts in this way furnishes a perspicuous way of ascertaining whether the proposition is true. Without the perspicuity the theory would have little to recommend it, since it would be subject to the accusation of being unconscionably vague. But just as the search for certainty along these lines is doomed to failure, so and for the same reasons is the attempt to find cases where truth must be perspicuous. Hence it seems as if the theory must remain vague or useless. Whether there is any more to be said for it is a question to which I shall return in section (d).

The rival coherence theory can be construed as an attempt to make capital out of the failure to find a satisfactory word-world relation that could be the foundation of truth. If truth cannot be founded on a relation of this kind, it can be founded only on a relation between the proposition in question and other propositions. The coherence theory can be found explicitly in this form in one surprising place: the view of the positivist, Otto Neurath;[10] it arises directly from a dissatisfaction with the idea of basic propositions in the sense of propositions whose verification comes through direct confrontation with experience. In Neu-

[10] See the papers by Otto Neurath translated in *Logical Positivism*, ed. A. J. Ayer (Glencoe, Illinois, 1959).

rath's theory, if there are basic propositions, it can only be a conventional matter which these are; but since there is no room for a correlation of propositions with reality, truth can consist only in the coherence of the body of propositions with each other. In more classical versions of the coherence theory, however, the theory has been associated with rationalist theories of knowledge and monist metaphysics (just as the correspondence theory has been associated with empiricist theories of knowledge and pluralist metaphysics). The point of departure is nevertheless the same as for Neurath: the impossibility of getting outside language or thought to a direct confrontation, unmediated by language or anything else, with reality. (This is less true of Spinoza, the seventeenth-century rationalist, than it is of the post-Hegelian idealists, e.g., Bradley. In Spinoza, apart from suggestions of a correspondence theory, the coherence theory follows from metaphysical views about the status of objects of experience, rather than vice versa. The issues are nevertheless fundamentally the same, since they turn on what is to be counted as an objectively existing substance, i.e., a substance that exists independently of how we conceive it.)[11]

Bradley's view (and this part of the theory is essentially the same as what is to be found in Hegel) is that judgment consists in subsuming reality under ideas. (Note the contrast here with the view to be found in the *Tractatus* that propositions are just concatenations of names.) Apart from our knowledge that we have experience, no knowledge of the reality so "given" is pos-

[11] For versions of the coherence theory see Spinoza, *Ethics*, II, 32ff., and his *Treatise on the Correction of the Understanding*; F. H. Bradley, *Essays on Truth and Reality* (Oxford, 1914) and *Appearance and Reality*, 2nd ed. (London, 1897) (though much of his view on truth stems from the treatment of judgment presented in his earlier *Principles of Logic* [Oxford, 1883], esp. Ch. 2). Cf. also H. Joachim, *The Nature of Truth* (Oxford, 1906 and New York, 1969), and B. Blanshard, *The Nature of Thought* (London, 1939 and New York, 1964), Chs. 25–27.

sible without the prior subsumption of it under ideas; knowledge of reality is always mediated, never immediate. There is thus no way of getting to reality in such a way as to make it possible to compare our judgments with it; all that we can do is compare one judgment or set of judgments with others. Hence the idealism and ultimately the monism, since what we build up in this way is a system of related and in some way cohering ideas; any divisions and distinctions that we take to exist within experience will not be objective distinctions, independent of our thought; they will be functions of that system of ideas. Indeed, in the end Bradley goes further than this, maintaining that judgment must always falsify reality, and produces specific arguments attempting to show that relations, even those presupposed in a system of ideas, are unreal because the notion of a relation tends to contradiction. I cannot go into these arguments here. The outcome is that absolute truth is an impossibility; there remains for judgment only partial and relative truth. All judgments are necessarily false to some extent, though they are also partially true; they have a higher degree of truth to the extent that they cohere with other judgments. Hence the coherence theory of truth goes with the doctrine of degrees of truth. (It should be clear that by "degrees of truth" is meant more than might be suggested by the use of a phrase such as I have used more than once in the foregoing: "It is less true of . . . ." By such locutions is meant merely that what is said is false in some respect or parts, not that the truth itself is a matter of degree.)

Critics of the coherence theory have often pointed in their criticism to the vagueness of the notion of coherence. The truth is that it cannot be elucidated without reference to the background of ideas from which it comes, any more than the parallel notion of correspondence can. It is useless to try to elucidate it in terms of other notions of a logical kind, like those of entailment or consistency. Entailment is too strong and consistency

too weak a notion to do justice to what is meant by coherence in this context. But the truth is that coherence
in this sense is not a logical notion at all. For a philosopher of this kind the most coherent system of judgments
or ideas is the one that seems to him most rational; hence
if grounds can be produced for the positive irrationality
of a given judgment these are *ipso facto* grounds for a
low degree of truth.[12] On the other hand, despite the
claim that there is no absolute truth, it is difficult for
the coherence theorist to escape all suggestions to the
contrary. I have already referred to suggestions of a correspondence theory in Spinoza. Analogously, Bradley
speaks about judgments about the Absolute, the sum to-
tal of experience, which are intellectually incorrigible.
They are so because they say in effect that the sum to-
tal of experience contains part of itself, and are therefore necessarily true like propositions about a true
substance or monad according to Leibniz.[13] It could be
said that whereas it is the tendency of empiricist thought
to postulate a number of brute facts, which we can
know for certain, there are no brute facts for the rationalist except the one grand fact about everything. But the
latter suggestion restricts truth, in genuine rationalist
fashion, to necessary truth, while the denial of facts of
any other kind seems to imply a denial of objectivity.
In fact, the idealist rationalist is right to stress the fact
that knowledge of things is a conceptually mediated
knowledge, since as was suggested in Chapter 3, section
(d), any knowledge of the world presupposes a system
of concepts; knowledge presupposes concepts. This does
not, however, imply any denial of the possibility of objectivity, since we can raise the question of what is objective and what is not only within the conceptual
scheme that we have. It may be that this fact prohibits
the possibility of the attainment of absolutely certain

[12] Cf. the slogan adopted by philosophers of the Hegelian persuasion that the real is the rational.

[13] Cf. Ch. 2, sec. (a), p. 31.

truth in the sense postulated in traditional epistemology, but this is a wild-goose chase in any case.

Thus the traditional correspondence theory and the coherence theory of truth are in effect misguided. They do not illuminate the concept of truth, nor do they provide adequate accounts of the conditions under which a statement can be said to be true. Their place is as part of the paraphernalia of traditional epistemology.

(c) Recent accounts of truth

Much recent discussion of truth has had as its points of departure the view expressed by F. P. Ramsey and the semantic theory originating from Alfred Tarski.[14] These two views have often been taken to be substantially the same, despite the fact that Ramsey's brief remarks on the subject in his paper "Facts and Propositions" amount to the view that the word "true" is redundant, while Tarski claimed that his theory was tantamount to the correspondence theory (although perhaps in the Aristotelian form not yet discussed). Ramsey said "It is evident that 'It is true that Caesar was murdered' means no more than that Caesar was murdered"; and he thought that in cases like "What he said is true" —where we cannot simply drop the "is true"—there were ways of paraphrasing the statement that would admit of the omission of the word "true." This view has become known as the redundancy theory of truth, and has been accepted by many who feel a reluctance to say that to ascribe truth to a statement is to ascribe a prop-

[14] F. P. Ramsey, "Facts and Propositions," *Proc. Arist. Soc.*, Supp. Vol. (1927), included in his *Foundations of Mathematics* (London, 1931). A. Tarski, "The Semantic conception of Truth," *Philosophy and Phenomenological Research* 4 (1943–44), pp. 341ff., reprinted in *Readings in Philosophical Analysis*, ed. H. Feigl and W. Sellars (New York, 1949). Tarski's earlier and more technical paper on the semantic conception of truth is included in translation in his *Logic, Semantics and Metamathematics*, ed. J. H. Woodger (Oxford, 1956).

erty to it. The resemblance of the semantic theory to Ramsey's theory is provided by the fact that Tarski expressed what is central to his view of truth in "equivalences" like " 'New York is a large city' is true if and only if New York is a large city." This is very like but not identical with Ramsey's " 'It is true that Caesar was murdered' means no more than that Caesar was murdered."

The background to Tarski's theory is his attempt to solve the paradox of the liar by distinguishing between what is said in an object language and what may be said about this in a metalanguage. According to the version of the paradox that consists of writing in a box on this page "What is written in the box on this page is false," it will follow that what is written in the box is false; and hence because what is written in the box is "What is written in the box on this page is false," it will be true that what is written in the box is true, and that therefore what is written in the box is false, and so on. Tarski takes the source of the paradox to lie in the ultimate self-reference of the sentence in question and therefore seeks to prohibit this by distinguishing what is said at level one from what is said about it at level two, and so on. Thus he takes " 'New York is a large city' is true" to be a second-order or metalinguistical sentence about the sentence "New York is a large city," which is a first-order sentence or one from the object language. Truth is thus a property ascribable to sentences, but it is not a grammatical property of them. According to Tarski it is a semantic property, since in effect a sentence has the property "true" if the sentence designates what is in fact the case. Tarski objects to the invocation of concepts like those of a fact or what is the case on the grounds that they are both vague and metaphysical; on the other hand, his assertion that his theory is a version of the correspondence theory makes clear that he has something like these ideas at the back of his mind. The problem is how to state the point without using these ideas. A series of equivalences like the one mentioned above might enable one to see what is at stake, but how can one state the general principle? It is impossible to substitute the variable p for the sentences that form one side or the other of the equivalence; it is impossible to say, for example, " 'p' is true if and only if p," since the conventions for the use of quotation marks entail that "p" is the name of the letter p and not the name of a variable sentence. One might be able to get round this by other conventions but not in a way that makes the resulting formula a straightforward sentence about an object language sentence. In a formal language one might provide an equivalence for a standard instance of a certain class of sentence and allow the idea that what is said be extended inductively (or, to use the technical term, recursively) for other members of the class, and so on for other classes. It is far less easy to see how anything similar might be done for ordinary language—a fact that Tarski takes as implying "So much the worse for ordinary language."

There are objections to this theory other than the intrinsic difficulties of applying it—though these difficulties are such that it might almost be treated as a *reductio ad absurdum* of *theories* of truth. The main objection is that it makes truth a property of *sentences*, without which it is not a *semantic* theory. But it is clear that truth cannot be a property of sentences for reasons given earlier. Indeed, this fact vitiates the account of the liar paradox that was given earlier; merely from the fact that a sentence is written in a box on a given page nothing can be inferred about its use. It may have been written there for decoration or as an example of something; only if we are given the additional information that it was written there to make a statement can we go on to make comments about its truth or falsity. On the other hand, meaning *is* a property of sentences; hence the idea of a *semantic* theory of truth is an incoherent hybrid. If one were to word the equivalences in the form "It is true that New York is a large city if and only if New York is a large city," they would not be subject to this kind of objection, but we would then have no distinction between metalanguage and object language, a distinction that Tarski thought necessary to resolve the liar paradox. There would also be no generating idea, like that of designation, that could be the foundation of a *theory* of truth.

It might also seem that we would in any case be reduced to Ramsey's position. This, however, is not so. What Ramsey said was something about what it *means* to say that a statement is true; our revised equivalence says nothing about the meaning of "truth," only about the necessary and sufficient conditions of truth. To generalize it by saying "It is true that p if and only if p" would not be to produce anything very illuminating or important, whereas to say that "It is true that p" says no more than that p is to say something about "true" that should have importance. For it implies that to say "It is true that p" adds nothing other than something of stylistic importance to saying "p"; as long as we have a theory of judgment we do not need a theory of truth in addition. The crucial question is whether stylistic considerations have any philosophical importance. Strawson, in the first of his articles on truth,[15] claimed that what Ramsey omitted to note was the specific *use* that "true" has, i.e., to confirm what has been said or what is supposedly said. Thus while "It is true that p" does not state any fact additional to that stated by "p," it does say more, in that it implies a certain context of use. On the other hand, Strawson said that the semantic theory allows that the statement asserting truth does more than the statement about which truth is asserted; but it misinterprets that "more." For the semantic theory says that to assert that something is true is to make an assertion about something, namely a sentence. And Strawson thought that it was wrong to say that it made an assertion about something, let alone about a sentence. Furthermore, Strawson said, the semantic theory does not really provide an explanation of the meaning of

[15] P. F. Strawson, ibid.

"true"; at the most it provides an account of the phrase "true if and only if," since an equivalence like "'New York is a large city' is true if and only if New York is a large city" can be taken as a degenerate case of those equivalences in which we might well read "means that" for "true if and only if" (e.g., "'New York est une grande cité' is true if and only if New York is a large city").

There are obvious objections to Strawson's position at this point. First (and Strawson himself admits this point), it does not appear that every use of "true" involves confirming an assertion, whether one actually made or one put up as supposition. (Cf. concessive uses like "If it were true that . . .") Second, the emphasis on the use to confirm an assertion seems to invite, though it does not actually entail, the conclusion that there is no such thing as *the truth*. If we take "It is true that . . ." as equivalent to the performative "I confirm that . . ." (and Strawson suggested in his original article that the utterance "It is true that" was quasiperformative), we might feel like saying to someone who insisted that that is all he meant in saying that something was true, "I do not want to know whether you confirm it, I want to know whether it is *true*." Attempts have been made to get round this kind of point by taking "true" as a term of logical appraisal, implying in its use not just that one confirms something but that it ought to be confirmed. This is more promising, although it does not completely evade the previous difficulty. Strawson said in a further article in reply to Austin[16] that the problem of truth was *how* we use "true." Whether or not "true" is a term of logical appraisal (i.e., whether or not this is its *function*) it would not be correct to say that we always use it in order to appraise another statement, let alone to confirm it. Finally, there is the point made in section (a), that references to confirmation or appraisal merely invite the

16 J. L. Austin and P. F. Strawson, "Truth," *Proc. Arist. Soc.*, Supp. Vol. (1950), pp. 111ff., reprinted in *Truth*, ed. G. Pitcher, pp. 18ff.

question "Confirm or appraise as what?" An understanding of the function of the expression "true" surely presupposes a knowledge of what it is to state a fact; it is *this* that requires elucidation. It might be held enough at this point to revert to a Ramsey-like position, and say that what this shows is the necessity of an adequate account of judgment, i.e., of what it is to state something, and that once this is done there is nothing else to be said about truth. In a certain sense this is so, but it may be so because our understanding of what it is for something to be a statement already presupposes the notion of truth, and not because "true" is redundant in any literal sense. Unless someone knew that the function of statements was to assert what is true, what is the case, or what is fact, what conception of a statement would he have? Indeed, one might say that a statement just *is* that form of linguistic expression that can be true or false.

In one of his more recent writings on this matter, written in reply to criticisms by Austin and G. J. Warnock,[17] Strawson admits that "someone who says that a certain statement is true thereby makes a statement about a statement" or at least does not dispute it; indeed, he refers to it as "the undisputed thesis." But he insists that this is compatible with a Ramsey-like thesis, taking this to be simply the thesis that "true" in its various locutions can be analyzed away. But he invokes as a possible way of analyzing away "true" in those cases where what is said to be true is not expressly formulated (e.g., "What he says is true"), the use of the formula "things are as . . ." (e.g., "Things are as he says they are"). He can thus say that a Ramsey-like paraphrase along these lines of predications involving "is true" says something not only about a statement but about "how things are in the world." How right one would be to take this as a Ramsey-like paraphrase is a matter for argument, but the point made seems to open the way to some version of the correspondence theory, since it implies a comparison be-

[17] In *Truth,* ed. G. Pitcher, pp. 68ff.

tween what is stated or said and how things are. It seems to me that some such move as this is inescapable. It is not enough to take the function of "true" to be that of confirming or appraising statements, not only for the reason already given (that of the implicit circularity involved), but also because there may be all sorts of reasons for confirming or appraising a statement in a given way that have nothing to do with its truth. We might confirm or appraise a statement in a given way for reasons of prudence, say, or to encourage someone in a certain direction of inquiry. If a statement is to count as true it must conform to fact, it must conform to standards of objectivity beyond itself and beyond the person who makes the statement.

(d) Can the correspondence theory be defended?

We have already noted objections to the classical correspondence theory, which attempts to found truth on some form of more or less direct matching between a statement and something in the world. But at the end of the previous section we also noted suggestions of a wider and less precise sense in which correspondence might have something to do with truth. Austin, however, defended a version of the correspondence theory that was somewhere between these extremes, against the kind of position that Strawson initially took. Austin's paper was, as already noted, replied to by Strawson; Austin wrote a further note entitled "Unfair to Facts," and the debate has gone on, with Warnock defending the Austinian position since Austin's death.[18] It would be pointless to pursue here all the intricacies of the argument. Some of the details of Austin's position are perhaps questionable and even inconsistent, e.g., his account of state-

---

[18] Austin's papers are included in his *Philosophical Papers* (ed. J. O. Urmson and G. J. Warnock). Most of the contributions to the debate, though not all of them, are to be found in *Truth*, ed. G. Pitcher.

ments. But Austin's central thesis is easy to state; it is summed up in his words "A statement is said to be true when the historic state of affairs to which it is correlated by the demonstrative conventions (the one to which it 'refers') is of a type with which the sentence used in making it is correlated by the descriptive conventions." Furthermore, though Austin is not as clear about this as one might wish, to say that a statement is true is to say that this relation obtains. Austin goes on to say that making his point by substituting "fact" for "state of affairs" may lead to trouble, since "fact" is regularly used in the locution "fact that," which may lead us to think that a fact just is a true statement; alternatively, it may lead us to think that for every true statement there is one fact that it fits. Austin thinks that both these suppositions are wrong. It is not altogether clear why the second is so objectionable; there may be one state of affairs that we can describe in various ways, but this need not imply that there is only one fact unless facts and states of affairs are to be equated. What Austin believes is that "fact that" is a phrase designed for use in situations where the distinction between a true statement and the state of affairs about which it is a truth is neglected; it is a "compendious way of speaking about a situation involving both words and the world." Austin's correspondence theory, therefore, is to be found in the statement quoted earlier about the correlation between statements and historic states of affairs.

Austin lays great weight on the conventions that underlie the word-world connection with which he is concerned. He says that these are of two kinds: (a) descriptive conventions, which correlate words (i.e., sentences) with the *types* of situation to be found in the world, and (b) demonstrative conventions, which correlate words (i.e., statements) with *historic* situations to be found in the world. And he goes on in one place to say that the relationship between a true statement and the world is itself a conventional relationship. Warnock, in a note to his article in *Truth* (ed. Pitcher), claims that this last remark and the one under (b) involve "slips" on Austin's part; the only conventional relationship of a demonstrative sort is that between a statement and the words used to make it, i.e., it is a conventional matter that we use the actual words "The cat is on the mat" to make the statement that the cat is on the mat. Hence Warnock prefers to word (b) by speaking of "*demonstrative* conventions correlating words as uttered on particular occasions with historic situations, etc." I do not think that these *are* simply slips on Austin's part; they are a function of the uncertainty and inconsistency in Austin's account of statements to which I referred above. But given these points, what Austin's account comes down to is that a statement is true when the state of affairs that it picks out is of the type that the words used purport to describe, given the descriptive conventions for the use of these words. Thus, if I use the words "The cat is on the mat" to make the statement that the cat is on the mat, then if the state of affairs that I pick out in making that statement is one of a kind that could be meant by the words that I use, then my statement is true. It is important here, as Warnock points out, not to be misled by the talk of demonstrative conventions into thinking that Austin is talking about conventions for demonstratives, and so to conclude that Austin's account will fit only affirmative subject-predicate statements— as Strawson was probably misled in his original reply to Austin. The scope of Austin's account is wider than that and will cover any statement concerned or plausibly to be taken as concerned with historic or empirical states of affairs. That of course still leaves a number of kinds of statement out in the cold.

Within these limits Austin's account has some claim to be considered seriously as an account of the conditions under which a statement can be considered true. Strawson originally claimed that this was not the problem of truth, the latter being the problem of how we use "true," but he has become considerably more liberal in his attitude in more recent writing. He claimed initially that

Austin was really concerned with the nature of fact-stating discourse, and made certain statements about the nature and role of facts themselves that I shall come back to in the next section. More recently (in the paper replying to Warnock in *Truth*) he has said that what Austin offers is "a (partial) account of what it is for a (true) statement to be made." There is some justice in this comment, or at least there is some justice in Strawson's more explicit claim that this is what Austin's account adds to what is also there in a Ramsey-like account—that the statement that another statement is true says that things are as this second statement says. In effect, Austin gives an account of what it is to state a fact, to state something that is true, about an actual situation in the world; if the stating is done successfully the statement will be true, and it will be done successfully if the general conditions noted are adhered to. But even if this is so, even if these things do constitute the necessary conditions of a statement (even if one of a certain restricted kind), it remains a question whether in saying that a statement is true one is stating that these conditions are fulfilled. Surely one is at most saying that whatever conditions have to be fulfilled in order to state a fact they have been fulfilled—or simply that a fact has been stated.

This does not mean that there is nothing left to the correspondence theory of truth; for it remains true that a statement will be true if and only if it corresponds to the facts. Indeed, if one considers what could be the general, necessary, and sufficient condition of any statement being true, it will appear that the only thing that it could be would be that the statement should correspond to fact. Moreover, any attempt to substitute some other term for "fact" is doomed to failure, since any terms that might be so substituted will be either synonyms for "fact" or so close to it that they could not be explained independently of the notion of fact without circularity. (Thus, if we were to say that a statement is true if and only if it corresponds to the states of affairs, we might be invited to say *which* states of affairs, and the only satisfactory answer to this question would be "Those states of affairs that actually obtain, or obtain in fact.") Thus a statement is true if and only if it corresponds to the facts, but nothing in this turns on anything to do with the word "corresponds." It is certainly not the case that every statement can be correlated with a fact in the way that the classical correspondence theory supposed. Austin claims in his paper, as we have already noted, that the suggestion that there is a fact for every true statement is objectionable; it is only so if one supposes in addition that there is an actual, specific way of picking out the fact from the true statement other than by saying that it is the fact that this statement states. The classical correspondence theory supposed that this last was possible, because it was supposed by its protagonists that this would provide a way of telling whether a statement was true. Without this the relationship of true statement to fact can still remain in some form.[19]

(e) Facts and objectivity

What then is a fact and what is the force of speaking of correspondence to fact? In ordinary language the word "fact" is used in a variety of ways, and it tends to get its sense via what it is opposed to; we may oppose fact to fiction, theory, supposition, and so on, and in each case there are different nuances to the use of "fact." Etymologically the word is, of course, connected with what is done (Latin *factum*; cf. Greek *pragma*), and this idea survives in the legal usages "before the fact" and "after the fact." These nuances mean that it is of little use to appeal to ordinary language for illumination about what is involved in speaking of a true statement corresponding to fact in the philosophical sense. In particular, it is irrelevant to point to the fact, as Austin

[19] See also my paper "The Correspondence Theory of Truth," *Phil. Quart.* XII (1962), pp. 193ff.

did in "Unfair to Facts," that we speak in ordinary language of a statement or theory fitting the facts. This tends to mean that the statement or theory fits in with what is already known to be true (i.e., "fact" = "known fact").

A further source of possible error is the fact that the word "fact" is characteristically used in a " 'that' construction," i.e., "fact that." Indeed, "It is a fact that . . ." is for most purposes synonymous with "It is true that . . . ." This may mislead people into thinking that a fact is just the same thing as a true statement; if this were so, to say that a statement is true if and only if it states a fact would be to state the most obvious tautology, and it would serve no useful purpose. That this is not so will appear later. It is true that a fact is what is stated by a true statement, but it does not follow from this that it is the same as the latter; nor would it be true to say that a fact is *just* what is stated by a true statement. This might suggest that facts do not exist until a statement is made that happens to be true, whereas it would appear that on the contrary there are countless facts that have never been stated and never will be. In his initial reply to Austin, Strawson did maintain that facts are what true statements state, while denying that true statements and facts are to be identified; he also asserted, however, that while *things* are the material correlates of referring expressions, facts are the *pseudo*material correlates of statements. He sought to excuse himself from the accusation of prejudice in favor of things over facts, but the use of *"pseudo*material" does suggest such a prejudice and also the point of view that facts as such do not really exist. Such a point of view would be mistaken. It is the facts that make true statements true, and it is this that makes it false to say that facts are just what true statements state; statements are true *because of* the facts. This is a point that Aristotle brought out when he said "If a man exists, the proposition by which we say that he exists is true; and conversely—for if the proposition by which we say that a man exists is true, the man exists. But the true proposition is by no means the cause of the fact existing; the fact is in some way the cause of the proposition being true. For it is by virtue of the fact existing or not that the proposition is said to be true or false."[20] It is noteworthy that Aristotle, who is often said to be responsible for the correspondence theory of truth, made no attempt to establish any detailed correlation between a true statement and the facts; he was not motivated by the same considerations as were Locke and his successors in the tradition of the search for certainty.

The problem is to make clear what is involved when it is said that statements are true *because of* the facts. It would not be right to say that a statement is true simply because of what is there in the world. For not all statements that are true are simply about what is "there in the world"; for example, the statement "$2 + 2 = 4$" is true and states a fact, but the fact in question cannot be said to be in the world in any obvious sense, though it does have objectivity. The force of speaking of objectivity here is to point out that a person's saying it cannot make it so; its truth is independent of *anyone's* saying it. It is the same thing that is involved in the "because of" used in saying that the statement is true because of the facts. The reason for the truth of the statement lies elsewhere than in its being stated. Strawson was right to say that facts are related to true statements in rather the way that things are related to names. Indeed, the notion of a fact is a *categorial* notion; it picks out a distinct category of entities (where by a category is meant here simply a class of entities picked out by a certain use of language or a certain mode of thought—the notion of a category in this sense arises at the frontiers of language or thought and the world and serves to point to all that is picked out by a mode of language or thought). A thing is what is picked out by a referring expression, a property what is picked out by a descriptive expression, and a fact what is picked out by a statement (granted that the

[20]Aristotle, *Categories* 12.

expressions concerned are all successfully used). It is only if there is something to be picked out in each case that we can speak of the successful use of the expressions in each case. Thus while the logic of these categorial expressions is linked with the roles of the corresponding forms of language and thought, the possibility of success in the use of these forms of language and thought implies a reference beyond these forms to something concerning which there can be objectivity. I put the matter in this way rather than by saying that there is a reference to what is in the world, since in neither case does objectivity necessarily imply that there literally exists something in the world in any concrete sense. It is possible to refer to a thing, without that thing being a concrete physical object (e.g., abstract entities, like justice); similarly for facts.

Thus while the category of fact picks out something that is involved in one particular word-world relationship, it is not true to say that a fact is necessarily something in the world in any concrete sense. Of course, there is *a* sense perhaps in which even, say, ethical facts are in the world; they relate to what is in the world. But they do not constitute a state of affairs that is in any sense concrete or even empirical. In saying that such facts relate to the world, I am bringing out the point that unless there were a world independent of ourselves, there could be no application to the notion of objectivity at all. A situation in which there was no world independent of me would equally be a situation in which there would be no people independent of me; my situation would be a solipsistic one. But there are grave objections to the possibility of such a situation if place is to be retained within it for objectivity. It would have to be a world consisting of myself and my experiences, and yet one where there were grounds for distinguishing between what was due simply to me and what was not. For reasons similar to those that Wittgenstein used in the *Philosophical Investigations* in arguing against the possibility of an intrinsically private language, such a situation would be impossible. Without the possibility of a public check there could be no way of distinguishing between what was a matter of decision on my part and what was a matter of recognition of a state of affairs independent of my decision. There could be no point of application for truth conditions.

Thus there would be no room for objectivity if there were not intersubjectivity. Not that objectivity and intersubjectivity are the same. The former implies the latter, but not vice versa. Intersubjectivity in turn implies the existence of a common framework against the background of which people can communicate; that is to say that it implies a common world. (The argument for this is complex; the essential point is that communication requires a common point of reference, a common framework within which things can be identified and reidentified.[21]) Thus talk of facts and talk of correspondence with fact implies a form of realism, not in the sense that facts are identical with concrete states of affairs, but in the sense that a necessary condition of there being objective truth is that there should be an independently existing world. To say that a statement corresponds to the facts is to say that the statement conforms to whatever standard of objective truth is applicable. What that standard is in any given case depends on what are the agreed truth conditions of that statement. I indicated in Chapter 3 how the kind of meaning that a statement has is dependent on its truth conditions; that is to say that there is an intimate connection between meaning and truth conditions. This also emerges from the present discussion. If there are no brute facts—and the present discussion also indicates that there are none —what is to count as fact depends on how we have come to see the world and upon the conceptual structure that is presupposed in our seeing it in this way. Because it in turn rests on our form of life, we cannot get completely

21 Cf. here P. F. Strawson, *Individuals* (Garden City, New York, and London, 1959), Part 1.

behind this conceptual ordering; but we can in principle question its applicability at any given point. That is why there can be no brute facts.

What we can state about the world depends on this agreed, intersubjective system of concepts. These bring with them criteria of truth, so that there must be points of agreement concerning the applicability of these criteria of truth. Hence there must also be points of agreement on what is to count as fact and what is not. That there must be facts, therefore, that make certain statements true is a precondition of any view about the world. What these facts are is something that we can raise questions about only from a point of view within what is agreed, and which provides the framework for intelligible discussions about what is fact and what is not. For a man cannot be said fully to understand a form of discourse if he does not know the truth conditions for what is said within it and if he has no idea of how these truth conditions might be satisfied; that is to say that understanding itself presupposes some knowledge of what counts as fact and how it might be ascertained what counts as fact. It is only against a common understanding of this kind that we can go on to ask what the facts are in a given case. A statement is true if and only if it corresponds to the facts. In one sense, this is to say no more than that it is true if and only if it satisfies the appropriate conditions of truth, if it fulfills the requisite standards of truth. But to use the language of *fact* here is to reflect all that stands at the back of this.

All this indicates, too, why, if correspondence with fact cannot be the *criterion* for the concept of truth (for truth and fact are too close for the concept of truth to be understood via that of fact), intersubjective agreement may be. I have said that it does not follow from the fact that people generally agree about something that it is true. On the other hand, since interpersonal agreement is the background against which we can speak of fact, it is to be expected that this agreement will provide the point of application for the concept of truth.

Or, in other words, if people agree on a matter it is to be expected that what they say will *normally* be true.[22] If it is not so, it is this fact that requires explanation. Just as people are normally expected to manifest certain forms of behavior when they are in pain, such that these forms of behavior therefore provide the criteria for the concept of pain, so it is with truth and intersubjective agreement. Interpersonal agreement provides the criterion for the concept of truth, the point of application through which the concept of truth becomes intelligible, and without which truth is impossible. That not everything that people agree about is true is no objection to this, but that they will *normally* agree on what is true is a precondition of the whole language of fact. This has considerable importance for knowledge and for all epistemological concepts, like those of perception and memory, which we must now proceed to consider.

[22] See my earlier discussion on pp. 69ff.

PART TWO

The Scope
of Knowledge

CHAPTER 6

Perception

(a) The argument from illusion

I began this book by indicating the way in which and the extent to which skepticism provides a point of focus for philosophical problems about knowledge. Similar considerations must apply to the various spheres in which knowledge is to be expected. It is obvious enough, and in the ordinary way no one would think of denying, that we do acquire knowledge through perception, and that often enough seeing is not just believing, it is also knowing. It is not that we cannot be mistaken in what we perceive; we clearly can. But we cannot be said to perceive something unless what we perceive is in some sense there; unless, within certain conventions about what is to be accepted as so, our claim to perceive such-and-such is correct.[1] Failing this, just as in the case of knowledge we have to withdraw the claim to knowledge when what we claim is not true and speak of belief instead, so in the case of perception we have to say not

[1] Cf. my *Sensation and Perception* (London, 1961), p. 193 (New York, 1961) and J. L. Austin, *Sense and Sensibilia* (Oxford, 1962), p. 95, n. 1.

that we actually saw such-and-such but that we thought that we did, that we seemed to do so, or something of the kind. This connection between perceiving and being in some sense correct would make skepticism about our ever being right in what we perceive extremely suspect, even if it were not so for other reasons. Skepticism could have a purchase here only if it had a purchase over the possibility of knowledge in general, and I surveyed the issues on that score in the opening chapters of this book.

Still, this does not prevent there being skepticism about *which* perceptual claims are correct, and it *might* be the case that our apparent right to claim perceptual knowledge of whole classes of things is unjustified. In ordinary usage we may speak of seeing people, so-called physical things, shadows, mirror-images, rainbows, people, and things on television or the cinema, stars that may have ceased to exist by the time that the light from them reaches us, ghosts,[2] and a variety of other kinds of thing. In appropriate circumstances it might be right to deny the right to speak of seeing many of these things, perhaps all of them in some circumstances. Many people would hesitate about whether it was right to speak of seeing ghosts at all; far fewer would dispute the right to speak of seeing someone on television. But what if the differences between or among these classes of phenomena were only ones of degree? In effect skepticism over the scope of perceptual knowledge arises from just this point —the belief that there is good reason for doubting certain kinds of perceptual claim and that there is only a difference of degree, not one of kind, between these and other, apparently more respectable, kinds. If this were accepted, the only hope would be to find forms and objects of perception that are different in kind from those already mentioned. This is the form of the so-called argument from illusion, though strictly speaking emphasis on illusion occurs in only one species of the generic argument and, as Austin maintained, even then it trades upon a

[2] See J. L. Austin, ibid.

confusion between illusion and delusion.[3] (A delusion implies a false belief on the part of the person who has it and the suggestion that there is nothing actually there corresponding to it; in the case of an illusion there is normally *something* there, and while the person concerned sees that something in a sense wrongly, he need have no false beliefs about it.)

H. H. Price distinguished two forms of the argument from illusion—the phenomenological and causal arguments.[4] It is the first that is the argument from illusion proper, and he thinks that this at least shows what he calls naïve realism to be false. (On his use of the term "naïve realism": This is the thesis that everything that we perceive is part of the surface of a material object—a thesis that is too naïve even to warrant consideration. Others, e.g., A. J. Ayer in *The Problem of Knowledge*,[5] have used the phrase to mean realism *simpliciter*, the thesis that we do in perception have direct knowledge of physical objects, a thesis that is not naïve but might be thought relatively uncontroversial.) The argument begins by pointing to the existence of illusions of various kinds, from sticks that look bent in water to double vision, thus indicating that we sometimes see things wrongly. It is then asserted that there is no phenomenological difference between cases of illusion and cases of veridical perception; that is to say that there is no difference from the point of view of the experience itself. How, then, can we be certain in the case of any given perceptual experience that it is veridical? And if we cannot be certain, there is room for doubt whether any perceptual experience is veridical. In some versions of the argument it is also said that in the illusory perception what we perceive cannot be a feature of a physical or

[3] J. L. Austin, ibid., Ch. 3.

[4] H. H. Price, *Perception* (London, 1932 and New York, 1950), Ch. 2.

[5] A. J. Ayer, *The Problem of Knowledge* (New York and London, 1956), Ch. 3.

material object, and hence, if there is no phenomenological difference between the illusory and veridical
perception, there are no grounds for saying that in the
case of a veridical perception what we perceive is a feature of a material object either. It is this last point that
is the main target of Austin's attack when he speaks, as
noted above, of the argument trading on a confusion
between illusion and delusion.

There is much else wrong in the argument too, and
Austin noted a number of deficiencies of this kind in
Chapter 5 of his book. There is, first, the point that
the notion of a phenomenological difference is obscure,
as is equally the notion of a difference in the experience,
since the notion of experience is itself unclear and perhaps ambiguous. (Does the man who experiences an
illusion and knows that he does so have the same experience as the man who does not know this or as the man
who sees whatever it is correctly?) Second, it is not at
all obvious that all cases of veridical perception and illusory perception are very much alike. Third, there are
obvious ways in which we can tell whether a perceptual
experience is veridical or otherwise, that have nothing to
do with any intrinsic features of the experience itself;
we can, for example, ask other people. It could be said
here that these ways of telling whether an experience
is veridical also involve perception so that we cannot
evade the difficulty in that way. There is nevertheless
a basic and erroneous assumption in the argument—that
perception is just a matter of having experiences, that
in any attempt to justify perception we have to justify
the move from those experiences to a world independent
of them (an idea that is written into the very notion of
an external world, a notion in terms of which the philosophy of perception has been so often discussed). Price
indeed starts from the point of view that we are always
directly aware of sense data, not physical objects, and
that the problem is to justify our claims to know about
physical objects on this basis. This presupposes an erroneous account of the concept of perception (a point

to which I shall return), and it begs the question in giving support to the idea that the only basis for a distinction between veridical and illusory perception must be some feature of the relevant experiences themselves.

The other argument, the causal argument, is one much favored by physiologists in *their* accounts of perception. It appeals to the causal conditions under which perception takes place. It is of course true that perception always depends upon certain conditions obtaining,[6] but this in itself could be no reason for doubting the fact that we do perceive physical objects and other things independent of ourselves. To reach this conclusion we need an extra premise of some kind. It could be argued that perception is simply the experience that results from a chain of causal processes starting from the form of energy change that affects the sense organs; this then sets up brain processes, and the experience is the last stage. Since the connection between this experience and the object that affects the sense organs is obviously indirect, it might well seem that we can have no direct awareness of that object. But without further argument, this point of view, which is the same as that noted at the end of the previous paragraph, simply begs the question. Why should perception be equated with this ultimate experience? Why should not a direct awareness of an object take place because of certain causal processes involving that object and our body? What is it that forces us into the position of saying that the awareness must necessarily be indirect? The point is surely that in those cases where perception is literally indirect, causal processes intervene that are taken to be similar in kind to those that are also involved in direct perception. Thus, once again, if there is a difference it is taken to be one of degree only. Seeing someone on television involves causal processes that differ only in complexity from those that are involved in seeing him in person. If this be ac-

---

[6] Cf. G. N. A. Vesey, "Seeing and Seeing-as," *Proc. Arist. Soc.* (1955–56), pp. 109ff.

cepted it is then possible to go on to insist that strictly speaking we do not see someone on television, we see only something that is the effect of processes set up originally by that person. If the situation is similar when we are directly confronted with him, in that similar causal processes are involved, then we should, strictly speaking, admit only that in that case too we see something that is the effect of processes set up by him.

A similar argument is involved in what is usually referred to as the "time-lag argument." This is the argument that relies upon the fact that light takes time to travel, and that there is therefore a considerable time lag between light leaving distant stars and arriving at the human eye. It can therefore result that we now seem to see something that has ceased to exist years ago, and how is it possible to see something that does not exist? It is surely part of the concept of perception that we cannot properly be said to perceive something if that thing does not exist. Whether or not this point in itself is persuasive, the argument is complete only with the further consideration that even in the case of things near at hand, light takes a certain though very small time to travel, and that in consequence an event that we now suppose ourselves to be witnessing has taken place a certain if very short time ago. What we perceive must therefore be the *results* of these and other causal processes, all of which take some time. In general, it is concluded from this that what we see must be a sense datum, the immediate deliverance of the senses, not the object responsible for it.

All these arguments rely on the consideration that there is a continuity of causal processes underlying any particular perception, such that there are only differences of degree between them; and the factor that is supposed to clinch the argument is our willingness to say at a certain point "We cannot properly be said to perceive *that.*" But in fact, where the perception is indirect, as in the case when we see someone on television, there is a discontinuity in the causal processes; they are not all of the same kind. It is that very fact that makes it plausible, though perhaps pedantic, to say that we do not really see *him* but only an effect set up by him. The fact that this is plausible by no means entails that it is also plausible to say that we do not see him when we are confronted with him directly. In the case of the time-lag argument, there is not the same discontinuity in the causal processes; hence it might seem that if we must refuse to allow that we see stars that no longer exist, we must also refuse to allow that we see everyday events, for the very same reason—that otherwise we should be seeing something that has already ceased to take place. But must we refuse to allow that we can see stars that no longer exist?

If it seems paradoxical if we do allow this, it is because we are invoking standards that were not meant to apply to cases of this kind. When it is said that we cannot properly be said to see something if it does not exist, the statement is made against the background of certain criteria of truth for the perceptual claims in question, criteria of truth that are applicable to statements about ordinary physical objects under ordinary conditions of existence. By those criteria it would certainly be false to say that we are seeing a star that ceased to exist years ago, just as it would be false to say that we see someone in our sitting room when he appears on television. It does not follow from this that it would be wrong to speak of seeing either of these things in any sense at all. It would be at least pedantic to claim that, when a certain person appeared to us on television last night, we did not see him, but only his image; it would be at least pedantic to claim that we do not see stars but only, say, the light that comes from them. The conventions involved in speaking of stars, of people on television, or the cinema, and the consequent criteria of truth for the perceptual claims in question, are different from those involved in speaking of seeing ordinary things in unproblematical conditions. Given this, it would be very misleading to say that we do not see stars, and if for special reasons we make the necessary qualifications and insist on saying this, it would be more than misleading to infer in consequence that it is wrong to speak of seeing everyday events; it would be an invalid application of conventions applicable in abnormal conditions to conditions that are anything but abnormal. There is a clear distinction to be made between the conditions in question, those that are normal and those that are abnormal, which introduces a discontinuity into the situation; and this prevents the argument making valid use of a continuity between the cases. Nothing in these arguments, therefore, makes it in any way plausible to say that what we perceive must be something directly given to the senses, in an absolute sense of "directly." The fact that there are conditions under which alone perception can take place in no way implies that we do not perceive a world independent of ourselves, and that we do not often see it rightly.

Neither form of the argument from illusion that Price distinguishes can, therefore, be taken as valid. The phenomenological version does not rob one of the right to make a valid distinction between veridical and illusory perception; the causal version does not substantiate the position that we never really perceive physical objects at all, although the possibility of unusual conditions for perception may indicate the need for caution in the case of some perceptual claims, if these are not to be misleading. Some philosophers have thought that what the argument shows is the need for some alternative theory to naïve realism in Price's sense—not that whatever we see is a feature of a material object, but that it is always something or other. Ayer reviews some theories of this kind in the first chapter of his *Foundations of Empirical Knowledge*, echoing a parallel discussion in Chapter 3 of Price's book. Thus Samuel Alexander is reported as maintaining that what we see must be characterized as a compound thing, things plus their contexts, not physical objects taken by themselves; in the familiar stick-in-water case, what we see is on this view not a stick that happens to be in water, but, as it were, a stick-in-water. This immediately raises the question how far the context is to be extended, but in any case the motivation behind the theory and similar theories is clear; it is to establish the existence of one kind of thing that can be produced as the answer to the question "What is it that we see?" in all cases and without qualification. This, as we have seen, flies in the face of our ordinary conceptions of the matter, and must be dictated by further considerations again. One such consideration might be economy, but what is the virtue of economy by itself in this context? Ayer suggested that all theories of this kind were really linguistic recommendations, in which economy in effect played a large part. The objection to a theory such as that of Alexander was that it could not cope with all cases (How, for example, could it cope with double vision?). Thus it was in effect too economical in its use of ideas; or rather the single idea that it used, that of compound things, did not give rise to an adequate account of the facts. Ayer himself recommended the use of the idea of sense data. "For," he said,[7] "since in philosophizing about perception our main object is to analyze the relationship of our sense-experiences to the propositions we put forward concerning material things, it is useful for us to have a terminology that enables us to refer to the contents of our experiences independently of the material things that they are taken to present." Austin[8] was suitably scathing about Ayer's claim that the philosophical issues about perception in general and sense data in particular are really linguistic in character, and there is indeed much to take issue with in Ayer's statement.

The main point at issue is Ayer's assumption that the main object of the philosophy of perception is to "analyze the relationship of our sense-experiences to the propositions we put forward concerning material things." In

[7] A. J. Ayer, *Foundations of Empirical Knowledge* (London, 1940), Ch. 1, p. 26.

[8] J. L. Austin, ibid., Ch. 6.

The Problem of Knowledge, where Ayer adopts views
that are in general somewhat different, though obviously
derived from, those of *Foundations of Empirical Knowledge,* he still claims that the introduction of sense data
provides insights into the analysis of perceptual statements. Moore made similar claims when, after declaring
a lack of interest in the usual skeptical arguments, he
went on to offer an analysis of what we mean when
we see physical things, which involved all the paraphernalia of sense data.[9] The assumption behind all this
is that in order to have knowledge of the world we start
from sense experiences, things that must be essentially
private, and somehow move from them to knowledge of
a public world independent of ourselves. Put in these
terms it is an obvious problem how this result is to be
achieved. But it is certainly implied that any adequate
understanding of sense perception must involve an
understanding of how this is to be done. And this implies in turn an account of the concept of perception,
which takes perception to be based on certain basic experiences. In those experiences we are given knowledge
on which our knowledge of the public world is somehow
based. If the objects of those experiences are sense data,
then these sense data are themselves more basic than
the physical objects with which they are contrasted.
Thus, as Austin says,[10] Ayer is, despite some disclaimers,
fully in the tradition of the British Empiricists for whom,
in a similar way, the basically existing things and the
basic objects of knowledge were ideas, impressions, or
sensations. The position involves both an ontological and
an epistemological claim, both a claim about what fundamentally exists and a claim about what is the basic
object of knowledge; though without the second claim

[9] See, e.g., G. E. Moore, *Some Main Problems of Philosophy*
(New York and London, 1953), Chs. 1 and 2, and "A defence of
common sense" in *Contemporary British Philosophy,* 2nd Series
(London, 1925), reprinted in his *Philosophical Papers* (London,
1959).

[10] J. L. Austin, ibid., p. 61.

the first would have little cogency. Hence the importance of an examination of the notion of a sensory experience, the "given," and of the general notion of a sense datum.

(b) The "given"

In *Perception*, Chapter 1, Price says, "When I see a tomato there is much that I can doubt. I can doubt whether it is a tomato that I am seeing, and not a cleverly painted piece of wax. I can doubt whether there is any material thing there at all . . . . One thing, however, I cannot doubt: that there exists a red patch of a round and somewhat bulgy shape, standing out from a background of other color patches, and having a certain visual depth, and that this whole field of color is directly present to my consciousness . . . . This peculiar and ultimate manner of being present to consciousness is called *being given*, and that which is thus present is called a *datum*."[11] It is clear from this account that the notion of the *given* is correlative with that of indubitability or freedom from all possibility of doubt. Price's description of what is "given" is more complex and three-dimensional than that provided by many other philosophers, but in his formal characterization of the notion he is much in agreement with them.

G. E. Moore attempted various ways of specifying sense data during his life. Sometimes he attempted to do it by way of examples such as that of an after-image, and I shall return to this kind of consideration in the next section. In one of his earliest accounts of sense data, however, that in *Some Main Problems of Philosophy*, Chapter 2, his procedure is very similar to that of Price, and he implicitly makes similar use of the notion of what can be doubted, despite his insistence, already noted, that he was not influenced by skeptical considerations. In the lecture given in this chapter he held up an envelope and asked the question, "What happened to

[11] H. H. Price, ibid., p. 3.

each of us, when we saw that envelope?" And he answers, "I will begin by describing *part* of what happened to me. I saw a patch of a particular whitish color, having a certain size, and a certain shape, a shape with rather sharp angles or corners and bounded by fairly straight lines. These things; this patch of a whitish color and its size and shape I did actually see. And I propose to call these things, the color and size and shape, *sense-data*, things *given* or presented by the senses—given, in this case, by my sense of sight."[12] (A footnote indicates that his later view was that only the patch should be counted as the sense datum. One of Moore's lifelong preoccupations was whether sense data should be equated with parts of the surfaces of physical objects.) Moore goes on to use the notion of "direct apprehension" for the awareness of the sense datum, and emphasizes the point that what each member of the audience directly apprehended, what sense data were "given," must inevitably differ because of the differences in their points of view. Moore does not explicitly say, as Price did, that the reason for invoking sense data was that these are the things over which there is no possibility of doubt. But his use of the phrase "actually see" and the notion of "direct apprehension" certainly suggests some such idea. Otherwise, why should not the members of the audience say that what they actually saw was an envelope? Why restrict the answer to something about patches of color? The only possible answer is that it might not have been an envelope after all, while there could be no doubt about patches of color. Of course, this last point might well be disputed. Why should there not be at least the *possibility* of doubt about colored patches, considering all the possibilities of illusion, hallucination, and perhaps even delusion? One possible reply to this complaint might be that there might well be argument and doubt about any description of the "given," but that something is given is beyond doubt. There must be some-

[12] G. E. Moore, *Some Main Problems of Philosophy*, p. 30.

thing that we actually see or directly apprehend. We do after all have sense experiences in which we are presented with data about the world; it is only by means of these that we make contact with the world at all. Such a reply must be considered further.

The form of the argument that is presupposed in the passages from Price and Moore has been characterized as one turning on the notion of the reduction of claims. When one claim about what there is to be perceived is shown to be dubious or at least not certain, a claim of reduced force is substituted for it. Instead of claiming to see a tomato or an envelope, we say that we at least see a shape of a certain color and size. This way of characterizing the move was invoked by R. A. Wollheim, and the procedure was adopted explicitly by Ayer in Chapter 3 of *The Problem of Knowledge*.[13] Ayer says there that because of the possibility of illusion, it may be that when I judge on the basis of present experience that my cigarette case is lying on the table in front of me, "I may, in saying that I see the cigarette case, be claiming more than the experience really warrants." He therefore suggests that in that situation one should say only that there seems to be a cigarette case there; and he moves from this position via that of saying that one is therefore seeing a seeming cigarette case to the final position of saying that one is directly perceiving a sense datum. Unlike Price, Ayer does not here wish to claim that such a perception is incorrigible (though he maintained this earlier, and there remain suggestions of that doctrine in the use of the phrase "directly perceive"). He does, however, wish to say that the sense-datum statement serves as a description of the content of one's sense experience, "irrespective of any larger claims that these experiences may normally induce us to make."

[13] R. A. Wollheim, "The difference between sensing and observing," *Proc. Arist. Soc.,* Supp. Vol. (1954), pp. 219ff., reprinted in *The Philosophy of Perception,* ed. G. J. Warnock (London, 1967), pp. 44ff.; A. J. Ayer, *The Problem of Knowledge,* Penguin edition (London, 1956), pp. 95ff. (New York, 1956).

There have been many criticisms of the steps in Ayer's argument, but the most pertinent one for present purposes is that it is not at all clear with what justification Ayer can speak of "the contents of our sense-experiences." This still presupposes that there is something basic that can be spoken of as the content of a sense experience. If I see a cigarette case, or even if I only seem to, why is not the content of my sense experience that I see a cigarette case? If a philosopher refuses to say this, it can only be because he still thinks that something is immediately given to the senses, something that is for that reason indubitable. It is impossible not to conclude that for a philosopher like Ayer, what one is directly aware of is not a world independent of ourselves but sense experiences that are in some sense private. And this view, the basic view of traditional empiricism, gives rise to equally traditional difficulties about how one can, in that case, ever justifiably claim knowledge of a public and objective world.

Idealists have generally rejected the notion of the "given," or if they have not rejected it altogether, they have certainly claimed that the contents of experience are mediate, not immediate. Immediate experience as such is incommunicable.[14] But this way of rejecting the "given" still involves an acceptance of the premises on which the argument leading to the "given" depends. It involves the acceptance of the point that any ordinary putative sense perception may be mistaken and *for that reason* cannot constitute a direct perception, an immediate apprehension of the deliverances of the senses. But ought one to speak of deliverances of the senses at all, and ought one to accept the point that any ordinary putative sense perception may be mistaken? That one should *not* accept that point has been urged by Norman Mal-

[14] Paradoxically enough, the same view has been adopted by some positivists who, like the Idealists, also accepted the coherence theory of truth, as indicated in the previous chapter, p. 122.

colm in discussing the idea of knowledge in the strong sense as we saw in Chapter 4, section (d). Malcolm would say of situations like that of Ayer's cigarette case that we just could not be mistaken, and we should not allow that anything could show us to be wrong. The fact that it is in some sense logically possible to be mistaken (though even this notion needs special care in its use) does nothing to show that we could in fact be wrong. There is much to be said for this kind of protest, and it serves to underline the point about what constitutes a description of our sense experience. It may indeed prevent us from embarking on the regress involved in the process of the reduction of perceptual claims, a regress which, it is supposed, leads to claims about the direct and immediate contents of our experience.

This brings us to the second point that I raised above: the question of whether one should speak of the deliverances of the senses at all. At this stage someone may feel like protesting: "But do we not have sense experiences? Surely we do receive sense experiences when our senses are stimulated, and it is by this means that we obtain information about the world at all." In other words, part of the seductiveness of the notion of the "given" lies in the belief that if nothing were given we would have no contact with the world at all; and we surely must have *that*. We here come up against the undeniable fact that perception depends upon the fulfillment of certain causal conditions. When these causal conditions are satisfied we undoubtedly have experiences, in the form of sensations, but it would be a mistake to identify these sensations with perception itself and then go on to argue that for that reason we must be "given" something. Sensations are not the basis on which we come to have knowledge about the world in the sense that they provide the basic information for a construction of a body of knowledge about the world. Ryle has argued that to make the contrary supposition is to confuse sensation with observation.[15] "Having a sensation," he says, "cannot itself be a species of perceiving, finding or espying," and to suppose otherwise is liable to produce an infinite regress. If perception (a better word than "observation" in this context) depends upon sensation, then if this in turn is a species of perception it will depend on a further sensation, and so on. So far the point is well taken, given that the philosopher under attack does identify or confuse sensation with perception in the way indicated. (Not every philosopher who invokes the notion of sense data does this explicitly; some, like Moore, have directly warned against such a confusion. Still it might be said that even these philosophers have sometimes covertly involved themselves in the confusion nevertheless.) Ryle goes on, however, in the postscript to Chapter 7 of the *Concept of Mind* (and also in his article, "Sensation") to have afterthoughts about the whole notion of, e.g., visual sensations. He thinks that "sensation" is in its primary sense a perceptual term, being the name for that by means of which we find out that things are warm, sticky, vibrating, and tough—i.e., a name for the faculty of tactual perception. There is another sense of "sensation" by which we refer to bodily feelings like pain, but to extend the notion to senses like vision is to introduce the notion of visual impressions as "ghostly impulses, postulated for the ends of a paramechanical theory." We speak of sensations in the case of senses like vision only when the senses break down, e.g., when we are dazzled.

It is not at all clear that this is right. Ryle is correct in his aim to demolish the idea of visual impressions in the traditional sense, but in achieving this aim he is in danger of throwing out the baby with the bath water. Nor is it easy to see the force of the observation that we

[15] G. Ryle, *The Concept of Mind* (New York and London, 1949), Ch. 7, esp. p. 214. See also "Sensation" in *Contemporary British Philosophy*, 3rd Series, ed. H. D. Lewis (London, 1956), pp. 425ff. (New York, 1956).

speak of sensations in the case of vision only when the sense breaks down, even granted that the observation is correct, which is itself dubious. The fact that we do not readily or usually speak of sensations in connection with vision may be due to the fact that we have normally no need to do so, not to any logical inappropriateness in the notion. On the other hand, Ryle is right in stressing the fact that the language in which we speak of sensations is, as he puts it, post-perceptual, and this is a matter of some importance. It is the same point as the one that Wittgenstein made in the *Philosophical Investigations*,[16] in attacking the notion of the private naming of sensations and the whole notion of an intrinsically private language. Indeed, it is a feasible suggestion that Wittgenstein himself was there criticizing the notion of sense data, since his comments are largely directed at the Logical Atomism that he and Russell had earlier espoused; that theory embraced the notion of sense data, explicitly in Russell's case, and implicity perhaps in his.

Wittgenstein's argument is that language depends on rules, and the notion of a rule depends for its application on the possibility of a public check. Where there is no such possibility, as would be the case with an intrinsically private language (as distinct from one that is a public one but used for private purposes, or that is private only in the sense that it happens to be used by one man only, though others could learn to use it), there is really no case for speaking of rules and none therefore for speaking of a language at all. Given this general argument, the private naming of sensations would be feasible only within an already established public language, since that language provides a means of giving sense to the words that we use; we would come to the sensations with an already established concept of sensation, which would bring with it criteria of identity, i.e., some way of giving

---

[16] L. Wittgenstein, *Philosophical Investigations* (Oxford, 1953), I, 242ff., esp. 293ff.

sense to the idea of speaking of the "same sensation again." Without this, there would be no way of distinguishing between a recognition that a sensation was the same one as we experienced before and a decision so to treat it. Without public criteria of identity the notion of "same again" fails to get any real purchase. Wittgenstein said that "an 'inner process' stands in need of outward criteria."[17] The public criteria for a sensation make it possible for a genuine sense to be given to the idea of a sensation being recognized as the same as one that occurred before. Any way of speaking of sensations must therefore be postperceptual, as Ryle maintains; it must, if it is to be intelligible, depend upon a prior conception and recognition of a public world open to perception. Indeed, a consideration of the typical forms of language by means of which we describe our sensations indicates that this is the case; the only words that we have, words like "burning" and "searing," are heavily dependent for their sense on analogies with previously recognized physical processes.

The importance of all this is that there is no possible way of building up a public world from immediately given sensations. It cannot be the case that we are given basic information in sensations from which we go on to construct a world independent of those sensations. There is not only the obvious difficulty of moving from the private to the public; there is the added difficulty that, to put the matter in a Pickwickian way, the information supposedly given in sensations would not be intelligible unless we already knew what it was to perceive a public world. But that knowledge is supposed, on the theory of the "given," to be derived solely from what is given in sensation. Thus Wittgenstein's argument is a *reductio ad absurdum* of the whole notion of the intelligibility of sense data. It is not enough to argue here, as Ayer

[17] L. Wittgenstein, ibid., I, 580. On this issue see further, Ch. 8.

does,[18] that a man on a desert island could construct a language to speak of his little world, since a language of that kind would not be private in the required sense; it would be a language that is in principle public, in that it could be learned by others. (But, in fact, the whole notion of a man born on a desert island and growing up in isolation from others, so as to develop a way of thinking and talking, is one that needs a great deal of critical philosophical attention.)

One of the crucial facts about perception is that it is concept dependent, in the sense that we cannot be said to perceive anything unless we have a concept of the object of perception as an object independent of ourselves, unless, that is, we understand what it is for something to be an object of some kind. This was seen by the eighteenth-century philosopher Thomas Reid, when he insisted that one of the things that marked off perception from sensation was that the former involved a "conception or notion of the object perceived."[19] To suppose that perception is founded on what is given in sensation is to suppose that this understanding, these concepts, could be derived from the sensations themselves (a view that lies at the heart of empiricism). But if what I have said is correct this is impossible, since the only *information* (something that itself involves concepts) that can be obtained in sensation must be postperceptual. This can be seen by considering an unequivocal sensation like a pain derived from a pinprick. One might come to know that the pain was caused by a pin from some feature of the pain, but only if we already knew what a pin was and what it was to produce a pinprick. Without all this we might still have the feeling, but merely to have a feeling is not to know anything about its cause, whereas

[18] A. J. Ayer, "Can there be a private language?," *Proc. Arist. Soc.*, Supp. Vol. (1954), pp. 63ff., reprinted in his *The Concept of a Person* (London, 1963), pp. 36ff. (New York, 1963).

[19] T. Reid, *Essays on the Intellectual Powers,* ed. A. D. Woozley (London, 1941), II, 5.

when we do know about the pin through feeling it we obviously do have this knowledge. Furthermore, whereas to have the feeling is to be aware of it, it is not *eo ipso* to be aware of it as a such-and-such, as a feeling of a certain kind. For the latter to be the case we need the concept of a feeling of this kind, and this, as we have seen, is not something that can be derived directly from the feeling itself. Thus nothing is "given" in having that feeling. This argument applies to any sensation and serves to undermine the whole notion of the "given."

(c) Sense data and appearances

Thomas Reid emphasized the distinction between sensation and perception in order to attack the notion of sense impressions, a notion inherent in British Empiricism, and one which, he rightly thought, involved a conflation of sensation and perception. But when he considered perception for its own sake, he still made a distinction between original and derived perceptions, the former corresponding in many ways to the more modern notion of sense data, without its dependence on what is given in sensation. Some modern philosophers also (e.g., Ayer) have insisted that sense data should not be identified with sensations. Without reference to sensations it is not altogether clear what is the force of speaking of *data,* but the suggestion remains that sense data are in some sense basic forms of perception, on which other forms are based. The questions that now suggest themselves are "In what way are they basic?" and "Does the sense in which they are basic enable them to serve as satisfactory bases or foundations for knowledge?" We have already seen that in *The Problem of Knowledge* Ayer makes no claim for the indubitability or incorrigibility of sense-datum statements (indeed, one might say that no perceptual statement could be incorrigible just because perception is a concept-dependent form of experience—it is always possible to misapply concepts). He nevertheless thinks that sense-data statements make the minimum claim about the world, and for that reason "serve as descriptions of the contents of our sense experiences." To the extent that it can be seen exactly what this last clause means in this context, the position adopted in it seems illegitimate. It is nevertheless undeniable that one can make a lesser claim by saying that "it now seems to me that I see a cigarette case" than by saying that "I see a cigarette case." And if "sense datum" is defined in terms of "seeming" or "appearing," one has thereby given a sense to the notion of a sense datum that makes it in one respect at least more basic than that of a material object. This does not mean, however, that the notion of a sense datum is basic in any absolute sense; it is merely that the statement about sense data makes a lesser claim, and its validation goes some way to providing grounds for the acceptance of a statement about a material object.

A further point is that Ayer has in effect simply given us an example of what he counts as a sense datum, and the difficulty with all explanations of a notion in terms of examples, like the difficulty with ostensive definition, is that we need to know the principle in terms of which the examples have been selected and that enables us to select other examples. The same difficulty applies to Moore's attempt, previously noted, to explain the notion of a sense datum in terms of the paradigm example of an after-image. Ayer's example is in effect the appearance of an object when I look at it (for the exposition of the case presumes that I start with an object, a cigarette case, in front of me). What justifies me, starting from either example, in going to the other or others yet again? It might be objected that Ayer does provide the necessary principle. Despite the fact that he starts from one example, he means in effect to define a sense datum as any appearance of an object. But in that case, our understanding of the notion of a sense datum presupposes and is founded on our understanding of that of a physical object, and this prevents the sense datum from serving as any kind of foundation of knowledge.

There is another kind of objection that has sometimes been made to any attempt to elucidate the notion of a sense datum in terms of an appearance or in terms of the notion of something appearing or seeming to be such-and-such.[20] This is that we use the expressions "appear," "appearance," and "seems" only where there is doubt as to whether we are really seeing what we think we are or where we wish to deny that we are really seeing this.[21] Ayer himself recognizes that "It would be considered odd for me to say 'it seems to me that I now see a cigarette case' if I had in fact no doubt that I did see one."[22] But he insists that the oddity is not so great that there need be excessive difficulty in understanding what is meant. It might be argued that in Ayer's case there *is* difficulty of this kind, since he has introduced the notion of a seeming-cigarette case only against the supposition that one might be wrong in thinking that there is a cigarette case there. However, whatever be the role of the notions of seeming, etc., in Ayer's own argument, it has been argued more recently by H. P. Grice that what he calls the "doubt or denial condition" (the presupposition in the use of "seems," etc., that there is doubt about the characterization or identity of the object perceived or that it is being denied that its characterization or identity is what is suggested) need not be fulfilled if the locution involving "seems," "appears," etc. is to be meaningful.[23] It is impossible here to go into the details of

[20] For this kind of approach see not only Ayer but also a notable article by G. A. Paul, "Is there a problem about sense-data?," *Proc. Arist. Soc.*, Supp. Vol. (1936), pp. 61ff., reprinted in *Logic and Language*, ed. A. G. N. Flew, I (Oxford, 1951), pp. 101ff. (Garden City, New York, 1951).

[21] See also J. L. Austin, ibid., Ch. 4, for more refined observations on these terms.

[22] A. J. Ayer, *The Problem of Knowledge*, Penguin edition, (London, 1956), p. 101. (New York, 1956.)

[23] H. P. Grice, "The causal theory of perception," *Proc. Arist. Soc.*, Supp. Vol. (1961), pp. 121ff., reprinted in *The Philosophy of Perception*, ed. G. J. Warnock (London, 1967), pp. 85ff.

Grice's argument, important though it is, but if he is right the objection from which we started in this paragraph cannot be maintained. This does not undermine the other objections, and it remains true that even if one can give a satisfactory paraphrase of the statements about sense data in terms of statements involving the locutions "seems," "appears," etc., this will not enable a philosopher to use the notion of sense data as a foundation for the philosophy of perception, if he presupposes, as he must, the notion of a physical object in identifying for us the relevant appearance.

If a philosopher cannot do the last, if he cannot without circularity tell us how to recognize a sense datum when we meet one, then his account must remain in a sense formal. It may be true that whenever I see some object I appear to see it, in Grice's sense, but that does not mean (nor, I think, did Grice intend it to mean) that I am in any way "given" that appearance and that my perception of the world depends on such appearances. In other words, the notion of a sense datum elucidated in this manner will not do the work that it has been traditionally intended to do. The same kind of criticism can be made of other attempts to give a formal characterization of a sense datum as the internal or intentional object of seeing, hearing, etc.[24] Don Locke indeed maintains that it is the whole point of the term "sense datum" that it is a term neutral between theories about perception, and that some of the defenders of the notion have been in this respect its worst enemies. Sense data are, he says, what we immediately perceive, and the term "sense datum" functions as an internal accusative of verbs of perception. Put in these terms, the account puts all the weight on the Berkeleian notion of

[24] A. R. White, *G. E. Moore* (Oxford, 1958), pp. 175ff. (New York, 1958); Don Locke, *Perception and Our Knowledge of the External World* (New York and London, 1967), Chs. 1 and 11; G. E. M. Anscombe, "The intentionality of sensation" in *Analytical Philosophy*, ed. R. J. Butler, II (Oxford, 1965), pp. 158ff. (New York, 1965).

immediate perception, which is just as problematical as that of sense data. What, after all, counts as immediate perception? To say, on the other hand, that to talk of sense data "is to talk about what we perceive without going beyond what we perceive, to describe what we perceive only as we perceive it to be, and only insofar as we do perceive it"[25] is to give a formal characterization of sense data only—as of course must be the case if the term "sense datum" is a theory-neutral one as Locke maintains. It then provides no clue as to how sense data are to be individuated; for this we need further details as to what is to count and what is not to count as an example of immediate perception. It is for good reason that the philosophers whom Locke describes as their own worst enemies in defending sense data have been so. Much more than a merely formal characterization of sense data is required if the notion is to do the work required of it in the traditional theory of knowledge.

It is essential to the notion of a sense datum as used throughout the philosophy of perception that it should cover what is seen in all cases of veridical perception, illusion, and hallucination. It *could* be argued that in hallucination we do not see anything at all, but only think that we do, while in the case of an illusion we do not see things as they are, but only as they seem to be. But a characteristic reaction to a case such as Macbeth's dagger is to say "But he was surely seeing *something*"; to say that he only thought that he was, does not differentiate the hallucination from a case of sheer delusion. There is something perceptual about both hallucinations and illusions, which there need not be about a delusion, the last being an aberration of belief; indeed, there need not be any erroneous beliefs involved in illusions and hallucinations. A man may be subject to either without any tendency to be deceived about the real nature of things (cf. the Müller-Lyer illusion and mescalin hallucinations). Even Macbeth was not sure whether it was

[25] Don Locke, ibid., p. 179.

a real dagger or not! To say that because there is something perceptual about illusions and hallucinations and that one must therefore be seeing something that is the same as what is seen in veridical perception is to invoke a feature of the phenomenological argument from illusion, which was criticized in section (a).

There is no harm, on the other hand, in reserving a term like "sense datum" to cover what is seen in illusions and hallucinations, if it is insisted that in illusion and hallucination the subject must see something. (This in effect is what Miss Anscombe does when she attempts to elucidate sense data as the intentional objects of perception, thus invoking Brentano's notion of something that exists only as the object of a mental act and toward which this act is directed—though the use of this notion may generate as many problems as it solves.[26]) To say that illusion and hallucination involve something perceptual is at least to say that in these cases the person concerned is having certain experiences, certain sensations, and because of these it is for him as if he were actually seeing something in a certain way. We need some way of characterizing what the object of his experience appears to him to be (and it is to be noted once again that it would be impossible for there to appear to him to be an object of this kind if he did not have the concept of such an object). Against this background there is no harm in saying that Macbeth saw a dagger. It was not of course a real dagger, and to say without reference to the background that Macbeth saw a dagger would be very misleading, though there need be no danger once that background of assumptions is recognized. Equally, to say that a sense datum is something of this kind would bring with it no dangers once the background story is recognized and accepted. But, once again, a notion of this kind could do no general work in providing the foundations for our knowledge of the world; it already presupposes that that knowledge exists.

[26] G. E. M. Anscombe, ibid.

(d) Traditional theories of perception

Apart from idealistic theories that have stressed the role of judgment in perception, sometimes to the exclusion of the merely sensory, most philosophical theories of perception have taken for granted some notion like that of a sense datum, and have gone on to discuss how our knowledge of a world of permanent and independent objects is built upon it. The two main theories have been the causal theory and the theory known as phenomenalism. These theories are in the main really theories about the nature of objects of perception. The causal theory maintains that material objects are literally material, and they cause impressions in us or cause us to sense sense data; phenomenalism in effect starts from the other end and argues that so-called material objects are really constructs out of sense data. To a large extent, phenomenalism constitutes a reaction against the causal theory, since this latter theory seems to have the obvious objection that if we perceive only the effects of physical objects upon us we are not in the position to have any direct knowledge of those physical objects. We are not therefore in the position to verify any statement about the causation of our perceptions, and in consequence physical objects as such are what Kant called "things in themselves," forever unknowable and outside our experience. Thus we have no real grounds for belief in their existence. It is this last consideration that leads directly into phenomenalism, a view very closely connected with the verificationist theory of meaning, as should be clear from the suggestion that the impossibility of verifying any statement about the causes of our perceptions makes any such statement meaningless. For that reason, if statements about physical objects are to have any meaning at all (and it seems that they do), they must really be about sense data themselves; statements about physical objects must therefore be reducible in meaning to statements about sense data. In cruder terms, physical objects just *are* collections of sense data.

Nonacceptance of the verificationist argument that leads to phenomenalism does not of course rid the causal theory of its difficulties, since the idea of something that is in principle unknowable is a very difficult one. In any case, both theories have a common premise—that we are "given" sense data. Without this there are no grounds for denying that we may, on many occasions at any rate, directly perceive physical objects. In what way this is so is something to which we shall have to return later. Meanwhile, it is to be noted that the causal theory has not received much support from philosophers with an empiricist turn of mind, for obvious reasons. Recently, a version of the theory has been defended in the article by Grice mentioned in the previous section. Grice depends on the conception of sense-data discussed there, and since this is not really the traditional one or cannot be used for traditional purposes, it is doubtful whether the Gricean version of the causal theory is to be considered anything like the traditional one either. Grice's formulation of the theory is as follows: (1) It is true that X perceives M if, and only if, some present-tense sense-datum statement is true of X which reports a state of affairs for which M, in a way to be indicated by example, is causally responsible, and (2) a claim on the part of X to perceive M, if it needs to be justified at all, is justified by showing that the existence of M is required if the circumstances reported by certain true sense-datum statements, some of which may be about persons other than X, are to be causally accounted for.

I shall say nothing about the second part of this statement, nor explicitly about Grice's additional claim that the first part is not obviously incompatible with phenomenalism. The difficulties in Grice's account lie in the "if and only if" and in the "in a way to be indicated by example."[27] It may seem obvious that in some sense or other objects cause us to see them—at least in the sense that it must be a necessary condition of our perception of them

[27] These are points that I think that I owe to Mr. F. R. Pickering.

that they cause us to have certain experiences. But we have seen already that there are other necessary conditions that have to be satisfied if genuine perception is to take place—we must, for example, have the relevant concepts. It seems highly dubious, therefore, that our being caused by objects to have certain experiences could be a sufficient condition of our perception of those objects, as well as a necessary condition. But just this is implied by Grice's use of the phrase "if and only if." It might be objected that in this I have ignored the qualification provided by the other phrase, "in a way to be indicated by example." Grice elucidates this[28] by saying, "For an object to be perceived by X, it is sufficient that it should be causally involved in the generation of some sense-impression by X in the kind of way in which, for example, when I look at my hand in good light, my hand is causally responsible for its looking to me as if there were a hand before me, or in which . . . (and so on), *whatever that kind of way may be.*" And he goes on to say that what that way may be is a matter for specialists. But when I look at my hand in good light my hand may not be causally responsible for it looking to me as if there were a hand before me; my eyesight may be bad, I may be daydreaming and not notice the hand, I may, *mirabile dictu,* not have the concept of a hand, and none of this is a matter for the specialist. Alternatively, my hand *may* be responsible for it looking to me as if there were a hand in front of me, but this might still be a hallucination, in certain very special circumstances where the presence of an object before my eyes brings on the hallucination. In order for my hand to be considered causally responsible for it looking to me as if there were a hand in front of me and for this to be a case of genuine perception, a number of negative conditions have to be fulfilled: the light must not be bad, nor my vision; I must not be absentminded; I must not be having an hallucination; and so on. Or to put the matter in another way, the hand will

[28] H. P. Grice, ibid., p. 105 in *The Philosophy of Perception.*

be responsible for my perception of it only under normal conditions. Without all this it is not true that "for an object to be perceived by X it is sufficient that it should be causally involved in the generation of some sense-impression by X," though it is clearly necessary that this should be so. If this criticism is valid, Grice's theory needs modification; but its modification will rob it of any claim to break new ground.

Phenomenalism, by contrast, has had a much longer run in modern times, though it has equally come under criticism and has all but been abandoned. The main objections are that it makes "actualities depend on possibilities" and that it has the consequence that any analysis of a material object statement will be infinitely long and therefore incapable of being carried out even in principle. The first objection is to the effect that the meaning of a statement about, say, the table in the next room will have to be given not only in terms of experiences that I am having now but also in terms of experiences that I would have if . . . The analysis of the statement about the table will involve not only statements about my present experiences but statements about what experiences I should have under certain conditions. In cruder terms, a physical object will not be just a collection of actual sense data, but also possible ones (or sensibilia, as Russell called them). How, it might be felt, can something actual involve or be largely constituted by mere possibilities? One possible reply to this is "Why not?"; there is, after all, much that is merely possible about more or less anything. Why, similarly, should not the analysis of a categorical statement about a physical object involve a whole host of statements about possible sense data? Ayer reacted in this way to an article by Isaiah Berlin[29] that criticized the proposed analysis of a categorical statement into hypotheticals, using the slogan "There is something

29 A. J. Ayer, ibid., p. 121; Isaiah Berlin, "Empirical propositions and hypothetical statements," *Mind*, N.S., LIX (1950), pp. 289ff.

hollow about hypotheticals." There is much to be said for this reaction if the criticism be taken by itself independently of the second objection to phenomenalism. This says that no finite list of sense-data statements is ever equivalent to a statement about a physical object. The number of possible points of view of an object are indefinite, and however many of these points of view are satisfied this will never amount to proof that the object exists. In other words, the nonexistence of an object is logically if not empirically compatible with any number of experiences that apparently witness to its existence. It could be argued that in practice we only require a finite number of experiences of an object in order to consider its existence confirmed; but this is irrelevant to phenomenalism as such, since it is not concerned with confirmation but with what will conclusively verify a physical object statement, this being presumed to be its criterion of meaningfulness.

Ayer, who was once the prime defender of phenomenalism in England, has gradually come to give it up. In the article "Phenomenalism"[30] he maintained that material object statements entail some statements about sense data, but not vice versa. Material object statements, he said there and in *The Problem of Knowledge,* constitute theories meant to explain the course of sensory experiences; the truth of the theory entails the truth of some statements about sense experiences, and the verification of the latter may go some way toward the confirmation of the theory, though it can never amount to strict proof. The snag with this is that, as we noted earlier, its point of departure is the idea that we are primarily "given" these sense experiences, and that the problem is to justify the move from these to a world independent of ourselves. If this is so it seems that the course of sense experiences could be compatible with the complete falsity of the

[30] A. J. Ayer, "Phenomenalism," *Proc. Arist. Soc.* (1947–48), pp. 163ff., reprinted in his *Philosophical Essays* (London, 1954), pp. 125ff.

theory about physical objects; they might not exist at all, and in that case we would be confined to our own experiences in complete solitude. The theory is unverifiable in principle, and on this account physical objects are in no better condition than they are on the causal theory. Both theories treat the link between ourselves and the world as a contingent one, and therefore as a link that cannot be *proved* to exist. Ayer tries to get around this point in the last section of Chapter 3 of *The Problem of Knowledge* by arguing that although the contingent relationship holds in the majority of cases, there are two limiting cases in which the relationship is more than contingent.

Ayer says,[31] "There may be no specifiable set of circumstances in which the fact that one does not seem to perceive a certain physical object entails that it does not exist; but given that it is the kind of object that is supposed to be perceptible, it surely would follow that it did not exist if there were no circumstances whatsoever in which it would seem to be perceived." Again, "Suppose it were the case that in what appeared to be the relevant setting the object would always seem to be perceived, no matter what further experiences were obtainable. Then, I think, it would logically follow that the object did exist." He does not think in either case that the relevant premise is one that could be conclusively established, or even be applicable to any ordinary situation, but he does think that we have here two limiting cases of a logical relationship between sense experiences and the world. "If the argument is correct, they prove that in this matter of perception it is logically impossible for appearances to fool all the people all of the time." Whether they are fooled in any given case, or whether some people are fooled all or some of the time, is something that has to be looked at on its merits; that is why perceptual statements have the status of theories. Unfortunately, whether or not

[31] A. J. Ayer, *The Problem of Knowledge,* Penguin edition, p. 130.

it is logically impossible to fool all the people all of the time, Ayer's own argument is invalid. There is much that is wrong with the two principles as set out.[32] For example, to say that an object is perceptible is to say that it can in principle be perceived; it does not follow from the fact that it can in this sense be perceived that it does not exist if there are no circumstances in which it would actually seem to be perceived; or at any rate it does not follow logically. There may be reasons why a perceptible object is never in fact seen in any circumstances whatever. One might protect the principle to some extent by arguing that we are concerned not with actual circumstances but with those that are logically possible. That is to say that the principle might be taken as saying that the object would not exist if it were logically impossible for there to be circumstances in which it would seem to be perceived. But this would make the principle logically true at the cost of depriving it of the chance of creating a link between actual sense experiences and the world (which is what is demanded). The same applies to the other principle. The truth is that if we take appearances as somehow basic and "given," and hope on that basis to forge a link with an objective world, it must be a forlorn hope. It is not indeed an intelligible enterprise, for the reasons I mentioned in discussing the "given" earlier.

With this failure, empiricism of the kind in question seems doomed. There is no way in which belief in an independent world can be justified or even made intelligible once we are committed to the idea that what primarily exist are sense experiences, and that it is up to us to show how we can go beyond them. Moreover, it is of no avail to go over, by way of reaction, to the idealist position and simply reject the idea that any determinate knowledge is "given" in sense experience, on the grounds that all such knowledge involves judgment on our part, judgment in which we may always be mistaken to some

[32] See A. P. Griffiths, "Ayer on perception," *Mind*, N.S., LXIX (1960), pp. 486ff.

degree or other. The idealist, such as Bradley, is right to emphasize the role that concepts play in perception, as noted in section (b). It is not right, however, to say that all perception involves *judgment*; perceptual judgment is comparatively rare, being limited to those cases in which we have to estimate or work out details of what is perceived. Moreover, it is not the case that in judgment, concepts are imposed upon a "given" which, just because it is nonconceptual, is indeterminate and incommunicable. The idealist does not reject the idea of something "given" in experience altogether; he merely holds that it cannot constitute knowledge. This merely has the effect of casting doubt on the very objectivity of perception. For what are the criteria of truth for perceptual judgments? It is no coincidence that the idealist normally rejects any form of the correspondence theory of truth in favor of the coherence theory.

(e) Perception and the world

The position that we have now reached is that it is impossible to accept the idea that we are "given" something in sense experience, and on its basis build up a world independent of sense experience; it is equally impossible to accept the idea that all that we mean by this world is something about sense experience itself. On the other hand, we are clearly not "given" the world ready-made in perception; each of us has to learn how things are, and we have to learn to see them very much as others do, even if we may differ sometimes over the details. The objectivity of perceptual judgments does not, however, consist simply in this agreement with others, since it is at least logically possible that we might all be wrong. This is so, however much agreement is to be expected in a whole variety of cases over what is to be counted as objective. As noted in Chapter 3,[33] Wittgenstein said that if

[33] See p. 69. The reference to Wittgenstein is to *Philosophical Investigations*, I, 242.

language is to be a means of communication there must be agreement in judgments as well as in definitions. This is an exceptionally important remark, which has many implications for the present issue. If agreement does not constitute the essence of objectivity, agreement at some points is a necessary condition of our giving any content to the notion of objectivity. Strictly speaking, the extreme empiricist is in the position not only of being unable to give an account of the objectivity of our perception of the world, but also of being unable to give an account of how this can be *our* perception, as opposed to its being mine or yours. To talk of the possibility of agreement in our perceptions presupposes a common framework, even a common world. Hence, once again, the suggestion that we start from our individual sense experiences and build up not only an independent world but a common one seems unintelligible; we have to *presuppose* that common world if the enterprise is to get off the ground at all.

The problem should not therefore be construed as one of how to build up a common and objective world from individual sense experiences, but one of the relationship of sense experience to that common, independent world, the existence of which is a precondition of the very intelligibility of discourse itself. That there is a common, independent world does not in itself show what place perception has in our conception of it, yet perception must clearly provide points of application for that conception. As we saw in Chapter 3, it is only from within a conceptual scheme of this kind that questions about objectivity can be raised. Thus perception must provide a basis for objective claims about the world. If the relationship between perception and how the world is were merely contingent, perception could provide no such basis. (It might thus be said that Ayer was quite right to look for a more than contingent relationship between experience and the world, but he approached the issue from the wrong end; he took experience as given and attempted to justify our conception of the world on its basis, instead of taking our conception of the world and asking what in experience makes this possible and what gives it application.) If the relationship between perception and the world *were* merely contingent, it would make sense to suppose that what we all see as, e.g., red is not red at all, even when there is nothing to suggest erroneous perception. It does, of course, make sense to raise the question whether what I see as red is so in fact, or whether what everyone sees as red in certain conditions is so in fact. For there may be special conditions that bring it about that I see things wrongly or that everyone does so in special circumstances. But to suppose that everything that we all count as red in any circumstance whatever is not so would be to rob the concept of redness of any point of application. Since our understanding of what red is presupposes some amount of general agreement about what is to count as red, to imply that nothing really counts as red is to suggest that there is in fact no understanding of what red is, that there is no such concept. Thus, to suppose that what we all see as red is not so would make sense only if there were really no understanding of what redness is at all. Our understanding of such a concept implies that the original supposition would not make sense and thus that there is not a merely contingent relationship between perception and the world, between how we see things and how they are. (It was, of course, a noncontingent relationship of this kind that Ayer was after in positing his two limiting cases, but his way of formulating the relationship was wrong.)

It is on grounds of this kind that it has sometimes been suggested[34] that it is a necessary truth that the majority of perceptual claims are correct. But the matter cannot be properly expressed in this statistical way. We have no real knowledge of the actual proportion of correct to incorrect perceptions. Indeed, the proportion might alter

[34] By, for example, Sydney Shoemaker in his *Self-Knowledge and Self-Identity* (Ithaca, New York, 1963), pp. 229ff.

from one period of time to another. After all, abnormal conditions of perception might become common, even if they are not so at present. In any case, I do not see how a philosophical argument that rests upon considerations about certain concepts could lead validly to a conclusion that involves as definite a matter of fact as a statistical claim. My use of the term "abnormal" gives a clue to the correct account of the matter. It is that people normally see red things as red, and indeed that a red thing is just what people see as red under normal conditions. Perception, as I have emphasized all along, is something that takes place under conditions—conditions that are of a variety of kinds, some causal, some not. In order for a man to see something correctly as X, what he sees must be an X, he must have the concept of an X, X must be in the position to affect his sense organs in certain ways, he must be attending to it, his sense organs must be functioning and not be defective, and so on. Each of these things constitutes a necessary condition for perception; they are not sufficient since we cannot eliminate the possibility that something else that we have not mentioned will prevent perception. What is sufficient may vary. One may manage to see something correctly despite circumstances that in the case of other people would prevent them from doing so. For these reasons we must have reference to the normal conditions of perception—just because we cannot say simply that a man will see red things as red when x, y, z, etc. The normal conditions are those that we take as appropriate to the proper functioning of the relevant sense, and therefore as those in terms of which the conditions for the recognition of a certain kind of object of perception are to be specified.

It has sometimes been said that what we mean by "red" is what appears red under these normal conditions. This cannot strictly be correct, since an understanding of "red" seems to be presupposed by an understanding of the notion of something's appearing red. Nevertheless, a full understanding of "red" implies, as we have seen, an ability to apply "red" to the right things in the right conditions; and this would be impossible without perception, and normal perception at that. People with abnormal vision may come to be able to apply "red" correctly, but this is possible only because other people have normal vision (and it is in terms of this that what is to be counted as red is specified). The situation is the same for people who can apply color words correctly without the use of vision, but by means of some other form of perception (e.g., as in the cases reported of people who can discriminate between colors by passing their hands over the colored objects, however this happens in fact). I have discussed this matter further in my "Seeing Things as They Are."[35] The most important passage is as follows: "To say that something is red is to say that the concept *red* is properly to be applied to it. It follows that if people have the concept *red*, in the full sense which implies an ability to recognize red things, then, other things being equal, they should apply the concept in this case, i.e., that, other things being equal, they should see the thing in question as red. From this in turn it follows that there is justification for the ascription of redness to something *only if*, other things being equal, people see it as red—and other things will be equal only if conditions are normal." There is a similar argument for the converse relation. What this amounts to is that there are certain concepts that have perceptual criteria; they get a sense only through their connection with perception, and it is perception under normal conditions that provides the point of application for these concepts.[36] What was wrong with traditional empiricism was that it insisted in defining red in terms of a certain experience, as if "red" were the name of that experience. Redness is a quality of an

[35] Inaugural Lecture at Birkbeck College (1965), reprinted in part in the new appendix (1967) to my *Psychology of Perception*, 3rd impression (London, 1969), pp. 116ff. (New York, 1969).

[36] Cf. my discussion of criteria in Ch. 3, sec. (d).

object, not an experience, but we would have no understanding of "red" without perception; thus, redness has perceptual criteria, and there is this much truth in empiricism.

This cannot be said of *all* properties of physical objects. Some of their properties, the so-called primary qualities, are detectable through more than one sense— characteristically through both sight and touch. Their criteria are thus more complex than with properties like those of color, which are normally detectable through one sense only. But a whole host of properties of things are not perceptual at all, or only indirectly so. It cannot be argued in their case that people will normally perceive them as such. The necessary connection between perception and the properties of things, between how we see things and how they are, holds only in some cases. But these cases are sufficient to constitute points of application for other concepts, and in a sense form a foundation for our knowledge of the world, though not in the way presupposed by traditional empiricism. For, to labor a point already made, traditional empiricism took for granted the intelligibility of the notion of something being "given" in sense perception as something prior to any understanding of and knowledge of the world to which perception is directed. My denial of the claim that the relationship between how we see things and how they are is altogether contingent undercuts that assumption. The very concept of perception implies some kind of awareness of an object independent of ourselves (something that is implicit, if one thinks of it, in the very notion of "how we see things"), and the only way of specifying sense experiences themselves is in terms of the features of public objects of perception, as we saw in section (b). The contrary idea is evident in the notion of an "external world," a notion that is often invoked in traditional empiricist treatments of perception, and a notion that should similarly be rejected. For it presupposes the idea that each of us is shut up in a private world confronted with private objects and that we have somehow to cross the gap to a world "external" to us. But the only valid sense in which one can speak of other objects being external to us is that they are external to our body; this sense of "external," however, is not sufficient for what is implied in the traditional notion of an external world, since "we" are not shut up in our bodies. Our bodies are public objects themselves and they are as much part of ourselves as our thoughts, feelings, and perceptions. There is no gap of the kind implied in the traditional notion of an external world to be crossed, and once this is recognized one foothold for skepticism is removed.

Once we are allowed to have perception at all, we must be allowed to have some conception of and some awareness of a public world, so that there is no longer a void between us and that world. This does not mean, of course, that we thereby necessarily see the world correctly, and certain things, of course, even things that are in principle perceptible and visible, we never or rarely see correctly, at any rate by a strict standard (cf. such very different things as very distant stars and our own faces—the latter we may see correctly on rare occasions, but most glimpses that we get of them in mirrors are certainly not correct, since they are transposed in the reflection). But since we have to build up our public conception of the world through perception, we can be sure that if we are to have any conception of things as red, for example, if there is to be any justification for ascribing redness to things, we must normally see red things as red. The only ground that the skeptic could have for denying that we ever see red things as red at all would be that redness itself was an unintelligible notion, or that we have no real conception of it. This, however, would be a very desperate measure, since a large part of the seductiveness of the skeptic's position lies in its suggestion that things may be other than they seem. To argue, on the contrary, that we have no real *conception* of things at all is far less plausible.

(f) Perception, knowledge, and belief

The argument given in the previous section shows that perception is a source of knowledge; it does not show that on each occasion that we perceive something we do have knowledge. That would be an absurd claim. Nor is it true that whenever we see something we believe what we see; seeing is not always believing. If it might be argued that if we see something as such-and-such we at least have a *disposition* to believe that it is such-and-such, this can only be because of our normal trust in perception as a source of knowledge. This means that we can have no understanding of perception except against the supposition that normally when we perceive something we have knowledge. In this sense the concept of perception is an epistemological concept, though it is not so in the sense that an analysis of perception inevitably involves a reference to knowledge as a constituent. The same applies to belief. It is impossible to say that what one *means* when one says that X perceives Y is that X knows or believes such-and-such about Y. There are even some cases in which we may be inclined to say that someone must have seen something even though the person concerned has no awareness of having done so. Furthermore, any attempt to analyze perception into knowledge, belief, or judgment, or to reduce it to knowledge, belief, or judgment will inevitably have the result of entailing the postulation of some cases of immediate perception where the knowledge, belief, or judgment has no further basis.[37] I may be able to justify certain perceptual beliefs or judgments by reference to other, similar beliefs and judgments, but any such chain of justifications must come to a stop somewhere with the remark that that is how I see it. If this is to be analyzed in terms of belief or judg-

[37] Cf. D. M. Armstrong, *Perception and the Physical World* (New York and London, 1961), Chs. 2 and 9.

ment, the regress must either go on ad infinitum (a very unsatisfactory idea) or it must come to a stop with a belief or judgment that has no basis (an equally unsatisfactory idea). If the latter is what immediate perception is, then either perception must ultimately lack a rationale and thus be arbitrary, or we must explain immediate perception in terms of the "given" (as in effect it is so explained in Berkeley), with all the defects and confusions that this involves. What is wrong here is the premise from which the argument has started—the position that perception must be analyzed in terms of belief, etc., so that we can say that perception is belief plus experience plus . . . .

What is true is that perception cannot take place except under the condition that we are having experiences (or at any rate this is true of sense perception—for we sometimes speak of perception of other kinds, as in those cases where we speak of a man of perception or of someone perceiving that a certain conclusion follows from certain premises). It also involves having and applying concepts—what we see we see as a such-and-such. But it is not that we apply the concepts to those experiences and thus come to have beliefs and knowledge about the world, for that view of the matter presupposes a notion of experience that used in this way is ultimately unintelligible, as we have seen in the foregoing. Hence we cannot suppose that the child develops its view of the world from initially private experiences, and that perception emerges somehow from those private experiences. The child certainly has to learn what the world is like, and it has to acquire and apply concepts of features of that world. But perception cannot take place at all unless the child has already in a certain sense the idea of a world independent of itself. This may sound like the rather discredited notion of innate ideas, a notion espoused recently by Noam Chomsky;[38] alternatively, it may sound

[38] Noam Chomsky, *Cartesian Linguistics* (New York, 1966), pp. 58ff., and *Language and Mind* (New York, 1968).

like the view put forward by William James[39] that what the child is initially given is the universe. But these are really ways, perhaps unhappy ways, of putting the crucial point that perception is basically an awareness of an object (using "object" in its most general, even formal, sense). Sense experiences make us aware of objects (and the object will initially be only an undifferentiated something or other), and they make possible further differentiations between objects and further ways of regarding and conceiving them. Thus a view of the world is developed through learning, because (causally because) we have experiences, and because we have the capacity to develop concepts and to apply them in accordance with the framework that we are in effect taught through our relations and communications with other human beings. The same applies to animals except that the possible relationships and forms of communication are limited—particularly because of the inability to develop and use anything that is properly to be called a language. It is this framework that provides the possibility of giving application to the concepts of knowledge and belief, and it is only in terms of it that we can speak of such things. (Hence the importance, already mentioned, of the notion of public agreement for those of truth and objectivity, and through them for that of knowledge.)

It is impossible that the awareness of an object of which I have spoken should be gotten through any features of sensations as such, or through such a factor as resistance to the will (something that some philosophers, from Maine de Biran onward, have thought could supplement the usual apparatus of empiricism, with its reliance on features of sensations as such). For this would imply that we had first to be aware of these features of our experiences, and then the notion of an object would have to be reducible to these features or would have to be derived from them by some process of inference.

[39] William James, *Principles of Psychology* (New York, 1890), Ch. 17.

Neither of these things is true or possible. We must, for all the reasons given in this chapter, forsake the apparatus of traditional empiricism, which has, after all, no sanctity. A correct developmental account of how knowledge of the world comes about cannot start from the position that we are "given" knowledge of certain things in experience. Knowledge is acquired; sensations do not in themselves and apart from other knowledge provide knowledge, but they do enable us to develop knowledge by making it possible to differentiate between different objects of which we may be aware. William James said that the experiences of a child constitute a "blooming, buzzing confusion"; the truth is that it can only become this when the objects of its experiences become differentiated. The primary awareness, if one can talk of such a thing, must be simple and undifferentiated. The Idealists saw this point, but they were unable to say how the differentiation takes place because they could conceive of it taking place only by way of the application of concepts to what is "given" in this way; and in that case any process of differentiation must, since it depends on how each one of us does it, be subjective and even arbitrary. But experiences, the sensations which we have, are not undifferentiated, even if the consequent awareness of objects is, and their multiplicity makes possible the development of a differentiated awareness of things. The Idealists' difficulty arose from too light an acceptance of the account of sensation provided by their empiricist opponents, with its identification of sensation with the "given." With the abandonment of this idea and the acceptance of the general notion of awareness of an object as something not reducible to sensation, a better account of perception becomes possible.

CHAPTER 7

Memory

(a) Skepticism about memory

In many ways the epistemological issues about memory are parallel to those about perception. Just as in the case of perception the skeptic relies upon the suggestion that there is a gap between us and the so-called external world, so with memory he may rely upon the supposition that there is a gap between us and the past at any one moment. The past is something that has gone and can never come again, and is thus irreclaimable. This supposition rests upon the idea that we are confronted at any one time with an experience from which we have to make the move to the past. This is a position that W. Von Leyden[1] calls the "present" view of memory, and he contrasts it with what he calls the "past" view, which implies that memory is a direct but somehow mysterious link with the past. The contrast is, I think, wrongly expressed by putting it in this way. The proper contrast is between those views that attempt to analyze memory in terms of present experiences and those that maintain that it cannot be so analyzed. In this respect the issues are similar

[1] W. Von Leyden, *Remembering* (London, 1961), Ch. 1.

the "philosophical system," the latter involving a belief in a distinction between experiences and the objects or events that produce them. Both philosophers think that, since this distinction cannot properly be made on the basis of those experiences, skepticism is philosophically justified, despite common sense.

A very similar attitude is to be found in Russell's *Analysis of Mind*.[3] Russell's main point is that there cannot be any logical connection between events at different times. "Everything constituting a memory-belief is happening now," and there is in consequence no logical connection between my present memory belief and the event or events that it is about. (Russell has indeed always taken for granted that the relation between past events and present memory experiences must be a causal one, and has even postulated a special kind of causality, mnemic causation, to account for the fact that the causal link is, to say the least, indirect. Von Leyden, too, speaks of a chain of causation, a point to which I shall return.) If there is no logical connection between a present memory belief and the past event that it is about, then it is conceivable that my belief should not be a memory belief at all, that the event in question should not have occurred, and indeed that the past should not have existed at all. "There is no logical impossibility," Russell says, "in the hypothesis that the world sprang into being five minutes ago, exactly as it then was, with a population that 'remembered' a wholly unreal past."[4] (Russell's placing of "remembered" within quotation marks is very significant, since it betrays a realization that it would, strictly speaking, be inappropriate to speak of memory at all, if there were not past events of the kind in question or no past events at all.) Russell goes on to say that he does not suggest this hypothesis as a serious one. "Like

[3] B. Russell, *Analysis of Mind* (London, 1921 and New York, 1954), Ch. 9. Cf. his *Outline of Philosophy* (London, 1927), p. 7 (New York, 1927).

[4] B. Russell, ibid., pp. 159–60.

all sceptical hypotheses, it is logically tenable, but uninteresting." It is uninteresting because the commonsense view is simpler and for that reason more acceptable. Nevertheless, the skeptic is not really answered, and, like Hume, Russell goes on to postulate a feature that serves to mark off memory experiences as such from other experiences. Memory images are, he says, accompanied by a feeling of familiarity. As with the Humean criterion of vivacity, there is some difficulty in understanding just what is involved in such a feeling of familiarity. It is not, for example, an obvious feature of memory images that they involve experiences of the kind involved in, say, déja vu. Nor indeed is it obvious that feelings, which could be represented as feelings of familiarity, accompany all cases of remembering. What both Hume and Russell are trying to get at is what makes the experiences in question *memory* experiences, such that they correspond in some way to what was previously experienced [as long, of course, as they are not cases of misremembering, and subject to certain qualifications about the restriction of memory to what has previously been experienced, qualifications into which I shall go in section (c)]. But whether memory experiences correspond to what has previously been experienced is not something that can be gathered from the experiences themselves.

This last point is an important one and has been emphasized by R. F. Holland in an important article entitled "The empiricist theory of memory."[5] Holland ends his article by saying "One cannot, as Hume thought, contemplate an idea of memory and an idea of the imagination and, *feigning ignorance of their origins*, begin to distinguish them afresh by means of a difference in their respective qualities." In those cases where one sets out to recall something or alternatively sets out to

[5] R. F. Holland, "The empiricist theory of memory," *Mind*, N.S., LXIII (1954), pp. 464ff., reprinted in *The Philosophy of Mind*, ed. S. N. Hampshire (New York, 1966), pp. 266ff.

imagine something, it is the relevant intention that determines whether the one is a memory experience and the other an experience of the imagination. But in those cases where an image just comes into one's mind, it may well be impossible to tell from the image alone whether it is a memory image or not. But this is no reason for skepticism about memory; for it may well be possible to tell whether it is a memory image from other considerations. Certainly there are considerations that will rule out its being a memory image, e.g., the consideration that one knew nothing whatever about the object of the experience before it occurred. But if one cannot lay down once and for all what would ensure that it is a memory image, the elimination of considerations counting against its being a memory image may in some circumstances go a long way to showing that it is one in fact. In deciding whether someone is actually remembering a given event we ask whether the person concerned was in a position to remember the event, whether he actually experienced it, whether he could have gotten to know about it in other ways, and so on. All this presupposes knowledge about past events independent of the putative memory experience under discussion. There might be an objection to this claiming that it presupposes the reliability of other memories, so that all that we are doing in this case is checking one memory experience against another. In that case there would still be no real grounds for accepting the general reliability of memory, except our reluctance to desert common sense.

It is this kind of consideration, I think, that makes Von Leyden prefer what he calls the "present approach" to memory rather than the "past approach," i.e., to prefer the view made explicit in Russell's claim that "everything constituting a memory-belief is happening now" to one that implies that access to the past is an essential feature of what is called "memory." For the latter view may suggest that we have a kind of direct acquaintance with past events, and how is this possible if past events are over and gone? Von Leyden counts Ryle's views on memory[6] (as well as those of Holland) as an example of the "past approach." Roughly, Ryle describes remembering as having learned and not forgotten; on this account a reference to the past is a necessary part of the concept of memory. Skepticism about a particular memory claim would then be skepticism about the applicability of the concept of memory in that instance. But if one accepts the applicability of the concept *in general,* there is room for skepticism only about particular memory claims and not about memory in general. Thus the real difference between what Von Leyden calls the present and past approaches to memory (or, better, the empiricist and non-empiricist theories of memory) is that the first takes remembering to consist of having a certain present experience, which happens to correspond to past events and which may also have other contingent features that distinguish it as memory, while the second says that remembering is essentially having knowledge of past events, so that it is not in any way a contingent matter whether, once given that we have memory, there actually were past events of the kind claimed as remembered. The latter *might* be taken to suggest a direct acquaintance with the past, but there is no necessary implication of that kind involved in it; all that is implied is that one is not entitled to call a claim a memory claim, or an experience a memory experience, unless certain conditions, including something about actual past events, are satisfied. Furthermore, there is no implication in this that one should be able to tell from the experience itself, without reference to other things, whether it is a memory experience.

Still, it might justifiably be objected that it does imply some kind of access to the past and thereby the possession of the concept of the past; otherwise there could be no way of establishing the claim of an experience to be called a memory experience, since the condition about

[6] G. Ryle, *The Concept of Mind* (New York and London, 1949), pp. 272ff.

reference to the past has to be satisfied. Von Leyden claims that all evidence for things remembered is ultimately based on memory, and that without memory there would be no concept of the past. This assertion presents a general challenge to the concept of memory, not just a challenge to particular memory claims. If it can be met, skepticism about memory cannot be based on this kind of consideration, i.e., on the general consideration that memory itself is supposedly the only basis for the applicability of the concept of the past. Von Leyden's claim indicates that a thoroughgoing empiricism must present not just an empiricist account of memory but also an empiricist account of our concept of the past. If the second implies the first, skepticism over memory will be invincible. The only hope for the empiricist is to give in his terms an account of the concept of the past that does not involve memory. Ayer gives such an account in *The Problem of Knowledge*,[7] and I shall return to it in the next section of this book and indicate where its unsatisfactoriness lies. Von Leyden, on the other hand, is content to rely on memory for the source of our concept of the past, and it is therefore no wonder that he emerges with skeptical conclusions.

There are, however, two components to his claim, of which only the second amounts to the view that our concept of the past is derived from memory. I shall leave consideration of that point until the next section. The first component of Von Leyden's claim is, as already indicated, that all evidence for things remembered is ultimately based on memory. The quick way with this part of his claim is to reject it outright. It is just not true that all evidence for things remembered depends ultimately on memory. There are such things as records, diaries, histories, archaeological remains, etc. It might be argued that our acceptance of these things as what they are, with their reference to the past, depends upon our

[7] A. J. Ayer, *The Problem of Knowledge* (New York and London, 1956), Ch. 4, iv.

prior awareness of the past as such, and that this in turn would be impossible without memory. It is true that our understanding of something as a record of the past presupposes an understanding of what it is for an event to be past, and it might even be the case that a creature without memory could have no such understanding. But this does not mean that the understanding is obtained from memory; nor does it mean that our knowledge that certain things are records of given historical events is based in any way on memory of those events. The evidence that something putatively remembered by Smith actually took place may be such strictly contemporary things as photographs or tape recordings. Our evidence for the fact that these *are* records of the events in question may be the fact that they say so in some way (the photograph may be dated, the tape recording may contain an indication of its timing). We have of course to understand the temporal reference, but this is not the same thing as requiring memory as the ultimate court of appeal on the truth of that reference. The ways in which the verification of statements about the past is arrived at may be very complex, but there is no necessity that memory should enter into the process *as a source of evidence*. Whether it enters into it as a source of the concept of the past—a very different thing—is a question to which we must now turn.

(b) The concept of the past

The empiricist account of concepts, e.g., that of John Locke, presupposes that a concept must have its origin in some feature of experience; we must get or derive the concept from experience in some way. Once given this general preconception, it is natural to suppose that our concept of the past must inevitably be derived from memory; we have memory experiences and thereby come to have an understanding of what it is for events to be past. There are objections to this conception of the matter on the general level of whether it is right in any way to talk of deriving concepts from experience, and whether it is right to speak of the source of our concepts in this way. I have discussed this question in Chapter 3 and shall not repeat the considerations here. But there is also a more particular objection to the idea that the concept of the past is derived from memory. It is put by Ayer[8] by saying, "We have seen that whatever the content of a memory experience, it acquires its reference to the past only through being so interpreted. But from this it follows that the identification of anything as a memory presupposes an understanding of what is meant by being past. And if this understanding is presupposed by memory, it cannot be founded on it." This is well taken. To remember something I must be aware of what I claim to remember as past, and thus I cannot be said to remember at all unless I have the concept of the past under which I subsume the events in question.[9] There is thus no hope of deriving the concept of the past from memory.

Unfortunately Ayer goes on in his discussion to seek a source for the concept of the past elsewhere than in memory. He argues that the notion of temporal precedence is given in experience, and that this, together with the notion of the present, will yield the concepts of both past and future. The notion of the present is definable ostensively as the class of events that is contemporaneous with *this*, "where *this* is any event that one chooses to indicate at the given moment." This will not do. No one could understand, simply from the use of the word "this," that it is the present event that is being referred to. What in any case limits the identity of the event through time? It is noticeable that Ayer has to use the words "at the given moment" to specify the event in question. In any case, anyone who could understand the notion of "contemporaneous" must understand not only the idea of two

[8] Ibid., Penguin edition, p. 151.

[9] I shall discuss qualifications to this statement in the next section.

events taking place at the same time, but, by contrast, the idea of different times. A whole schema of understanding about time is presupposed in this, which prevents it being at all plausible to speak of temporal notions being given in experience. To the extent that we can be said to perceive one thing following another, to that extent we must already have some concept of time, and for this reason the argument that Ayer uses to rule out the possibility that the concept of the past might be derived from memory applies, *mutatis mutandis*, to the idea of deriving the notion of temporal succession from experience.

One way of putting this result would be to say that the concept of time and thereby the concept of the past is a priori—a claim made by Kant. The snag with this suggestion is that the notion of an a priori concept is one that gets a sense only by contrast with that of an a posteriori concept, and the latter is equivalent to that of a concept derived from experience. In other words, the notion of an a priori concept is one that presupposes the whole framework according to which concepts can, at least in some cases, be spoken of as derived from experience; and this is the very point at issue. The criteria of someone having the concept of the past would be provided by his ability to make temporal distinctions at all.[10] In a normal, language-speaking human being this would be indicated in his ability to use tenses or other similar temporal indicators. It is a reasonable question to ask what makes this possible. Given what was said in Chapter 3 about the conditions under which someone can be said to have a concept F—namely that he must not only be able to give a formal account of what it is for something to be F but also recognize instances of it—it would seem that someone who has the concept of the past must inevitably be in the position to pick out events as past rather than as

[10] Cf. G. E. M. Anscombe, "The reality of the past" in *Philosophical Analysis,* ed. Max Black (Ithaca, New York, 1950), pp. 38ff.

present and future. Ayer was right when he went on
to say that the past can be defined as the class of events
earlier than the present, whether or not he was right in
claiming that the notion of the present might be defined
ostensively. Certainly to understand the past a man must
also understand the relation of past events to the present
and future. In forming the notion of the present he has
to recognize that events in time exist for him as it were
from a point of view in time, which is always changing
in an ordered way relative to those events, though it is
always his. Does this understanding and the recognition
of certain events as past demand the existence of memory? Is the possession of memory, that is to say, a condition of having the concept of the past, even if that
concept is not derived from memory?

One thing that should immediately be noted in considering this question is that we do not need to have something parallel with memory, but concerned with the future rather than the past, in order to have a concept of
the future. We have, that is, the concept of the future
without precognition, or any form of knowledge about
the future.[11] The concept of the future is involved in expectation, hope, fear, etc., as well as in analogous cogni-
tive states; similarly, the concept of the past is involved in
states like regret and remorse, as well as in memory. One
might possibly conceive of a being who had various expectations, but no memories, and who might come to a
concept of the past by contrast with the concept of the
future that he had; he might even have vague regrets
that for him the past was empty. The objections to such

[11] My late colleague, Mr. D. J. Shillcock, introduced in un-
published writings the concept of prememory in this connection,
the state of premembering being related to future events as remembering is to past events, particularly in respect of the causal
relation between those events and the state of mind in question.
In precognition, if it exists, there is no necessity that the knowledge of the future be because of any causal relation between
future events and present states of mind, as is the case with
memory and past events.

a supposal come not from any formal difficulties with this idea, but from difficulties in the idea that such a being could have anything that might validly be called experience at all. For to have the notion of an object he would need the idea of identity through time, and it is difficult to see how he could have this without memory in some form. (This is one feature of Kant's "transcendental deduction," a step in the so-called threefold synthesis; objective experience requires the subsumption of the manifold of experience under a concept as a unity, both in itself as a manifold and in its identity through time. Objects are indeed just things that have these kinds of unity and identity.[12]) Thus a being who had *no* memory could have no idea of an object, in which case it is doubtful what sense could be attached to the idea that he might also have expectations; for the concept of expectation implies the idea that the object of expectation should have an identity. Thus it seems that memory may after all be a necessary condition for having the concept of the past, though not in the obvious way that at first seemed worthy of consideration.

Norman Malcolm has recently tried to argue for what is in effect a much closer relation between memory and the concept of the past in the course of a discussion of Russell's skeptical hypothesis about the possibility of the world having sprung into being five minutes ago.[13] Malcolm's suggestion is that Russell's "hypothesis" is inconceivable on the grounds, not simply that the population in question could not have memories because there was no past, but that it could not even seem to them that they remembered things because in these circumstances they could have no concept of the past. Malcolm argues for this last point on the basis of Wittgenstein's remark that "if language is to be a means of communication there must be agreement not only in definitions but also . . . in

[12] I. Kant, *Critique of Pure Reason*, the Transcendental Analytic, A 98ff.

[13] N. Malcolm, *Knowledge and Certainty* (Englewood Cliffs, New Jersey, 1963), pp. 187ff.

judgments."[14] He takes this to mean that if people are to have the concept of the past they must agree upon the application of that concept; they must, that is, agree about things that have happened in "a multitude of cases." This, he thinks, brings in truth in turn, so that for there to be a concept of the past there must be a multitude of cases in which it is true that such-and-such happened. This is excluded, ex hypothesi, in Russell's suggestion. The argument seems to me to be mistaken. And the situation is made even worse by a further suggestion of Malcolm's—that if people began to manifest memories of "a wholly unreal past" only after they had lived for a considerable time with genuine memories (so that there were grounds for attributing the concept of the past to them), then it would not be intelligible to suppose that this "unreal past" was unreal, since the "apparent memories" would be verified as true.

There is a manifest implausibility about Malcolm's argument. The ability of the populations in these two cases to use sentences in the past tense would itself seem to indicate an understanding of the concept of the past. Of course in normal circumstances one would expect of someone who had a concept of the past rather more than a mere ability to use sentences of this form; one would also expect him to use them in the appropriate circumstances. In Russell's example there are no appropriate circumstances for the use of these sentences (at any rate for any event that took place more than five minutes ago, and this itself is an important qualification). But the situation is ex hypothesi very abnormal; and for that reason one is hardly in the position to apply ordinary considerations. Again, as we saw in Chapter 5, since agreement is the criterion of truth, one would expect that in normal circumstances what people are agreed about will be true; but on the "hypothesis" that Russell puts forward the circumstances are not normal. Finally, there does indeed have to be agreement over the application of concepts

[14] L. Wittgenstein, *Philosophical Investigations* (Oxford, 1953), I, 242.

(what Wittgenstein referred to as "agreement in judgments") if these concepts are to be properly intelligible, though not necessarily over any or every concept and not over any or every form in which that concept might be expressed; but in Russell's example this is not really at issue, since there is no dispute over whether the population in the example agree in what they say.

The real issue is whether people could be said to understand what they say, if what they said were never true. The answer to this is that if this state of affairs were pervasive, they could not be said to understand; and there would be room for doubt on this matter if they never said what was true within some limited sphere, unless there were some special explanation for their failure to state the truth. But there *is* such an explanation in the case under consideration, and it must therefore be concluded that there is no reason to doubt the suggestion that the Russellian population might be said to have the concept of the past. If it is not necessarily true that a failure to attain truth entails the lack of the relevant concept, the contrapositive need not be true either; that is to say that it need not be true that the possession of the concept entails the truth of what is said by its means. Yet this is what seems to be implied by Malcolm's second case; for the fact that the population has the concept of the past and is agreed about its application in various ways (i.e., both in connection with memory and in connection with the interpretation of "records") is taken by him to entail the correctness of the population's judgments about the past. I conclude, therefore, that there is no reason to accept Malcolm's suggestions about the connection between memory and the concept of the past, prima facie implausible as they are in any case. Such connections as there are remain as I stated earlier.

(c) *Types of memory*

I have so far made no systematic distinctions between types of memory phenomena or between the different objects of memory. It has become customary, however, for philosophers discussing memory to make such distinctions —and for good reason—even if it is not always obvious what such distinctions amount to. There are, first, distinctions between the kinds of object that the verb "to remember" can take—distinctions parallel to those made with respect to "know." Thus one can be said to remember a thing or event, to have a memory of it; one can also be said to remember that such-and-such; and finally one can be said to remember how to do such-and-such. The last two are sometimes said to be dispositional by contrast with the first; Ayer, for example, in *The Problem of Knowledge,* Chapter 4, refers to "remembering that" as "habit memory," in distinction from memory of events. One can find similar distinctions with minor differences in Bergson's *Matter and Memory,* Woozley's *Theory of Knowledge,* and Ryle's *Concept of Mind.* Yet differences between the kinds of object that "remember" can take are not coincident with such distinctions as that between dispositional and occurrent memory, or between those occasions of occurrent memory that are the result of intention on our part and those that are not, but in which, as we say, a recollection comes to mind. Furthermore, there may be other distinctions to make in terms of what, if anything, comes into a person's mind when he recalls something, or in terms of whether he had personal experience of the event or thing recalled.

Not all of these distinctions are as important as some of the others. Malcolm, for example,[15] selects three forms of memory for special consideration. These are what he calls factual memory, perceptual memory, and personal memory, and he discusses their mutual dependence or independence, putting greatest weight on factual memory. Factual memory is just memory that such-and-such is, was, or will be the case. Perceptual memory is the memory of something that involves seeing, hearing it, etc., in the mind's eye; it essentially involves imagery.

[15] N. Malcolm, ibid., pp. 203ff.

Personal memory is that form of memory that depends on the person's previous perception or experience of the thing remembered. It is certainly not clear that these forms of memory are on the same level, but to mention them does bring out the fact that not all memory is explicitly memory of facts; although it may be the case that in recalling an object we must also remember it as a such-and-such and thus remember that it was a such-and-such. Similarly, the reference to perceptual memory does bring out the point that the occurrence of images is certainly not a necessary feature of memory; and the reference to personal memory brings out the point that it is not always necessary in order to remember A that we should have experienced A ourselves in the past. We can, for example, be said to remember an event because we read about it in the papers at the time, or got to know of it in the past in some other way. On the other hand, we certainly cannot be said to remember something if we had no knowledge of it previously, and we cannot be said to remember being involved in something if we had no experience of that something at the time. Malcolm argues[16] that perceptual and personal memory of something involve at least some factual memory of the remembered thing, and this seems valid to the extent that memory of events or things in general implies knowledge about them. Since that knowledge is knowledge by memory, we can admit that memory of things or events implies factual memory.

There is, therefore, a special importance to be attached to factual memory, or "memory that." Such memory can be dispositional in the sense that a man may be said to remember that such-and-such is the case whether or not he ever positively recalls that this is so or even thinks of it. If he does recall it, whether intentionally or spontaneously, his recollection must inevitably involve some thought concerning the matter in question—at best the thought that the such-and-such is the case. But if

[16] N. Malcolm, ibid., p. 204.

he does not, he may still be said to remember that p, as long as he is in the position to recall that p in relevant circumstances. Thus there is much in Ryle's dictum that basically memory is having learned and not forgotten. This is unsatisfactory as a *definition* even of this basic form of memory, since forgetting is the opposite of remembering, and could hardly be intelligible if the idea of remembering were not intelligible. Still, as a slogan, it has much to commend it. I shall consider a more formal definition directly. One further question that must be considered first is whether if I remember something, I must know that I do. Must I, that is, know that I have learned something in the past, if I now remember it (whatever that "it" is)? This question is parallel to a similar question about knowing, which I discussed in Chapter 4—must I, if I know p, know that I know p? The answer must again be "No." A man may quite properly be said to remember something if he himself has no idea how he came by that knowledge—as long as *we* know how he came by it, or at any rate as long as *we* know that he learned it in the past. Similarly, a man who remembers how to swim is one who can swim and knows how to swim because he once learned, whether or not he remembers the learning or even knows now that he did once learn. Furthermore, given that a man who remembers p knows that p, even if he does not know why, it is possible for him not to know that he knows; and hence for that reason too he may not know that he remembers p. (By contrast, to say in the first person "I remember p" is, as with "I know," to commit oneself to p, even to give one's warrant to the truth of p, although the force of saying explicitly "I remember . . ." is also to make clear how one knows.)

I have emphasized these parallels between "remember" and "know" advisedly, for memory is basically a form of knowledge or, in some cases, a bringing to mind or a coming to mind of such knowledge. In the latter cases where knowledge is brought to mind or comes to mind the knowledge that one has is utilized in one way or another in thought, whether or not that thought involves imagery in addition. If the thought in question involves an awareness that the knowledge is memory knowledge, it must involve some reference to the past, since one cannot be said to *remember*, as opposed simply to know, that something is going to happen unless one's knowledge that it is going to happen was acquired in the past. But of course one can think of something in such a way that this involves the utilization of memory knowledge, without being aware of this. One may think that one is not remembering at all or one may not know whether one is; and in that case there is obviously no reference to the past in the thought itself. Yet no one could be in this position if he *could* not refer to the past in thought, if he did not, that is, have the concept of the past. What, however, of the cases in which there is no question of the knowledge in question coming to mind or being brought to mind, so that there is equally no question of the memory involving any explicit thought about what is remembered? We speak, of course, of animals remembering things, and it may seem implausible at first sight to suggest that they have a concept of the past. If we did not allow them that concept, cases of animal memory would be exceptions to the general rule about the dependence of memory on the concept of the past. In the cases where we speak of human beings remembering things in the dispositional sense, without there being any suggestion of anything coming to their mind, we can explain this by saying that they *could*, at any rate in principle, recognize that what they now know is because of something in the past; and in doing so we acknowledge that they have the concept of the past. But this course is not open to us in connection with animals, unless we are prepared to allow them the concept of the past.

Many of the cases, though perhaps not all, in which we are liable to speak of animals remembering, are cases of recognition of things on their part. To speak of an animal recognizing something is to say that it knows the

thing in question and that it does so because it has come
to know it in the past; there is no necessary implication
in this that the animal knows that it knows the thing
because it came to know it in the past. Thus it is not necessary in cases of recognition to invoke in addition the
idea that the animal actually recollects anything in any
sense that would imply an awareness of the past. This
in itself, however, would not rule out altogether memory
of any kind, and there are undoubtedly other cases where
the animal exhibits in its behavior what has all the appearance of genuine memory—cases that are more than
the mere manifestation of skills or abilities acquired in
the past. A dog may indicate in its behavior, for example,
that it remembers where its food is kept—or so it seems.
It is not easy to make a decision on what we should say
here. Are we to say that memory does not necessarily presuppose a concept of the past—in which case, what marks
off memory from other forms of knowledge due to what
has happened in the past? Or should we preserve the
title of memory for those forms of knowledge where the
knowledge either is or could in principle be explicitly of
something as past? I am inclined to think that the latter
is the course to adopt, and we must then either acknowledge that animals can have a concept of the past if we
are to ascribe memory to them, or we must allow that
we speak of memory in their case only by courtesy. If
we do allow them the concept of the past we shall have
to allow them some recognition of other temporal distinctions. We tend to allow some animals hopes, fears, and
expectations that would suggest the attribution to them
of the concept of the future, in the sense that what we
allow them is a state of mind that has reference to the
future. Why not, then, a concept of the past? In all these
cases, of course, the temporal consciousness that we would
allow them would be simply such as has immediate relevance to their behavior.[17] It would be another matter,

[17] Cf. C. Taylor, *The Explanation of Behaviour* (London,
1964), p. 68 (New York, 1964).

as Wittgenstein in effect suggests,[18] to attribute to them refined temporal concepts such as that of the day after tomorrow. In sum, I am inclined to allow that some animals can have memory in the full sense, and thereby attribute to them also the concept of the past, thus making the possession of the concept of the past a necessary condition of having memory.

Malcolm defines factual memory with respect to persons and without this explicit presupposition of the concept of the past by saying that a person remembers that p if and only if he knows that p because he previously knew that p.[19] This definition of factual memory thus involves reference to present knowledge, past knowledge, and a relationship between the present knowledge and the past knowledge that is to be expressed by saying that the present knowledge exists *because* of the past knowledge. If this were sufficient one could go on to account for other so-called forms of memory by specifying the additional factors necessary in their cases. But is it sufficient? I have already indicated my belief in the necessity of a reference to the concept of the past, but it could be argued that this was catered for in the restriction of the definition to the memories of persons. Apart from this I think that the definition is satisfactory provided that an adequate account can be given of what is meant in saying that the present knowledge exists *because of* the past knowledge. Certainly the past knowledge does not entail the existence of the present knowledge; otherwise forgetting and misremembering would be impossible. Prima facie, the most plausible account of that "because of" is that it is a causal one; the present knowledge is causally dependent on the past knowledge. Malcolm, however, rejects that suggestion on the grounds that it implies, as Von Leyden suggests,[20] an unbroken causal chain stretching from the initial experience or acquisition of knowledge to the present.

[18] L. Wittgenstein, ibid., p. 174.
[19] N. Malcolm, ibid., pp. 222ff.
[20] W. Von Leyden, ibid., p. 42.

Such a causal chain is problematical, and if its existence is made a condition of having memory, the possibility of its nonexistence gives rise to skepticism about the possibility of genuine memory. Moreover, we do not need to be satisfied about the existence of the causal chain in order to be justified in ascribing memory to someone. In place of this notion, Malcolm suggests that all that is required is that the "because of" should be taken as essentially negative. Its force is to rule out other reasons why the person in question may now know that p—reasons such as that he has relearned or been told that p. In effect, this is to say merely that when a person remembers that p, he knows that p and he would not know that p if he had not known that p at the time to which there is (at least tacit) reference in the memory attribution. Thus the previous knowledge is merely a necessary condition of the present knowledge.

Such an account is insufficient. It is easy enough to produce cases in which present knowledge has past knowledge as a necessary condition without this constituting memory. There might be someone who knows something that he has once known but has forgotten, but he knows it now because he has since been told about it, and for some reason it was possible to tell him about it only because he *had* known about it previously. (One can imagine some social institution prescribing this condition.) It might be replied that this is an objection to Malcolm's formal definition only, and that it is not an objection to the spirit of his account since that account is meant to rule out such things as being told later about the thing supposed to be remembered. But what is included under the heading "such things"? This is the trouble, for what has to be ruled out is anything that could make it false that one knows that p now because one has previously learned that p and not forgotten. One's previous knowledge has to explain one's present knowledge, and it is not a sufficient explanation to say that one would not know now if one had not known at the previous time, because this is compatible with a number of different possible relations between past and present knowledge. It seems therefore that if X remembers that p, X's knowledge now must be causally dependent upon his having come to know that p in the past. How that causal dependence is to be further specified is another matter. Since the person who remembers must be the same person who previously knew, it is to be expected that the details of the causal story are to be looked for in that which provides for us the grounds for speaking of the same person—the spatio-temporal continuity of the body and bodily processes. (If disembodied persons are possible, it may very well be considered a problem whether and how they can have memories, and it is no coincidence that philosophers concerned with immortality and personal survival have often been prepared to allow that memory is something that belongs essentially to the embodied soul.)

Does this view give rise to the skepticism that Malcolm suggests that it does? It is difficult to see why it should, any more than the fact that perception takes place under complex conditions gives rise to skepticism about perception. It is a fact that someone cannot be said to perceive something if certain processes of a physical and physiological kind do not take place; he cannot be said to perceive unless the experience that he has is causally dependent upon other factors. Since these processes are complex in nature, it is always possible in a given case to suggest that some part of them may not have taken place, and thus that the person concerned did not really perceive what he thought he did. We do not normally take these vague and hypothetical possibilities as reasons for skepticism about perception, and we do not think that we have to be satisfied that the causal processes have in fact taken place on every occasion on which we speak of perception. The same applies to memory. However we are to explain the causal dependence of the present knowledge involved in it on past knowledge, we are normally prepared to say that someone remembers that p as long as there are reasonable grounds for thinking that his present knowledge that p is due to his past coming to know that p. We may come to believe that there are such reasonable grounds if we can eliminate alternative explanations for his having the present knowledge; but that does not mean that the nonexistence of alternative explanations is *all* that we mean by the "due to."

It should be pointed out, finally, that nothing of what I have said about forms of memory is meant to exclude misremembering and delusions of memory. It does not exclude, that is, the possibility of making mistakes about what one remembers or of thinking that one remembers something when one does nothing of the kind. Memory, as we have seen, may fail for many reasons and in many respects, and someone who thinks that he remembers something may not in fact do so because what he thinks that he remembers did not take place at all or did not take place as he thinks. This is to acknowledge what is implicit in the account already given—that one cannot be said to remember that p if it is not true that p. If this condition fails then the person concerned does not remember that p. But other conditions may fail as well. It may be true that p, but it may not be true that the person concerned knows that p, or it may not be true that he knows it now because he once knew it, and so on.

(d) Is memory a source of knowledge?

Given what I have already said, this question can be dealt with in a relatively summary fashion. The temptation to think that memory is a source of knowledge comes from assimilating it to perception, which undoubtedly *is* a source of knowledge. One is liable to think that memory is the way in which we come to know about the past, just as perception is the way in which we come to know about the world around us. Of course, perception is not the only way in which we come to know about the world around us; we may, for example, come to know certain things about the world by way of inference from other things. Nevertheless, if we did not find out certain things about the world through perception, there would be no way in which we could find out about it in other ways. In this sense perception is the ultimate source of knowledge about the world around us. Nothing like this is true of memory. It may be that, as I suggested toward the end of section (b), memory is a condition of experience of objects in general, so that the acquisition of knowledge depends in some way on memory; but this does not make it true to say that memory is a *source* of knowledge.

The reason for this is the fact that to remember something is either to know it for the reasons discussed in the previous section or, as in the case of occurrent memory, to think of it in such a way that that knowledge is exercised in the thought. One cannot really find out something by recalling it, although one may, by recalling something and reflecting about it, make explicit to oneself the knowledge that one already has. One who recalls an event and thereby realizes something about it that he has not realized before must be said to have known implicitly what he now realizes all along, unless what is realized is no more than can be realized on the basis of *any* kind of reflection. I may reflect upon a certain matter and come to realize something as a result that I had not realized before. In that sense I may be said to have acquired new knowledge, although the new knowledge is likely to be something inferred from what I previously knew. Similarly, if I recall something, my realization of something that I had not realized before will be the result of a parallel reflection on what I knew by memory, and is likely to be something inferred from that. I can therefore gain new knowledge by using my memory, either by making explicit to myself what I previously knew implicitly or by drawing further conclusions from the knowledge that I previously had. None of this makes memory a source of knowledge in the way that perception is. Although it is possible to say to someone who asks how he can find out about some matter of fact, "Look and see," it is not similarly possible to say to someone "Recollect and see," unless this means, as I have mentioned above, "Recollect and reflect upon what you recall." To ask someone to recollect something is normally to ask him to make explicit to himself what he already knows in effect, and he cannot obey the instruction if he does not have that knowledge.

One further reason why it may be supposed that memory must be a source of knowledge about the past is the belief that if memory is not such a source there cannot be any way of finding out about the past. I discussed some of these issues at the end of section (a). The quick and straightforward answer is that, provided one has the concept of the past, there are many ways of finding out about the past: looking up records, archaeological remains, and so on. The possibility of history depends on this fact. Still, it might be replied that the situation with memory might be like that with perception in the sense that it is the ultimate source of knowledge about the past, just as perception is the ultimate source of knowledge of the contemporary world. This suggestion must again be rejected. There is nothing in the case of memory that is parallel to looking. To look involves turning one's eyes and directing one's attention on to an object of vision. In the case of the past one can recollect, in the sense of trying to remember something, but there is nothing in this corresponding to turning one's eyes in a certain direction; and if in this process one does direct one's attention, it is merely to the past in the light of the general description of what one is trying to remember, not to something that is already an object of memory, as the object looked at must be already an object of vision. The image conjured up in this connection is that of the searchlight illuminating an object, but while this metaphor has something to be said for it in the case of perception, it has no force at all in connection with memory.

This is a function of the fact that the past is past, and for that very reason there is no way of finding out about it by any form of direct acquaintance with it, such as is available through perception with the contemporary world around us. One can find out about the past through indirect evidence, of course; this must not be denied. But memory's role in this is not a direct one. Memory is not a source of knowledge about the past; it is basically already a form of knowledge. That is one reason why I entitled this part of the book "The scope of knowledge" and not "Sources of knowledge" or "Ways of knowing." The fact that we have memory, and thus knowledge of a certain kind, says something for the scope of knowledge, namely that we do have knowledge about past events, etc., and we have it because we came to have that knowledge in the past. But to remember something is not itself a way of coming to know it.

CHAPTER 8

Knowledge of
Oneself and Others

(a) Privacy and solipsism

The problem of our knowledge of other minds has become one of the classical problems of twentieth-century Anglo-Saxon epistemology. Its point of departure, however, is farther back in considerations about the extent to which what I know about myself is private in some sense or other. For if, for example, my states of mind are essentially private to me, how can others have any knowledge of them? The logical extreme in connection with assertions of privacy is solipsism, the doctrine that everything that I am aware of is private to me, so that I am in some way locked up in my own experiences and have no way of getting through them to a public world. Just as skepticism has been the bogey against which traditional epistemology has been carried on, so solipsism is the special bogey in connection with discussions in the area with which we are now concerned. Indeed, it is fair to consider solipsism one kind of skepticism—a skepticism about the existence of a public world in which each of us finds a place.

There are at least two kinds of solipsism, and these

present issues that arise also over the more general issue of privacy. There is first the solipsist who says that the idea of a public world independent of himself is meaningless, so that it is logically true that there is only him and his experiences.[1] Second, there is the solipsist who acknowledges that it is meaningful to speak of a world independent of himself, and admits that there might indeed have been such a world, but who claims that (alas, alas!) there is no such thing. In some ways the second position seems the more interesting one, because presumably such a philosopher must have reasons for maintaining what appears on the face of it to be a view that is manifestly though contingently false; the reasons that he has for maintaining this view are therefore likely to be of interest in themselves. Yet, *is* it merely contingently false that there is nothing independent of oneself? That is to say, is the second kind of solipsism really independent of the first? The second kind of solipsist allows that it is meaningful to speak of a world independent of himself, but it might well be questioned how he *can* attach meaning to such a suggestion. For is not meaning something public, something that presupposes interpersonal rules and standards?

I have said something on this issue in Chapter 3; it is best discussed here in the context of a consideration of the general notion of privacy. As far as concerns solipsism, it is necessary only to say that if meaning *is* something essentially public, then the very intelligibility of the solipsist thesis of the first kind entails its own falsity. Solipsism of the second kind could, for similar reasons, be maintained only in some such form as the assertion that while the public conditions necessary for meaning and thus for the intelligibility of the thesis once obtained, they do so no longer. It is of course a fair question why anyone who believed this should want to insist on saying it, since there could on his own thesis be no

[1] P. F. Strawson, *Individuals* (Garden City, New York, and London, 1959), Ch. 2, p. 73, calls him the "true solipsist."

one to listen to him. Such a reply is an argumentum ad hominem. Perhaps a stronger point is that someone who insists (perhaps irrationally in the circumstances) in maintaining such a thesis, must, if his thesis is to be at all interesting, let alone acceptable, be able to provide reasons for his paradoxical beliefs. A mere insistence without reason that there is nothing apart from oneself is of no philosophical interest, and someone who engaged in such behavior might justifiably be considered mad. (There is the further question of what, in this context, is meant by "oneself." If one's body is a necessary part of oneself, is not this a public object? This is a question that I shall not consider further here, although I shall return to it to some extent later.)

Let us turn now to the general notion of privacy, because it is considerations about this notion that lead to possible skepticism about our knowledge of other minds. This is a less radical skepticism than that involved in solipsism, but nonetheless one that requires an answer. Once again there is more than one thesis involved in the claim that our states of mind are private to us and indeed necessarily private to us. My states of mind are certainly private in the sense that since they are mine no one else can have them. This is not true of a number of other things that are private to me: my private property or even my private beliefs, for example. Other people could come to have things that are now my private property, and other people can have or come to have beliefs that are private to me, in the sense that they can have identically the same beliefs. In the latter sense, too, there are many other states of mind that I have that other people could also have. Nevertheless, there is equally a sense in which those states of mind are mine in such a way that they could not be others'. This is not so merely in the sense that those states of mind are to be identified only by reference to their owner, although that is true enough.[2] It is also that I am aware of *my*

[2] Cf. P. F. Strawson, ibid., p. 97.

states of mind, or can be, in a way that others are not. This can be put by saying that I *have* my states of mind; I *have*, for example, my pains, while others do not, although they have theirs. It is impossible that anyone else should have my pains in the way that I do; they could not feel my pains.

The last point has sometimes been denied on the grounds that it is possible to imagine circumstances in which I could feel another's pain.[3] Thus Don Locke supposes that it might be possible to connect another person's nervous system with mine and thus for me to feel his pain. But this would be his pain only in the sense that it is because of something happening in a nervous system that is not normally mine. The consequences of a supposal such as that which Don Locke makes in this connection raise a number of issues about personal identity. Would we, as Locke in fact asks, say that there was here one person with a complex body? Perhaps not, but in that case would nervous systems, under the supposition in question, belong to persons in any sense other than that in which other property belongs to them? However we decide these questions, it is not at all clear that we should have the right to say that when the nervous systems were connected in this way we should be feeling another's pain. There is a very good sense in which it would be *our* pain. For one thing, we should locate the pain differently from the way in which the person to whose body ours was connected would locate it. This does not apply of course other than to bodily feelings to which the question of their localization applies. Even so, states of mind of other kinds do not simply stand by themselves, and if it were possible to connect our nervous system with that of another so as to enable us to have certain emotions, say, when he does, it is not at all clear that we should be forced to say that we were experi-

[3] E.g., by Don Locke, *Myself and Others* (Oxford, 1968), pp. 9–10, although Locke makes a number of useful distinctions between different senses of "private."

encing his emotion; for the significance of the feeling to us would be likely to be different from its significance to him. The issue of the criteria of identity for states of mind raises large questions. Even if it were possible for us to have an exactly similar experience to that had by another, and in identically the same circumstances, owing to some such bodily connection as Don Locke supposes, it does not follow that it would be right to say that we were then having that other's experience or even experiencing it.

It is easy to see in all this how questions about having other people's experiences merge into questions about personal identity. To put the matter in the strongest way, I could not have another person's experiences, in the sense in question, unless, *per impossibile,* I could become that other person. This does not mean that I cannot imagine what it is like to have another person's experience or even imagine having that other person's experience. This is a feat that some people find more difficult than others; to put oneself in another's position is to imagine *oneself* in that position, and this is something that cannot be done in its entirety. But neither an inability to put oneself to some extent in another's position, nor the previously discussed inability actually to have his experience entails that I cannot know about another's experience. That we *can* know about other people's experiences and states of mind seems obvious enough, although how it is possible is a question that I shall return to in a later section. At any rate, the fact that states of mind may be private in the senses so far discussed does not entail that others cannot know of them in principle, however difficult it may be on occasion to tell what state of mind someone is actually in. Even if it is logically possible for someone so to disguise his state of mind that no one else knows about it (and this gives a special point to the claim that our states of mind are private), this does not mean that states of mind are in general unknowable by others. Thus to the extent that the impetus toward skepticism about our knowledge of other minds starts from the position of "Only I know what I feel, think, etc.," that impetus can be checked by a rejection of the starting position. It is just not true that only I know what I feel, think, etc.

It is nevertheless possible to reinforce that skepticism by means of the consideration that even if I can know what another person feels, thinks, etc., what I know in this case is different from what I know when I know what *I* feel, think, etc. And if this is so, I understand something intrinsically different when concerned with another's state of mind from when I am concerned with my own. This brings us back to the question of private vs. public meanings. To say that what I understand when concerned with my own feelings is quite different from what I understand in connection with the feelings of another is prima facie implausible. When we attribute feelings to others we do not suppose that we are saying something different of them from what we would say in speaking of our own feelings. This is not to say that the force of saying "I am in pain" may not well be different from the force of saying "He is in pain." There are certainly differences in this respect, and Wittgenstein laid great stress on the extent to which first-person avowals of feeling can be assimilated to expressions of feeling.[4] This can be summed up in the slogan that first-person avowals of pain are to be construed as pain behavior. But such a slogan cannot be taken as literally true, as Wittgenstein knew, and as Malcolm too admits[5] when he points out that an assertion like "My leg hurts" has a contradictory and can be true or false. To say that an avowal of pain has the force of pain behavior and to say that it just *is* pain behavior are different things. Given this, it remains a plausible position

[4] L. Wittgenstein, *Philosophical Investigations* (Oxford, 1953), I, 244ff.

[5] N. Malcolm, "Knowledge of other minds," *J. Phil.* LV (1958), reprinted in *Knowledge and Certainty* (Englewood Cliffs, New Jersey, 1963), p. 140.

that what I attribute to myself when I assert that I have a certain feeling is the same as what I attribute to others in comparable assertions, and moreover that what I understand by "feeling" in these two cases is the same. It may be that I attribute feelings to others on the basis of the expressions of feeling that I perceive in them, while I certainly need no such reference to my expressions of feeling in my own case. (It would be absurd to suggest that I have to wait to see how I react before I know what I am feeling.) But this does not mean that what I understand when you speak of other people's feeling is something about their expressions of feeling, something, for example, about their behavior. To suppose this is to accept a verificationist theory of meaning, to confuse what is meant in speaking of other people's feelings with what would count as verifying the statements so made.

To give way to this suggestion at all is to involve oneself in the misunderstanding that Wittgenstein describes as that of studying "the headache I have now in order to get clear about the philosophical problem of sensation," or of supposing that I know what the word "pain" means only from my own case.[6] To refute this suggestion Wittgenstein uses an analogy. He asks us to suppose that everyone has a box with something in it, but such that no one can look into anyone else's box. We call what is in each box a "beetle," and "everyone says he knows what a beetle is only by looking at *his* beetle." Wittgenstein points out that it would be possible for what is in each man's box to be different, or even for there to be nothing there, and yet for the word "beetle" to have a use. (Indeed, what that use is has been specified in the setting up of the situation; a beetle is whatever is in the box, even if there is nothing there.) Then he adds, "If we construe the grammar of the expression of sensation on the model of 'object and name' the object drops out of

[6] L. Wittgenstein, ibid., I, 314 and I, 293. The beetle analogy is to be found at I, 293.

consideration as irrelevant." That is to say that *if* we construe talking about our sensations as if all that were at stake is the reference to a private, inner object, the use of the language under consideration would be consistent with the existence for each of us of any or even no object. That "if" is important, for Wittgenstein does not mean to say that it does not matter whether there is anything in particular there when we speak of our sensations. He is trying to refute the suggestion that what we mean by, e.g., "pain," is something that we know solely from our own case by reference to a private object. On the other hand, there is no public object involved here, so that our understanding of the word "pain" cannot simply be an understanding of the word's application to an object. What else, then, is involved?

To answer this question we need to refer back to what I said about concepts and criteria in Chapter 3, section (d). For a concept of a private object there must be public criteria. There must be public and intersubjective agreement on the conditions under which the concept gets a use. Someone who did not know, for example, that pain is a feeling that is normally found unpleasant and that is normally expressed in certain sorts of ways, and that these behavioral expressions provide the agreed points of application for the concept, would not really know what pain is. The passage from Wittgenstein to which I have already referred is part of an extended argument against the possibility of what is often referred to as "private languages." I have discussed the argument before,[7] but I shall go over some of the ground again here. The argument is in fact one directed against the possibility of the sense of expressions being given by a private reference or a reference to a private object. Wittgenstein's general line of argument is that language presupposes rules of use. The notion of a rule implies the possibility of a check upon its observance, and where the sense of an expression is given by a private

[7] Cf. Ch. 6, sec. (b).

reference there is no possibility of such a check. It is of no avail to say that the individual could himself check upon his observance of the rule, since without reference to a public standard there is no real distinction to be made between the recognition that it is correct to apply the expression and a decision so to apply it. It might be objected that a similar difficulty applies to any attempt to pick out private sensations. How do we know that we are in fact picking out the same sensation in each case? May not our recognition of the sensation as the same one as that which we experienced before be in reality a decision so to treat it? Do we not need criteria of identity if we are to be justified in speaking of a sensation as the same as one previously experienced, and how are criteria of identity to be established for private experiences?

In the case of ordinary experiences we can generally determine the answer to the question "Is it the same one as . . . ?" by reference to features of the experience. But this presupposes that our understanding of the experience and its features is something that can be expressed in terms of the language that we already have. There is nothing objectionable in the idea of the private use of language which is parasitical upon our ordinary public language. What is objectionable is an intrinsically private language, or, as I put the point above, expressions whose sense is given by a private reference. Such expressions would be like Wittgenstein's "beetle." It would be an illusion to suppose that we really understood the word "beetle" in that example, except as meaning whatever is in the box (including the case where there is nothing in the box). And in the case of an expression whose sense is given by a private reference, in the sense of privacy that is relevant to sensations, there is not even the context provided by the box to help us. (Indeed, Wittgenstein's example not only trades on an inadequate sense of "privacy," it relies upon a public object, a box, which all can in principle see and understand; its use of "beetle" is thus to some extent parasitical upon a publicly understood use of words. But, of course, this kind of inadequacy in providing a complete parallel with the privacy of sensations is typical of analogies, and it is inevitable here if the use of "beetle" is to be intelligible to us at all.) Thus sensation language must presuppose a public understanding of a public world. To understand a concept like that of pain involves the understanding of the way in which the concept of a private object fits into that understanding of a public world. That is where the behavioral criteria for the concept come in. To understand the word "pain" one needs to understand the normal expressions of pain and the way in which they are expressions. Hence the importance of an understanding of the kinds of force that avowals of pain can have.

Given the publicly determined sense that is to be given to words connected with private experiences, there can be no valid suggestion that what we mean in speaking of our own feelings is quite different from what we mean in speaking of the feelings of others. (Nor, of course, can there be anything in the more radical position against which it is possible that Wittgenstein was arguing, the position to be found in Russell's *Philosophy of Logical Atomism*,[8] that what we understand by *any* expression is something private. Russell tries to save himself against the suggestion that for this kind of "private language" no one would understand anyone else by saying in effect that no one really does understand anyone else. Fortunately, however, words are ambiguous, and even if they do mean something different for each of us we get along because of that very ambiguity. But this is no ordinary ambiguity, and the whole situation described is really an absurdity.) If we are not locked within a private understanding, there is no obstacle to the possibility of having knowledge of other people's

[8] B. Russell, "The Philosophy of Logical Atomism," *Monist* (1918–19), reprinted in his *Logic and Knowledge*, ed. R. C. Marsh (London, 1956). See esp. p. 195.

states of mind.[9] Whether there are other obstacles is a matter to which we shall return.

(b) Knowledge of one's own states of mind

I spoke earlier of my being aware of my states of mind in a way that others are not, a point that might be put by saying that I *have* them. It is possible for some states of mind to be unconscious, but even in that case it must in principle be possible for me to be aware of them in a way that is not possible for others. To that extent one cannot have a state of mind without either knowing that one has or being able in principle to know that one has, and in each case the knowledge is not in any way inferential. This point has sometimes been put by saying that whereas one needs criteria for ascribing states of mind to others one does not need them for ascribing them to oneself. Indeed, the very idea of using criteria in order to ascribe states of mind to oneself makes no sense. So it is argued by, e.g., Sydney Shoemaker.[10] But to put the matter in this way is misleading, since if the notion of a "criterion" so invoked is the Wittgensteinian notion, it should have something to do with meaning, not with grounds for making truth claims. To say that one does not ascribe private sensations to oneself on the basis of bodily criteria is surely to say something about how statements about oneself are to be verified. It is perfectly true that one does not need to know anything about bodily conditions in order to know about one's feelings, but this is not well put in terms of criteria. (It has to be admitted, however, that Shoemaker's account of the concept of criterion, to the effect that a

[9] See J. W. Cook, "Wittgenstein on privacy," *Phil. Rev.* LXXIV (1965), pp. 281ff., reprinted in *Wittgenstein*, ed. G. Pitcher (Garden City, New York, 1966; London, 1968), pp. 286ff.

[10] S. Shoemaker, *Self-knowledge and Self-Identity* (Ithaca, New York, 1963), Ch. 6.

criterion is something that provides direct, noninductive grounds for the truth of a statement, is in conformity with his subsequent account, whether or not it is faithful to what Wittgenstein intended.) As it is, Shoemaker goes on to say that being entitled to assert a first-person statement about pain, for example, "consists simply in the statement's being true."[11] He means by this presumably that if I am in pain I have all the entitlement that I need to say that I am. But the point would be better put by saying that what we must do is to resist any temptation to speak of grounds for first-person statements about one's feelings, for, as we have already seen, their normal role is as avowals, and it makes no sense to ask someone for the grounds for his avowal. To ask someone who says "God, I am in pain," what his entitlement is to make that statement would be ludicrous.

At all events, one is one's own authority for the truth of first-person avowals of feeling. What this means exactly, however, is something that needs further investigation. It has often been claimed, for example, that such first-person avowals are incorrigible, that one cannot be mistaken in making them. And with this has sometimes gone a thesis, thought to be derived from Wittgenstein, that where there is no possibility of error it is inappropriate to speak of knowledge. It might well be thought that these two theses are incompatible. For, how can there be incorrigibility where it is inappropriate to speak of knowledge at all? Yet Malcolm, for one, takes the two theses to be two sides of the same thesis and maintains that they are taken from Wittgenstein.[12] As far as concerns the second part of the combined thesis, Wittgenstein does say, "One says 'I know' where one can also say 'I believe' or 'I suspect'; where one can find out" (and

11 S. Shoemaker, ibid., p. 216.

12 N. Malcolm, "Wittgenstein's Philosophical Investigations," *Phil. Rev.* LXIII (1954), reprinted in his *Knowledge and Certainty,* pp. 96ff., esp. p. 110.

the possibility of finding out something also implies the possibility of being wrong about it).[13] This remark is, however, preceded by another that reads, " 'I know what I want, wish, believe, feel . . .' (and so on through all the psychological verbs) is either philosophers' nonsense, or alternatively *not* a judgment *a priori.*" In other words, for a philosopher to say, as a remark about the concept of feeling, that we know what we feel, implying that we can come to know what we feel, is nonsense (and there are other remarks in Wittgenstein emphasizing the meaninglessness of saying this sort of thing). But this does not mean that a use could not be given to "I know what I feel," when this is not meant to be a remark about the concept of feeling. Thus someone to whom it is said "You cannot possibly be feeling *that* in these circumstances" might well say "I know what I feel," and this would be perfectly intelligible, though not a remark about the concept of feeling. One needs therefore to go very carefully with the thesis that it is inappropriate to speak of knowledge of one's own feelings, let alone other states of mind such as beliefs, where there does not seem even a prima facie difficulty with regard to the suggestion that one may on occasion find out about what one believes. I shall return to this point directly, along with the question of whether it even makes sense to talk of our coming to know or finding out what we feel.

In a way, similar considerations apply to the incorrigibility thesis. There would indeed be a kind of absurdity in the suggestion that a man who felt intense pain in a certain part of his body might be mistaken about this fact. He could not be mistaken as to the fact that he was experiencing pain nor as to the part of his body in which he was experiencing it. (Where the cause of the pain was to be found is another matter, and it is sometimes the case that the cause of a man's pain is to be located elsewhere than where he feels the pain itself to be.) But this kind of absurdity is no different from that involved

[13] L. Wittgenstein, ibid., p. 221. See also Ch. 4, sec. (d).

in the suggestion that a man might be mistaken about what is directly in front of his eyes when the conditions of perception are entirely normal. It is not that error is logically impossible, but that it is inconceivable how error of this kind could arise in these circumstances. But not even this much is true of less intense feelings. In some circumstances a man may genuinely be in doubt whether what he experiences is properly to be called a pain or not, or whether it is in one precise part of his body rather than in another part nearby. It may also be that he comes to decide that he was formerly wrong in characterizing his experience as a pain. In that sense his description of the experience is corrigible by him, and in some circumstances by others too, since they may justifiably come to the conclusion that he does not know what it is to have an experience of a given kind. The point at issue here is that descriptions of experiences involve the subsumption of the experience under a concept, and it is always possible to misapply concepts.

This may seem to imply that the only mistakes that we can make about our own experiences are because of defects of understanding; there are no simple errors of fact in this area. This conclusion is correct up to a point. When I am mistaken about the color of an object, for example, I may have an entirely adequate understanding of color; my error may be because of defects of vision or because of a failure to note the peculiarities of the situation. There is nothing corresponding to this in the case of private experiences. This is not to say that one cannot find out things about our experiences by paying close attention to them (by what is sometimes referred to somewhat grandiloquently as introspection). But this is not really like paying close attention to material things, since in the latter case there are objective and interpersonal criteria of truth for what we claim to find out, while in the case of our own experiences what each of us says goes, unless there are grounds for positing a defect of understanding on our part. Thus instead of saying that it is possible for us to discover that we were wrong about our feelings, it may be less misleading to say that it is possible for us to *decide* this. There is indeed no real distinction between discovery and decision here. Not that the word "decision" suggests that the conclusion to which we come need be in any way arbitrary. Our decision that what we have been experiencing during the last few seconds was an irritation rather than an itch may be well advised and completely rational, based on considerations about what it is for something to be an itch. The decision may be the result of just reflection. There is after all a certain kind of necessary connection between particular feelings and particular wants; it is, for example, part of the concept of an itch that it is a feeling that brings with it wanting to scratch the part of the body where the itch is located. Thus a way of deciding whether a feeling is an itch, if such a decision is required, is to ask oneself whether one has any desire to scratch.

This kind of consideration is even more obvious in the case of more complex feelings, like the emotions. Someone may quite genuinely ask themselves whether what they feel is love. Such a question is indeed a commonplace of the romantic novel or the popular song.[14] To answer the question may again require decisions of a kind, since there may be no obvious way of finding out the answer in a way that could properly be called objective. Yet here too there begin to be cases in which the opposite may seem to be true. It may be obvious to others that someone is in love before it is clear to that person, and the realization on the part of that person that he is in love may come as a genuine discovery. This is because emotions of this kind involve attitudes and beliefs on our part, and it is quite possible for us to be ignorant of the fact that we have these attitudes and beliefs. Such an error is not just a defect of understanding; it is a genuine mistake of fact about ourselves. We

[14] Cf. Cole Porter's "Is it a cocktail this feeling of joy, or is what I feel the real McCoy?" in the song "At long last love."

saw in Chapter 4 that it is quite possible for us not to know that we believe certain things. It is equally possible for us to discover that we do so believe. Even so, some cases of this sort might well be better construed as cases of *deciding* that we believe, e.g., cases of religious decision, the decision on the part of someone that he believes in God. For deciding that one believes things in this way is in part a matter of deciding whether one can give one's assent. In deciding whether one believes, one reviews the grounds for the belief, but the decision that one so believes involves commitment to the belief, and this has implications for future action. In these circumstances it is not really up to others to say "No you do not." The situation is different when the question is whether someone has believed something over a period of time, or when the question is whether he really does believe something even though he is not prepared to admit it. Since beliefs may manifest themselves in many ways, it is possible for us to discover beliefs in others that they themselves do not know about. Similarly, the person who has a belief of this kind may eventually come to see that he *must*, as we say, believe this. This may be a genuine discovery, although the final step to the realization, not just that he *must* believe this, but that he actually *does* so, may, because it involves the assent already referred to, be best construed as a decision that he believes.

The actual relations between discovery and decision in respect of differing states of mind may be complex ones. In some cases it is possible for someone to stand back from himself, as it were, and observe himself to the extent that he may make discoveries about himself in the same or in similar ways to those in which others may do so. Yet since the person who makes the discovery in that case is the same as the person about whom the discoveries are made, it is always open to him to say to himself some such thing as "I can see from my behavior that I must believe that, but do I really believe it?" And the import of this last question is whether here and now he is prepared to commit himself to the position at issue; he *may* decide that he is, and in doing so he is deciding that he so believes.

Similar considerations apply to emotions to the extent that beliefs or attitudes are involved in them. A person may reflect in a similar way to that which I have just reviewed when considering whether he really loves someone, whether he is really proud of someone, or jealous, and so on. Here, however, there may be other factors also, since in the case of certain emotions, conditions have to be satisfied before a person can be said to have the emotion in question. A person cannot be said to be proud, for example, of something that he has nothing to do with; he cannot be said to be jealous of someone if he does not stand in a certain relation to that person.[15] Nevertheless, it may still be possible for someone to *feel* proud or jealous when these conditions are not satisfied, since it is possible for him to take up attitudes to people and things that are quite unreal and to have beliefs about them that are completely irrational. Hence, as I said earlier, a person may discover what emotions he feels by reviewing the beliefs and attitudes that he has. Where those beliefs and attitudes are not justified he may content himself with that realization in some circumstances; but in others he may say to himself, for example, that although he feels jealous he is not really jealous at all.

I cannot go further into these matters here. They are largely the concern of the philosophy of mind. I shall say a little more about knowledge of our intentions in section (c). My concern here has been to indicate the complexity of the situations involved in knowledge of our own states of mind. There has, however, been a common thread running through these situations. Increased complexities in states of mind (in the sense of an in-

[15] Cf. E. Bedford, "Emotions," *Proc. Arist. Soc.* (1956–57), pp. 281ff., reprinted in *Essays in Philosophical Psychology,* ed. D. F. Gustafson (Garden City, New York, 1964), pp. 77ff. and *The Philosophy of Mind,* ed. V. C. Chappell (Englewood Cliffs, New Jersey, 1962), pp. 110ff.

crease in the complexity of the conditions that have to be
satisfied before the state of mind can properly be attributed to someone) lead to increased possibilities of
making genuine discoveries about one's own states of
mind; for one can in these cases discover that the conditions referred to are satisfied. But there comes a point
with all these states of mind when the satisfaction or
otherwise of publicly determinable conditions no longer
remains in question. At this point the person concerned
can, in principle, still ask himself, "Do I feel pain?" "Do
I believe that?" "Do I love her?" and so on. All that he
can do at this point is reflect on the situation in the light
of his understanding of the appropriate concepts. He
can, for example, ask himself, "Do I really want to get
away from the situation that produces this feeling?" "Do
I really want to commit myself to that position?" "Do I
want to be with her all the time?" and so on. His *decisions* on these questions will determine for him the nature of the state of mind that he has. There are, of course,
circumstances in which it would be ludicrous that these
questions should ever arise, but, as I indicated earlier,
such a consideration equally applies to the question
whether in given circumstances there really is a certain
object in front of us. Hence the important point that is
peculiar to states of mind is the point about decision,
and it is this that is involved in saying that we ourselves
are ultimately the authority for statements about our
states of mind.

(c) *Knowledge of other people's states of mind*

Once the issues about privacy have been cleared up,
the issue about knowledge of other people's states of
mind falls into place. The assumption that "Only I know
what I feel" leads directly to the belief that I can know
about other people's feelings only in an inferior sense
and in an indirect way. One more or less traditional account of this situation is that we know about other

people's states of mind by analogy with our own. It is supposed that we note the connection between our own states of mind and their bodily expression; we also note this bodily expression in others and therefore argue that there must be a similar connection between this bodily expression in others and states of mind that they must have. The quick way with this argument is to say that an argument from analogy cannot be used when there is no possibility even in principle of determining independently whether the fourth term exists. If the only case in which I can really know of states of mind properly is my own case, I can have no justification, even in principle, for the supposition that a body in front of me belongs to someone who has states of mind. An argument from analogy is valid only where and to the extent to which the analogy can be established independently. But in the present case there is no such possibility ex hypothesi. As James Thomson points out, the situation is not like that of whether the windows in houses across the road have rooms behind them like the one which we are in, for it is in principle possible in the latter case to go and find out the truth directly.[16]

I have no wish to claim that analogy plays no part at all in any case where we have to decide whether what is in front of us is a creature with feelings, etc. I shall indicate later a class of cases where analogy may be relevant. But it cannot be the only thing that we go on in any case whatever. Hampshire has made an attempt to invoke a more respectable version of the argument from analogy.[17] He argues that we are in the position to verify directly the statements made by others about our feelings and thus learn the reliability of certain methods

16 J. Thomson, "The argument from analogy and our knowledge of other minds," *Mind*, N.S., LX (1951), pp. 336ff. See also N. Malcolm, "Knowledge of other minds," *J. Phil.* LV (1958), reprinted in *Knowledge and Certainty*, pp. 130ff.

17 S. N. Hampshire, "The analogy of feeling," *Mind*, N.S., LXI (1952), pp. 1ff.

used by people in order to ascertain the feelings of others. We can then justifiably use the same methods in order to arrive at conclusions about other people's feelings, on the basis of an analogy that exists between the conditions under which the statements in question are made and verified. As far as concerns the traditional problem of other minds, this argument is, as Malcolm points out, an ignoratio elenchi;[18] for it is presupposed in the argument that we know about other people, that we know that these others are people. It is an extremely important and indeed fundamental point that once given that we are confronted with a person the question whether he has a mind can no longer arise. To raise the problem at all we have to suppose that the question is whether the *body* in front of us belongs to such a person. But this question is already begged in Hampshire's argument. It might be said that Hampshire is not concerned with the traditional problem of other minds at all; what he is concerned with is the circumstances in which alone we come to an understanding of feeling-words. But if that is so it would seem to be supposed that the story about meaning must be given in terms of conditions of verification; that is to say that it is Hampshire's concern to show how statements about other people's feelings can be verified in ways analogous to those in which we verify their statements about our feelings.

This suggestion seems to receive confirmation in his use of the point that there is no class of statements about other minds, a point that is also made by Ayer, who undoubtedly has verification conditions in mind.[19] The point that there is no class of statements about other minds can be taken in a variety of ways, depending on

[18] N. Malcolm, ibid., p. 133.

[19] A. J. Ayer, "Statements about the past," *Proc. Arist. Soc.* (1950–51), reprinted in *Philosophical Essays* (London, 1954), pp. 167ff. See also his "One's knowledge of other minds," *Theoria,* XIX (1953), also reprinted in *Philosophical Essays,* pp. 191ff., and *The Problem of Knowledge,* Penguin edition, (London, 1956), pp. 214ff. (New York, 1956).

whether the emphasis is put on the words "class," "statements," or "other." But both Hampshire and Ayer certainly want to say that other minds are always other to someone, and any given mind may be "other" to other people though not to the person whose mind it is. Thus, it is claimed, it is not part of the content of a statement about a certain mind that it is other, since it is only other to people who do not own it. Ayer puts this by saying that it is not part of the meaning of a statement about anyone's feelings that they belong to someone other than the person who makes the statement. There seems to be a confusion in this about meaning. Meaning belongs to sentences, not statements (the latter being the use of sentences). Still it might be said that when I say "I am in pain" and someone else says in the same circumstances "Hamlyn is in pain," we have both said the same thing, both made the same statement; hence it cannot be part of the content of a statement that it is made by a particular person and with a particular form of reference (i.e., by using the pronoun "I" or a proper name, etc.). This raises large questions about the criteria of identity for statements, which I cannot go into here.[20] On the face of it, it certainly seems to make a difference for the question of what is said whether the statement is made by a person about himself or about another.

However, Ayer's view is that the entire content of a statement using demonstratives or proper names is that someone answering to a certain description possesses the property ascribed thereby to him. Thus, when I make a statement about Ayer, the content of my statement is that a person answering to a certain description is such-and-such. It is only a contingent matter that I do not myself satisfy that description and so cannot verify the statement directly. Hence any statement about another person's feeling is verifiable in principle by the maker of the statement, though not in fact. Thus it transpires that

[20] See, for example, L. R. Reinhardt, "Propositions and Speech-Acts," *Mind*, N.S., LXXVI (1967), pp. 166ff.

the aim of the argument is to show how statements about other minds are verifiable in principle. They are so because it is only a contingent matter that what answers to the specifications provided by the content of the statement is other than the person who makes the statement. As I have said, this raises large questions about the criteria of identity for statements, and also about such notions as "meaning" and "content," into which it would not be profitable to go now. Nevertheless, it is evident that the argument would have an appeal only for one who thought that the problem of other minds was that of showing how statements about other minds are verifiable in principle, on the hypothesis that this is required for their meaningfulness. That is to say, that the thesis put forward brings with it the relics of the verification theory of meaning, if not the full-blown theory itself.

The same or similar relics can be found in a generally more powerful argument to be found in Chapter 3 of Strawson's *Individuals*.[21] Strawson there puts forward the principle that a condition of ascribing states of mind to oneself is that one must be prepared to ascribe them to others, and indeed that one should actually do so. The argument that follows is (in very, very brief form), that one could not ascribe them to others unless there were in fact a way of doing so such that in ascribing them to others one was ascribing them to the very same kind of thing as in ascribing them to oneself. For this to be possible the expressions of states of mind must count as more than mere signs of those states of mind. The behavioral expressions must count as logically adequate criteria for the ascription of states of mind to others. Since all this is a presupposition of ascribing states of mind to oneself directly, skepticism about the existence of other minds is impossible. It is not possible to do justice to all the complexities of Strawson's argument in a short space,

[21] P. F. Strawson, *Individuals* (London, 1959), pp. 99ff. (Garden City, New York, 1959).

and I shall not try to do so here.[22] I say that the position adopted reveals the relics of the verificationist position because Strawson to some extent speaks as if his account is meant to explain the meaning of what he calls "P-predicates" (predicates that can be ascribed to persons alone), and as if the meaning in question is to be explained in terms of the ways of ascribing those predicates. (There is, however, an important passage on page 110 of his book that emphasizes the point that the meaning of predicates is not given solely by the logically sufficient criteria for their ascription but also by "the rest of the language-structure to which they belong." This suggests a more Wittgensteinian approach in terms of the context of use within which the predicate is intelligible.)

Apart from this, Strawson's argument seems defective in at least two places. First, the initial principle seems valid only in the form that a condition of ascribing states of mind to oneself is that one must be *prepared* to ascribe them to others, not that one need actually do so. In a footnote on page 99 of his book, Strawson says, "The main point here is a purely logical one: the idea of a predicate is correlative with that of a range of distinguishable individuals of which the predicate can be significantly, though not necessarily truly, affirmed." Since, however, there is nothing wrong with the idea of a uniquely instantiated predicate—a predicate applicable in fact to one thing only—it cannot be argued from the fact that a mental predicate is applicable to me that it must necessarily be attributable to anyone else. Hence despite some protestations by Strawson earlier in the note, it cannot be inferred that one who ascribes states of mind to himself should actually ascribe them to others. He may insist that he is perfectly prepared to do so; only there are, unfortunately, no others to whom they can be as-

[22] See G. Bird, *Kant's Theory of Knowledge* (London, 1962), pp. 181ff. (New York); A. J. Ayer, *The Concept of a Person* (New York and London, 1963), Ch. 4; Don Locke, *Myself and Others* (Oxford, 1968), Ch. 7.

cribed. The argument does not deal with this form of skeptic. It may, however, deal in part with another form of skeptic: the one whom Strawson calls the "true solipsist", who says that it is meaningless to talk of states of mind other than his own; for the logical principle invoked entails that it must make sense to ascribe them to other subjects than oneself, whether there actually are any.

Second, there is the point about logically adequate criteria. This is an obscure notion in itself and seems on the face of it to imply that certain behavioral manifestations entail the existence of certain states of mind in the person concerned. This does not seem to be true, and it involves the same confusions about criteria to which reference was made in Chapter 3, section (d). (The point is connected with the relics of verificationism already mentioned.) It is true that if a mental term is to be meaningful there must be criteria for the concept in question, and this implies in turn that a given state of mind must normally be expressed in a given way. But this cannot rule out the possibility that a person may be dissembling or disguising his feelings; hence there cannot be any entailment between the existence of a certain form of behavior and the existence of a certain mental state. One can say indeed that a form of behavior does in particular circumstances count merely as a sign of a certain mental state, even if the connection between behavior and mental states cannot be merely contingent in general. The truth is, as is implied by Wittgenstein's discussion, that mental terms require public interpersonal criteria, and would not be intelligible without this. Thus the acceptance of the intelligibility of the terms in which the skeptic raises the question of other minds implies the acceptance of the impossibility of rejecting the existence of other minds on the grounds of the meaninglessness of the suggestion. But this does not mean that it is similarly meaningless to doubt either the current existence of other persons with minds or the existence of particular states of mind in particular persons who behave in particular ways. The first possibility cannot be ruled out because a determined skeptic can say that the conditions necessary for his having the concepts of states of mind were indeed once present; unfortunately, persons have now ceased to exist and have been replaced by automata. Such a suggestion would be ridiculous, and without good supporting reasons entirely empty, but it is not meaningless. The second possibility cannot be ruled out because it is not part of the story about the behavioral criteria for mental concepts that the manifestation of the appropriate behavior must be taken to *entail* the presence of the relevant state of mind. There is no entailment relation between behavior and states of mind.

The truth is that we ascribe states of mind to others neither on the direct, noninductive basis implied by talk of logically adequate criteria nor on the basis of an analogy from our own case. The former implies that the meaning of a given mental concept is to be given entirely in terms of certain forms of behavior; the latter implies that it is given in terms of our own private experiences (in terms of our own case, as Wittgenstein puts it). The meaning of concepts of this kind certainly depends on interpersonal and public behavioral criteria; it presupposes characteristic and normal ways in which states of mind are expressed, and for this reason it is not open to any of us to doubt the possibility of other minds existing at all; such a doubt would be unintelligible. To doubt that other minds actually exist now (even allowing that they once existed) would be absurd in another way, as already indicated. Once given that what is in front of us is a person, doubt as to his having states of mind cannot validly arise. But given an understanding of the concepts under which various states of mind fall and an understanding of their criteria, there is opened up a way of ascribing particular states of mind to particular persons, not on the basis of an analogy from our own case but on the basis of what is normally to be expected of a person who has a given state of mind. This is not to say that our own personal experiences have no part to play in our understanding of what is normally to be expected in this way, and to this extent analogies with situations in which we have found ourselves may provide the basis for an inference to another's state of mind in similar situations. But this is not the kind of analogy presupposed in the use of the argument from analogy to provide a general basis for knowledge of other minds.

Analogy may play a part in another way too in rather different circumstances. I have indicated that once given that we are confronted with a person, the existence of another mind is not problematic, and analogy can play a part only in argument from one situation to another—argument of the form "I felt that in this situation, so he probably does too." (And this argument has a suppressed premise to the effect that the speaker is typical of people generally, or of some class of people.) But what of what might be called the other worlds problem—the problem of whether creatures to be found on other worlds are conscious and have minds? In fact the problem is little different from that which confronts us over certain animals and insects. Do ants have feelings? Up to a point analogy can have a part to play here—analogies between our behavior in certain situations and the behavior of the creatures in question. Of course it may be held to beg the question to speak of behavior at all, if by "behavior" is meant anything like what we mean by action. Similarities between the movements of creatures in varying situations and the movements that we make may be indicative of something, but such considerations are not likely to be clinching, any more than analogies between the structure and composition of their bodies and that of our own. Hence if all that we know is that we are confronted with a body, there is little hope of clinching the issue, whether or not it is also conscious. Wittgenstein said "The human body is the best picture of the human soul,"[23] and for

[23] L. Wittgenstein, ibid., p. 178.

that reason Malcolm[24] argues against the possibility that any sounds coming from, e.g., a tree, or indeed any other phenomenon in this connection, "could create any probability that it has sensations and thoughts." What is required, he says, is human behavior or something similar, and this requires something like a human form. (This is not to say that we could not *give sense* to the idea of a tree feeling or thinking things, as happens in fairy stories, but this is ex hypothesi not the ordinary sense.) But the question that immediately arises is how great the relevant similarities have to be. What of ants, as I asked earlier? It is a feasible suggestion that we should invoke here Wittgenstein's notion of a form of life, and say that we should be prepared to attribute consciousness to something nonhuman in anything like the human sense to the extent that we are prepared to consider sharing the same form of life with it, to the extent that we can contemplate it calling out human responses from us and responding to us in any analogous way, to the extent that we can contemplate a form of relationship with it that is anything like a human relationship. Not that this will solve all problems. It may still leave us, for example, with the question of whether ants are conscious in any sense at all.[25]

(d) Knowledge of one's own body

There are many things that one can know about one's body only by means of the ordinary processes of observation. But as I noted in Chapter 4, section (d), there is a form of knowledge of our own body, the knowledge of the place of our limbs and possibly the knowledge of the location of bodily sensations, that is not ordinarily ob-

[24] N. Malcolm, ibid., pp. 134ff.

[25] The difficulties here stem from the fact that, since consciousness represents a *category* of states, there cannot, as was indicated in Ch. 3, n. 18, be criteria for it, as there can be for the states that fall within the category.

tained in this way. One does not normally have to look to
see what is the position of a leg. In cases of paralysis, of
course, we have to do just that, and this indicates that
sensations from the limb play some part in our knowledge of its location. On the other hand, we do not normally have to note the sensation that we are having and
make inferences from this to the position of the appropriate
limb. Hence, as I noted in Chapter 4, section (d), Anscombe has called the knowledge in question "knowledge
without observation." Whether or not this term is a happy
one and whether or not it applies in the same way to all
the things to which she applies it, it is certainly the
case that knowledge of the position of our limbs is normally noninferential. It is not based on inferences from
further observations. Under normal conditions we just
know the positions of our limbs, and we know them because they are where we feel them to be. We could not
feel them to be there unless our body was sensitive, and
the sensitivity of the body is the reason why we feel our
limbs to be there; it is, it might be said, the cause of the
awareness that we have, although not the grounds for
the knowledge in question. Thus this form of knowledge
is a form of direct awareness of our body, mediated by
the sensitivity of the body. We can be mistaken in it,
we can sometimes be deceived about the position of
our limbs, and often enough we can be quite ignorant
about it, if the body happens for some reason to be insen-
sitive. Psychologists have sometimes spoken in this connection of a "body schema" or "body image," since in being
aware of the position of a given limb or part of one's
body we are aware of it relative to other parts. But to
speak of a body image overintellectualizes the matter; it
is not that we have an idea of this schema and locate a
limb in it, like a point on a system of co-ordinates, for the
awareness in question is not a conceptually mediated
awareness. An animal can be said to know where its tail
is if it goes straight to it and bites at it when it irritates.
The animal has the knowledge in question just to the
extent that it has the ability to manipulate the part of its

body in appropriate circumstances. Concepts come in only when the awareness is to be formulated.[26]

Similar considerations apply to our knowledge of the location of bodily sensations, to the extent that it is appropriate to speak of knowledge here at all.[27] This knowledge is again a function of what has been called "the body *qua* sensitive."[28] There are no data from which we infer the location of the feeling. We simply feel the feeling to be wherever it is. This counts in particular against the thesis that has been known since Lotze as the local-sign theory. This is the thesis that sensations bring with them certain characteristics that serve as signs of their origin. If this were true, we should have to infer the location of a sensation from some other feature of it. Apart from the fact that we do not have to make inferences of this kind, such an account would succeed only in shifting the problem one stage farther back, for a satisfactory account would have to be given of how the characteristics of the sensation *could* act as signs of its origin. What kind of characteristic of a sensation could show that it was a sensation in the leg, apart from a prior understanding of what it is for a sensation to be in the leg? To know *in this way* that the sensation is in the leg would demand the possession of the concept of a leg and its relationship to the body. But an animal can be said to know that the sensation is there in the same way as it may know where a certain part of its body is. It knows it to the extent that it can go straight to the point of the irritation, or whatever feeling it is; and this is not something that it has to learn to do. Our awareness of the place of our sensations, like our awareness of the place of

[26] For similar reasons M. Merleau-Ponty calls the awareness a form of experience that is "preconscious" and "pre-objective." See his *The Phenomenology of Perception*, trans. C. Smith (London, 1962), *passim*, e.g., p. 242 (New York, 1962).

[27] Cf. Ch. 4, sec. (d), and sec. (b) of this chapter.

[28] See G. N. A. Vesey, "The location of bodily sensations," *Mind*, N.S., LXX (1961), pp. 25ff. Cf. his *The Embodied Mind* (New York and London, 1965).

our limbs, need not be conceptually mediated. We simply feel the sensations to be where we experience them. On the other hand, whereas one can be wrong about the positions of our limbs, it is not so obvious that one can be wrong about the location of a sensation; although one can sometimes be in doubt about it, and one can certainly be mistaken about the location of the physiological cause of the sensation. I have discussed this matter in section (b), and I shall say no more about it here.

One other point requires mention: the issue of our knowledge of our own actions and intentions. I have said something about this in Chapter 4, section (d); a full account of the matter would require an investigation of the concept of human action in detail, a subject that is outside the province of this book. Suffice it to say that some distinction must be made between the concept of an action and the concept of a straightforward bodily movement that simply occurs (i.e., one that is not to be construed as *made by* the person whose body it is). Many movements in our body are movements that have to be observed to be known at all, e.g., the movements of organs within our body; others can be felt so that our knowledge of them is akin to knowledge of the position of our limbs. But knowledge of our actions is of a quite different kind; we do not in the ordinary way know of them because we observe them to take place or because we feel them to take place. We can of course discover that we have performed an action of a certain description, and we may in this sense observe the fact, in that we did not realize at the time that what we were doing answered to that description. This is characteristically the case with unintentional actions. And it may be that in certain more recherché cases we can be unaware of the fact that we are doing something of a certain kind intentionally. But all of these cases presuppose that there is *something* that we are doing *knowingly*, and this knowledge is not based on any kind of data. When we perform an action intentionally, it is not that we do something and thereby know it; in doing it we know what we are doing, and if we ask how it is that we know this, the answer must be that it is because that is what we intend doing. It is of course possible to be mistaken in this; we may think that we are doing something of a certain kind and not be doing it at all. But in this respect the claim to knowledge involved is in no different position from other claims to knowledge, which may turn out to be false. On the other hand, if we do intend something we cannot be mistaken as to *that* fact; though we may well fail to carry out what we intend. It is part of the concept of intention that we cannot be said to intend something without knowing that we do, and it makes no sense to ask *how* we know this.

(e) Self-knowledge and knowledge of other persons

This section must be considered as something of an appendix to what has gone before. The question of what it is to know oneself and what it is to know other people is a very difficult and complex one, to which I can give little by way of an answer here. I wish merely to point out that while some philosophers might be content in a treatment of these matters with the sort of thing that I have discussed in previous sections,[29] what is ordinarily taken to be meant by self-knowledge is far more than this; and the same applies to knowledge of other people. For a man to have self-knowledge he has to have some kind of insight into himself; and here knowledge merges into understanding. When Socrates demanded "Know thyself" he was not demanding a mere awareness of feelings, intentions, and so on. He was demanding that we try to acquire a kind of insight into our character and personality, an understanding of the springs of our action. Self-knowledge is indeed often taken to require more than this; it is sometimes taken to have as its end and goal a kind of acceptance of and commitment to a certain way

[29] Cf., e.g., S. Shoemaker, ibid., Ch. 6.

of life. For it involves the abandonment of delusions and prejudices about oneself and one's relationship to the world at large. Perhaps for that reason self-knowledge is often taken to involve the recognition not merely that one is a person of a certain type and kind but that one is just that person that one is, and not another. Socrates probably felt that only by this recognition and by the abandonment of delusions that are an obstacle to it was there a chance that people could act with what subsequent philosophers have called a good will. It may seem an odd and extravagant view that self-knowledge should involve all this, but it is certainly true that knowledge of oneself is impossible without an awareness of one's relationship to other people; and this in turn presupposes some conception of what a proper relationship of this kind should be like.

Knowledge of another person is similarly not just a matter of knowing what sort of person he is; it is not even a matter of knowing how, so to speak, he is likely to jump, and thus of knowing how to react to him. That kind of knowledge could be obtained in principle by studying a person from afar. It is the kind of knowledge that we think we have of people whom we see, for example, only on television. Yet if pressed, I think that we should have to admit that the impression that we have of knowing people who appear regularly on television is just an illusion. We might even say that in truth we do not know them at all. This is not just a function of the fact that we have not met these people in the flesh, that they do not, as we sometimes say, know us. For while we may say in some contexts that we know people whom we have met—casual or even regular acquaintances—there are equally contexts in which we should be forced to admit that we do not really know them. This, too, is not just a matter of not having met them enough, of not knowing enough about them; for it is at least logically possible for someone to have met a person regularly and to know a vast amount about him, but still to insist that he does not really know him. Philosophers like Sartre might insist that this is because of the individual's freedom, the possibility that he has of varying his personality and character. But there are clearly limits to the extent to which a given individual can do this, and it is not just a matter of there being an extra degree of freedom behind, as it were, the seventh veil. I think, in fact, that the notion of knowledge of other people cannot be understood in independence of the notion of personal relationships. If it is not really true that to know all is to forgive all, it *is* true that a person who could not feel sympathy toward others, who could not establish relationships with them with all the dimensions of feeling that this presupposes, could not ever be said to know people in the full sense. We distinguish people from things largely in terms of the kind of relationships that we can have with them. Sometimes we say that someone treats people as things, meaning to point out that his attitudes toward people are not of the kind that we think appropriate toward them. Thus we can have no full understanding of self-knowledge and knowledge of other people except against an understanding of human relationships, and against a conception of what is to be expected of such relationships. Some people have a kind of intuitive appreciation of these things, and are in consequence good at getting to know people. But a philosophical elucidation of this knowledge is clearly a complex matter, toward which I have given, and can only give, hints.

There is, however, a general point here. Knowledge of anything demands an understanding of the kind of thing that the object of the knowledge is, and full knowledge requires full understanding. Part of what is involved in speaking in this way of "the kind of thing that the object of the knowledge is" is the sort of relations it can have with us and we with it. The kind of relationship that material things have to us is relatively contingent. Even if a conception of a material thing involves often enough a conception of its use, its function, or what can be done with it, the concepts under which we subsume these things are concepts that have relatively little to do with what is human. This is far from true of the concept of a person, and a case can be made for the thesis that no proper understanding of the concept of a person can be had in independence of an understanding of the concept of a human relationship. If this is so, it is not surprising that a philosophical elucidation of knowledge of persons, whether ourselves or other people, is a complex matter. Relatively little has been done by philosophers in this direction, and the reader who is interested in these matters will have to be content with following up such hints as are available.

CHAPTER 9

A Priori Knowledge

(a) What is a priori knowledge?

The kinds of knowledge that I have so far been concerned with have all had some connection with experience. Not that they are all directly concerned with experience or even directly derived from it, and not that an empiricist would be happy with all that I have said. On the contrary. Nevertheless, an empiricist would feel that he was at least on his home ground, that the range of knowledge claims involved are of the sort that empiricism has traditionally felt it could cope with. The sticking point for the traditional empiricist has been the suggestion that there can be forms of knowledge that are in no way derived from experience or that have nothing whatever to do with experience. This could alternatively be put by saying that what the empiricist rejects is any suggestion that human reason or thought can by itself produce new knowledge. But, it might be objected, cannot a man produce certain kinds of new knowledge by thinking and reflecting, and deriving conclusions therefrom? The strict empiricist would have to reply to this by saying that this is possible only if the reasoning in question starts from premises that are derived in some way from experience. Not many empiricists have been as strict as this, since the obvious exception is mathematical knowledge, where there seems little or no appeal to experience, unless one maintains, as Mill did, that mathematical propositions are just very highly confirmed generalizations.[1] This last move has little plausibility; hence the modern empiricist is inclined to say that all propositions that can be known are related in some way to experience, *apart from* the propositions of logic and mathematics. The latter depend for their truth solely on the meanings of the terms involved and thus in effect merely make explicit what is already in those terms. Although what is produced in this way may have a psychological novelty, we are not really provided by means of it with really new information. The propositions of logic and mathematics are trivial in this sense.

Kant put the issue in terms of the question whether and to what extent a priori knowledge is possible. The term "a priori" and its counterpart, "a posteriori," have a complex history going back to medieval philosophy, but they have their roots in certain notions of Aristotle.[2] This history is unimportant for present purposes, and in any case by Kant's time the term "a priori" had come to mean "independent of experience," and the term "a posteriori" to mean "derived from experience." These terms could be applied either to concepts or to judgments or propositions. As applied to concepts, the issue is whether all our ideas are derived from experience.[3] As applied to propositions or judgments, the issue is whether all the knowl-

---

[1] J. S. Mill, *System of Logic*, II, Chs. 5 and 6 (London, 1843; 8th ed., 1872).

[2] See my article on "A priori and a posteriori" in *The Encyclopaedia of Philosophy*, ed. Paul Edwards (New York, 1967). Two other articles that I contributed to the same encyclopedia, those on "Analytic and synthetic statements" and "Contingent and necessary statements" cover ground that is relevant to the discussion in the present chapter.

[3] Cf. Ch. 3, sec. (a).

edge that we have—all the knowledge that is expressible in propositions—is derived from experience, or, in other terms, whether all propositions are verifiable in terms of experience. Kant's own position was that although all knowledge presupposes experience, not all is derived from experience. Hence a priori knowledge is certainly possible. Empiricists like Hume had not really disagreed about the possibility of some a priori knowledge, since they admitted knowledge based on "relations of ideas," although they claimed that all the ideas themselves were ultimately derived from experience. But they also claimed that this knowledge was not substantial knowledge; it did not provide really new information. Rationalists had claimed that reason could provide substantial knowledge, and Kant was to ask what were the limitations upon such knowledge if it existed at all. He himself thought that mathematics provided substantial knowledge of an a priori kind. Science and experience in general also had certain necessary presuppositions, knowledge of which was a priori. On the other hand, a priori knowledge about the world of the kind demanded by rationalist metaphysics was impossible.

Kant claimed that there were associations between the concept of the a priori and certain other concepts, such as those of the universal and the necessary. If a proposition is known a priori it must also be strictly universal and necessarily true. Other philosophers have held that if a proposition is known a priori it must also be certain. It is of some importance to examine these putative connections between the concepts of the a priori, the universal, the necessary, and the certain. It cannot be maintained that these concepts are to be identified with each other, but it may well be the case that they have implications for each other. Our present concern may be limited to the question of whether a proposition's being a priori implies that it has the other properties. Certainly propositions can be universal in character without being known a priori; generalizations of science are universal in character, but it is not normally believed that they are known a priori. Kant would have claimed that these statements are not *strictly* universal; the very fact that they are generalizations only might indeed suggest this conclusion. But the use of the adverb "strictly" suggests that something like a persuasive definition is being used here; that is to say that we are to be persuaded to accept the conclusion because nothing else is to be counted as acceptable. On the other hand, the reverse connection, the implication that if a proposition is a priori it is universal, seems prima facie to have some plausibility. This is because of the very natural belief that knowledge about particular things cannot be arrived at as a result of an exercise of reason. Yet it is not completely obvious that this is true. If numbers are particulars, then a proposition like "2 + 2 = 4" would be a proposition about certain particulars, and yet it would surely be a priori. This raises large questions about the status of numbers, and even if it were decided that numbers are technically particulars it might still be held that there is something universal about the proposition in question, given the way in which numbers get application to classes of things. Still, presumably what Kant means to say in claiming that a priori judgments are strictly universal is that they are not and cannot be invalidated by any particular matter of fact; and that, at any rate, seems true.

That consideration also has a bearing on the claim that a priori propositions are necessary. They are necessarily true not just in the sense in which any proposition must be true if it follows necessarily from established premises, but in the sense that nothing could conceivably count against them; it is impossible for them to be otherwise, as Aristotle put it in explaining the notion of necessity. If these propositions cannot be invalidated by any particular matter of fact, that goes some of the way toward the claim that they are necessarily true. It does not go all the way, however, since they might be invalidated by other means. If a proposition is known a priori, its validation must come not by way of experience but by way of thought alone. Hence, if it is true, its falsity must be in some sense unthinkable; its falsity would give rise to one kind or other of absurdity, and might in some cases lead to a contradiction. There is thus an obvious sense in which if a proposition is a priori true it is necessarily true; it could not be otherwise than true. Whether the converse relation holds is not so clear. There is *a* sense in which if something is the case, it could not be otherwise than the case; since it just *is* the case. (The necessity involved here is what the medieval logicians called necessity *de re*, as opposed to necessity *de dicto*; Parmenides invoked a notion of this kind and perhaps confused it with the other kind of necessity in his [invalid] proof of the impossibility of thinking of what is not, and Aristotle invoked it in his argument concerning the possibility of future contingencies in *De interpretatione*.[4]) A similar necessity is sometimes attached to laws of nature, although there is much argument about this and about the reasons why laws of nature are to be taken as necessary, if they are. Nevertheless, there is an obvious temptation to believe that where a proposition is necessarily true it is because its falsity is in some sense inconceivable or unthinkable, and hence to believe that if a proposition is necessarily true it is also a priori true. Whether or not the temptation is ultimately justified I shall consider later, but there are prima facie reasons for the belief in question, and most philosophers would probably accept them. In sum, there are good grounds for saying that a proposition that is a priori true is also necessarily true, and *some* grounds for holding the converse. Nevertheless, the situation here is very like that with respect to the relationship between the a priori and the universal. Just as Kant was led to say that a priori judgments are *strictly* universal, and conversely, so one

[4] Parmenides, fr. 6, line 2; Aristotle, *De interpretatione*, 9. See also G. E. M. Anscombe, "Aristotle and the sea battle," *Mind*, N.S., LXV (1956), pp. 1ff., reprinted in *Aristotle*, ed. J. Moravcsik (New York and London, 1968), pp. 15ff.

might be led to say that all and only a priori propositions are *strictly* necessary. The qualifications may have some importance.

With respect to the notion of certainty, the situation is somewhat different. There are no real grounds for holding that only a priori propositions are certain. There are no propositions that are absolutely certain in the sense required by the "search for certainty" discussed in the opening chapters of this book. On the other hand, many propositions are certain in the sense that there is every reason to be certain about them, that there is no reason at all to suppose them false (whether or not it is *logically* possible that they might be false). In that sense there is no reason for restricting certainty to those propositions that are a priori true. In a way it is just as certain that the paper on which these words are written is white, as that 2 + 2 = 4. It has sometimes been suggested that very complex a priori propositions, like complex arithmetical truths, are not certain, since we might make mistakes in working them out.[5] What this means in fact is that we might be mistaken about the identification of the a priori proposition in question, and may thus be mistaken in claiming as an arithmetical truth something that is not, just because of our failure in carrying out arithmetical procedures correctly. This in no way reflects upon the point that if a proposition is a priori true it is certain. It is certain just because it is necessary. Although not all propositions that are certain are necessarily true in the sense that we are concerned with here (though they are, necessarily, true if they are certain), it is clearly the case that if a proposition is necessarily true it is certainly true, and it is for that reason certain.

I have assumed in the foregoing that an a priori proposition is one that is known as true or false independent of experience. It might be objected that propositions involve words and that one cannot come to an understand-

[5] See, e.g., A. J. Ayer, "Basic Propositions" in *Philosophical Essays* (London, 1954), pp. 105ff. (New York, 1954).

ing of the meaning of words without experience of some kind. This is certainly true. On the other hand, it is not to be taken as implying that no proposition is a priori. So to understand it would rob us of a useful distinction, since there are certainly propositions that are such that, given that we understand the terms involved, their truth is ascertainable by a procedure that makes no reference to experience; equally, there are propositions of which this is not true. Once we understand arithmetical truths, it is absurd to suggest that we need any kind of appeal to experience in order to ascertain their truth. There may be other kinds of proposition, the truth of which can be ascertained without appeal to experience, once given the general point that the terms involved and the relations between them presuppose certain very general facts about experience. I have in mind here truths like the one that something cannot be red and green all over at the same time and in the same respect. It would show a misunderstanding to look to experience for the verification or falsification of such a truth. Yet such truths depend on the general nature of experience—that we distinguish colors in the way that we do—in a way that is not the case with arithmetical truths. This is in the main due to the ways in which words like "red" and "green" get a meaning, by contrast to that in which words like "two" and "plus" and "four" get a meaning. (Kant tried to make a parallel distinction by distinguishing between a priori judgments simpliciter and *pure* a priori judgments.) In the light of this it may be useful to make a further distinction between the relative and absolute a priori. The latter, consisting of truths founded on thought alone, or, as Leibniz called them, truths of reason, are, to use a further notion that is also Leibnizian, true in all possible worlds. The former are in a certain sense relative to this world—not because something about this world alone makes them true but because their very meaning can be understood only in relation to the world and our experience of it. I shall say more about such truths later.

(b) The analytic and the synthetic

So far in discussing the a priori I have not mentioned another notion with which it has been associated since Kant. This is the notion of the analytic, with its contrasting notion, the synthetic. Kant introduced these terms as technical ones, so that he could establish a general thesis by their means. He defines an analytic judgment as one in which the concept of the predicate is contained (though covertly) in the concept of the subject, while in a synthetic judgment the concept of the predicate stands outside that of the subject. He added that analytic judgments are such that their denial involves a contradiction, whereas this is not true of synthetic judgments. In appealing to the consideration that certain judgments are such that their denial involves a contradiction, Kant was following some of his predecessors, particularly Leibniz. But in his first, and main, account of an analytic judgment he was, though building on the previously accepted notion that one idea could be included in another, introducing a new concept. The distinction between analytic and synthetic judgments cuts across that between a priori and a posteriori judgments, because while according to Kant there are synthetic a priori and synthetic a posteriori judgments, there are no analytic a posteriori judgments, but only analytic a priori ones. This view is intelligible, since if a judgment is such that the concept of the predicate is included in that of the subject (if, in other words, the meaning of the subject term includes that of the predicate term), we need no appeal to anything other than meanings in order to validate it. Kant argued for the existence of synthetic a priori judgments, though he claimed that they were not to be found where the rationalist metaphysicians had looked for them; they existed only in the form of presuppositions of possible experience. The first half of the *Critique of Pure Reason* consists in an argument for the recognition of truths that must be accepted as necessary if there is to be objective experience—truths such as the one that every event has a cause or that space and time are unitary forms within which every perception must fit. Empiricists both before and after Kant have opposed the possibility of such truths, since they seem to be truths that are necessary and yet afford information about the world in some sense quite independent of experience. We shall return to this question in the next section; here we shall be concerned only with the general distinction between the analytic and the synthetic.

Many criticisms have been directed against Kant's way of making the distinction. It is confined to judgments of subject-predicate form, for example. Thus there have been many subsequent attempts to give an account of analytic truths in such a way that the definition can be applied to propositions, and propositions of varying logical form. One of the difficulties is that most philosophers have been inclined to accept that there is an intuitively recognizable class of analytic truths, and that the problem is simply one of arriving at a satisfactory definition of the class; this is despite the fact that Kant introduced the term "analytic" as a more or less technical term. Gottlob Frege, for example, defined an analytic truth as one in the proof of which one finds only general logical laws and definitions, and he thought that arithmetical propositions are analytic in this sense.[6] It was in arithmetical propositions that Frege was primarily interested, and it is in such a context that talk of proof has a place. One would not, however, ordinarily think that a proposition such as that which Kant produced as an illustration was one capable of proof—"All bodies are extended," where it is supposed that extension is part of the meaning of "body." Nevertheless, it is along these lines that analytic propositions have come to be defined.

[6] G. Frege, *Foundations of Arithmetic,* trans. J. L. Austin (Oxford, 1950), p. 4.

Friedrich Waismann, for example, says that they are propositions that reduce to logical truisms when appropriate definitionally equivalent terms have been substituted for terms of the original proposition.[7] Thus "All bodies are extended" might be reduced, given the definition of "body" as "extended thing," to "All extended things are extended," which seems to be an exemplification of a proposition conforming to the law of identity. Similarly Willard Quine puts forward, as an account of the usually accepted class of analytic truths, the thesis that they are truths such that when synonyms are substituted for synonyms they may be turned into logical truths (which he defines as those that remain true under all reinterpretations of their components other than logical particles—a definition that raises further questions concerning what counts as a logical particle).[8] On these views analytic propositions are in an important sense trivial. (Kant indeed had said that they were not ampliative—they do not enlarge our knowledge.) They are trivial in that while there may be psychological novelty in a given analytic proposition, in the sense that someone may not have realized before that *this* proposition was true, and necessarily true at that, such propositions nevertheless provide no really fresh information that was not implicit in the meanings of the very words involved. All that can be learned from them in the way of genuine matter-of-fact information is something about the meanings of those words, and such acquisition of information must be incidental. The last is so because analytic propositions are not themselves definitions, and so are not explicitly about words or their meanings, however much they may incidentally help us to become clear about these meanings. (Thus Ayer is wrong in *Language, Truth and Logic* to say that analytic truths record our

[7] F. Waismann, "Analytic-synthetic," *Analysis* X (1949), pp. 25ff.

[8] W. V. Quine, "Two Dogmas of Empiricism," *From a Logical Point of View* (Cambridge, Massachusetts, 1953), Ch. 2.

determination to use words in a certain way, if this is meant to be a statement about the main function of analytic truths.[9])

Given this last point, there is something in the suggestion that analytic truths have no real point, since, if making clear the use of words is only an incidental function that they may have, it is difficult to see what else they might be used for. In that case, it might seem feasible to suggest that there are no actual analytic statements, since statements are the uses of given sentences, and an analytic statement would thus have to be one in which a sentence was used without any real point. But this is not in itself a crucial objection to the possibility of analytic truths, even if it indicates that they have no great importance; they will have to be truths the statement of which is pointless, except in an incidental way. But this is just what is implied by their being trivial, as indicated above.

More fundamental objections to the idea of analytic truths have been put forward by Quine, among others. Quine puts forward two different, though perhaps connected, lines of argument in his paper "Two Dogmas of Empiricism."[10] The first turns on certain difficulties about synonymity that he thinks exist. As already indicated, Quine distinguishes between analytic truths in the sense here in question and logical truths proper, the former being reducible to the latter by substituting synonyms for synonyms. I have already noted the difficulty of specifying what is to count as a logical truth —one that turns on the further difficulty of determining what counts as a logical particle. There are other difficulties into which I cannot go here; suffice it to say that in the end Quine takes logical truths to be merely those that are most entrenched, in the sense that they are the truths that we are the least willing to give up in the

[9] A. J. Ayer, *Language, Truth and Logic,* 2nd ed. (Gloucester, Massachusetts, and London, 1946), Ch. 4, esp. p. 84.

[10] W. V. Quine, ibid.

face of apparently falsifying circumstances. The same would be true of analytic truths generally, were it not for the fact that there are additional difficulties about synonymy in Quine's view. For this reason he maintains two theses by way of objection to analyticity—the first turning on synonymy, the second turning on an alleged difficulty in drawing a hard and fast line between analytic and synthetic truths, so that the distinction, if it occurs, is one of degree only.

Quine's objections to the notion of synonymy turn on the difficulty of giving an account of it that does not presuppose the notion of analyticity or something close to it. He explores the possibility that synonymy might be explained in terms of the idea that two expressions are synonymous when they are interchangeable, leaving the statements in which they occur unchanged in truth value, so that they are interchangeable *salva veritate*. There has to be some restriction on this general thesis since, if, for example, "bachelor" is taken to be synonymous with "unmarried man," we cannot take as a counterexample to the general thesis the fact that you cannot substitute *salva veritate* "unmarried man" for "bachelor" in some statement about, say, bachelors of arts. Since "bachelor of arts" has to be taken as a single expression that has a meaning only as a whole, Quine formulates the restriction by speaking of interchangeability *salva veritate* in all contexts *except within words*. There are other examples that present the same difficulty and that can be dealt with in the same way. But even with a restricted thesis, Quine points out that there seems to be an objection to equating synonymy with interchangeability *salva veritate*; for the interchangeability may be due to accidental factors, as with "creatures with a heart" and "creatures with kidneys," if it happens to be the case that all and only creatures with a heart are creatures with kidneys. Might not this be the case also with "bachelor" and "unmarried man"? If we think not, it is because we think that interchangeability *salva veritate* is not a sufficient condition of synonymy. If we try to get around this point by saying that it is necessary that all and only bachelors are unmarried men, and not a mere accident, we are presupposing the concept of necessary truth in our account of synonymy; whereas the whole point of the appeal to synonymy was to afford a definition of at least one kind of necessary truth—that involved in analyticity.[11]

A fair rejoinder to Quine on this issue would be that he is prescribing an impossible task. He is in effect insisting that nothing counts as a sufficient account of synonymy unless that notion is explained in terms of something quite different; but there is nothing that is both sufficiently different and satisfactory as an analysis of synonymy. Yet it is taken that one of the criteria of satisfactoriness here is that the analysis should serve to mark off an intuitively acceptable distinction between what is analytically necessary and what is accidental. The truth is, as Grice and Strawson point out,[12] that "analytic" and "cognitively synonymous" (as Quine puts it) are terms belonging to the same family, and Quine is unwilling to accept terms drawn from the same family as providing a sufficient account of any other member of the family; yet to go outside the family, as Quine does in considering the claims of interchangeability *salva veritate* as criteria of synonymy, is to have recourse to terms that are too remote to offer a satisfactory account. Surely the notion of meaning, which is presupposed in that of synonymy, ought to be taken as presupposed in this exercise.

Quine now goes on to argue that other accounts of

[11] Quine's argument is more complex and tortuous than I have represented it, but the substance of the argument is as I have given it. Quine's worries about synonymy have much in common with those of Nelson Goodman in his attempt to outline a nominalist theory of meaning. See Nelson Goodman, "On likeness of meaning," *Analysis* X (1949), pp. 1ff., reprinted in *Philosophy and Analysis*, ed. M. Macdonald (Oxford, 1954), pp. 54ff.

[12] H. P. Grice and P. F. Strawson, "In defence of a dogma," *Phil. Rev.* 65 (1956), pp. 141ff.

synonymy, such as that employed by Carnap in having recourse to the idea of a semantic rule, are equally unsatisfactory by his standards. He also suggests that one may suppose that there must be analytic propositions on the basis of the intuitively obvious consideration that propositions normally contain a factual and a linguistic component; hence it may seem that there must be propositions where either the linguistic or the factual component will be null. Analytic propositions will be those in which the factual component is null. This takes him on to the second dogma—that of reductionism. For this is the second dogma that he claims to be a feature of classical empiricism, and is in that context matched by the first dogma of the existence of analytic propositions. It is involved in the verificationist theory of meaning, with its assumption that there are basic propositions that can be directly verified, so providing the units of meaning; these propositions will be those with null linguistic component. Quine argues that to suppose that there are such propositions involves an unwarrantable dogma of empiricism. He then goes on to assert his main thesis on these issues that even if a distinction could be drawn between the analytic and the synthetic it could be drawn only in a relative way. There is no sharp boundary between the analytic and the synthetic, and the distinction can be drawn at all only within the bounds of a particular system. Otherwise the only distinction to be made is in terms of the relative degree of entrenchment of any given propositional belief. There are no propositions that depend for their truth on a direct confrontation with experience.

Whatever can be said about the pragmatist tendencies that are evident in this general thesis of Quine's, it is certainly not evident that an acceptance of his point about the dogma of reductionism and of the point that there are no basic propositions has as an immediate consequence that there are no analytic truths. There could be propositions with null factual component even if there were no propositions with null linguistic component.

Indeed, Grice and Strawson describe a method of making the general distinction between the analytic and the synthetic, in terms of the idea that the responses to the attempt to falsify statements of each kind would be different. In the case of analytic statements, an apparently falsifying situation would be likely to lead to a revision of our concepts, while in the case of synthetic statements it would be likely to lead to a revision in our view of the facts. The former tends to happen sometimes in science, where a theoretical statement is sometimes made immune to falsification by altering the status of the concepts involved, so making it logically true. This suggestion of Grice and Strawson's would not be acceptable to Quine, since it presupposes that a definition of analyticity is possible—something that goes against his first line of argument—and it presupposes a firm distinction between what is conceptual and what is factual. Nevertheless it indicates that Quine's two lines of argument are not completely independent of each other.

Quine's assertion that it seems intuitively obvious, even if, he thinks, ultimately unacceptable, that there are propositions in which the factual component is null, might be put by saying that, language being what it is, it must always be possible to construct sentences that could be used to state analytic truths—whether or not there would be any point in this. The point is analogous to one that Wittgenstein made in the *Tractatus* about the logical notion of tautology—that they are a necessary part of our symbolism in the way that "o" is part of the symbolism of arithmetic.[13] But just as "o" cannot be used in counting (or at least not directly), so tautologies cannot be used to state any fact. They are thus, he says, senseless but not nonsense (senseless in that they do not state any conceivable fact of a determinate kind about the world). It seems intuitively obvious that it is possible, and

13 L. Wittgenstein, *Tractatus Logico-Philosophicus*, new trans. by D. F. Pears and B. F. McGuinness (New York and London, 1961), 4.461ff.

must be possible, to construct sentences by means of which one can say nothing. This is especially compelling in the case of sentences that are tautologies in the straightforward sense. But, where considerations of meaning are involved, as they must be in the case of analytic truths as classically conceived, there are additional complications. I pointed out earlier that the Kantian account of analyticity presupposed the idea that one concept can be contained in another. If a given statement is to be determined as analytic it must be possible to determine also whether the concepts involved in understanding the statement are so related. Empiricism holds that there are basic ideas that provide the units of meaning, in terms of which the meaning of more complex ideas is determined. If this view were to be acceptable it would be easy to see how it could also be determined whether a given statement was analytic. Any given concept could be analyzed into its constituents, so that it would become apparent whether it included any other concept in question. But on a theory of meaning that rejects the idea that there are, as it might be put, atomic concepts into which other concepts may be analyzed, the notion of an analytic proposition in anything like the Kantian sense may have to remain as an ideal only; which examples, if any, count as analytic propositions might be arguable.

The same applies to an attempt to explain analyticity in terms of definitions; for, once again, what the proper definition of any given term is might be arguable. And exactly the same thing applies to the suggestion that analytic propositions are those expressed by means of sentences through which one says nothing. It is possible to attach a use in ordinary language even to sentences of the form "A is A"; there are idioms in terms of which to say something of this kind is to say something more or less determinate (cf. Kipling's "East is East and West is West . . ."). But exactly what one is saying thereby will depend on things like context; hence, whether or not one is saying something determinate will be arguable.

This, however, does not mean that there cannot be analytic propositions, only that one cannot tell whether any putative example really is one merely from the characteristics of the sentence that expresses it. The notion of an analytic proposition is thus something of a limiting case. It might be argued that the notion of an analytic proposition is an uninteresting one too, since the interesting cases of necessary truths, if there are any, will be those in which the proposition concerned states a necessary truth of an informative kind. This raises the whole question of the synthetic a priori, to which we must now turn.[14]

(c) Synthetic a priori truth

As we saw earlier, Kant claimed that there are genuinely informative truths that are both necessary and a priori. These are, in his view, truths that it is possible to arrive at by means of the understanding. Metaphysicians claim to put forward further truths of this kind through the use of reason alone. These, Kant thinks, are spurious and lead only to contradiction, since reason tries to go beyond the bounds of possible experience to which the understanding is limited. Thus the only genuine sphere for synthetic a priori knowledge is that which the understanding, not reason, can provide, and it is limited in one way or another to the conditions of possible experience. Thus Kant claims to show a priori the truth of certain propositions about space and time (viewed as forms of experience), and the truth of such principles as that there must be a permanent substance and that every event must have a cause—all in application to ex-

[14] It should be noted that the difficulties I have raised at the end of this section are not the same as Quine's. He is concerned with the explication of the notion of synonymy itself, not with the question of what are the criteria of synonymy and how one determines whether the meaning of one term includes, or is similarly related to, that of another.

perience as we have it (and no other form of experience, no other form of sensibility, as Kant puts it, is conceivable by us). To try to go beyond experience, to what Kant calls things-in-themselves, as metaphysicians do by appealing to what reason can tell them, is to involve oneself in contradiction and paradox.

Empiricists have always been opposed to the idea of synthetic a priori truth in any form—not only to the claims of the rationalist metaphysics to which Kant was opposed, but also to Kant's own claims. Yet Kant was not really claiming to be able to arrive at truths about the world as such by a priori means, let alone to arrive by such means at truths that are strictly empirical. The reference to possible experience in Kant's argument is very important. To say that the truth of the proposition that every event has a cause, for example, is a condition of possible experience is not simply to say that in every experience we have of the world we find that every event has a cause; it is not an inductive claim about experience as we have it. Indeed, Kant's claim can be validly interpreted only as a claim about what can conceivably be taken as an experience. It is thus something about the conditions of application for the *concept* of experience. Such a claim is synthetic because what is maintained about the conditions of the application of that concept, the conditions under which something can properly be called "experience," is not in any sense part of what is meant by that concept. It is not part of the concept of an experienced event that it is caused, let alone part of the concept of an event per se. It is thus not analytic that every experienced event has a cause. Yet Kant wishes to say that causality is a necessary feature of objective experience; it is not, as Hume supposed, that we just happen to believe that one event is the cause of another because the imagination, because of the constant conjunction of the events in our experience, takes us from the one event to the other. The existence of causality is necessary if anything is to count as an objective experience; and this can be known a priori. It is in this sense that the principle of universal causality is claimed as synthetic a priori.

This can be seen from the way in which Kant argues about the principle of universal causality in the Second Analogy of the *Critique*—without prejudice to the question of whether or not that argument is valid.[15] For he attempts to argue for his conclusion by reference to a pair of examples. Surely no one could reasonably be taken as arguing for a general truth about the world in any ordinary sense by means of a small number of isolated examples. Kant's examples are what he takes to be the case with the perception of a house and of a ship going down a river. It is important that Kant assumes that in each case we are given a series of perceptions, a series of experiences as Kant construes them in his epistemology; moreover, it is taken that one series of perceptions constitutes a series that is objectively determined while the other does not. That is to say that the series of perceptions of a ship going down a river constitutes the perception of a series of objective events, while in the case of the perceptions of the house the series is dependent on us, since we can choose how and in what order to view the house. Put in this way, the examples may be considered rather unfortunate, since what Kant wants in order to provide a contrast with the series of objective events is a series of *subjective* events, and the series of perceptions of a house is subjective only in the sense that the order depends on our decision. It is true that the series has the order that it has for me and not for all men; and Kant sometimes puts the contrast between the subjective and objective in terms of what is true only for me and what is true for all men. Nevertheless the series of perceptions of a house is not subjective in the sense that a flight of the imagination would be. However that may be, Kant next argues that the series of perceptions of a ship going down a river is irreversible—something that is not true of the other series.

15 I. Kant, *Critique of Pure Reason*, A 189, B 232ff.

It is thus subject to a rule or law, and Kant infers that the objective series necessarily implies causality.

There is much that is questionable about the details of this argument, and I have no wish to defend it in all those details. There are better examples of the sort of thing that Kant is trying to arrive at than this one. The important thing to bring out is the character of the truth that he is trying to prove. It has often been pointed out that the principle of universal causality is doubly general; its formulation contains two general words, not just one—*every* event has *some* cause.[16] This makes it neither verifiable nor falsifiable in terms of any set of particular states of affairs. Any proposition that is asserted of *every* such-and-such is not completely verifiable, and any proposition that asserts that *some* things hold good is not completely falsifiable; hence any proposition that asserts both these things is neither completely verifiable nor completely falsifiable.[17] If this is true of the principle of universal causality, it must be nonempirical by any criterion that determines what is empirical in terms of either verifiability or falsifiability. It does not follow that the principle may *for that reason* be said to be a priori, since a proposition that is a priori is one whose truth is *known* independent of experience. All that the point about verifiability or falsifiability implies is that the principle cannot be known to be true or false on the basis of experience; it says nothing about whether or how it *is* known. It would thus appear that the nonempirical character of a proposition (by the criterion under consideration, at any rate) is not a sufficient condition of its being a priori. If a proposition has any claim to be a priori true

[16] See S. N. Hampshire, "Multiply general sentences," *Analysis* 10 (1950), pp. 73ff.; G. J. Warnock, "Every event has a cause," *Logic and Language*, ed. A. G. N. Flew (Garden City, New York and Oxford, 1953), II, pp. 95ff.; J. W. N. Watkins, "Between analytic and empirical," *Philosophy*, XXXII (1957), pp. 112ff.

[17] Cf. K. R. Popper, *The Logic of Scientific Discovery* (London, 1959), pp. 68ff., 193 (New York, 1959).

it must be possible for its truth to be known. It would appear that Kant's claim to know a priori the truth of the principle of universal causality must depend on what lies in our understanding of what it is for a series of phenomena to be a series of objective events. This suggests that if there are synthetic a priori propositions their necessity turns on concepts in a way different from that in which analytic propositions depend for their truth on the concepts involved.

This point may be brought about by reference to a more ordinary and perhaps more perspicuous example than that provided by Kant in his consideration of the principle of universal causality. Let us consider an example that has been, despite its apparently more ordinary character, almost as much the subject of controversy: the proposition that something cannot be red and green all over at the same time and in the same respect. Although this example is the subject of controversy, it is not so in the same way as the principle of universal causality; for the *necessity* of that principle has often been disputed, while it has been far less often disputed that it is in some sense a necessary truth that something cannot be red and green all over at the same time and in the same respect. It seems that someone who looks for a counterexample to that thesis has not really understood what is at stake. The problem is not whether it is necessary, but why. Yet, on the face of it, such a proposition is not analytic, since it does not seem to be part of the meaning of a term such as "green" that it excludes "red" in such a way that something that is red cannot be green. There is nothing, of course, to prevent something being both red and green in the way that shot silk may be. But such a thing would not be red and green all over *in the same respect*. I have said that it is not part of the meaning of the term "green" that it excludes "red." I mean by this that "red" does not mean "not green," or vice versa. I do not want to imply that the exclusion of the two terms has not something to do with the concepts involved. Thus if the proposition in question is to be called synthetic a priori, it will be synthetic because the proposition does not conform to the technical specifications of an analytic proposition. How this is so can be seen by a consideration of the kinds of difficulty that empiricists have found in a proposition of this kind.

According to the empiricist terms like "red" and "green" will be ostensively definable, and in a way it is just this consideration that raises the difficulties. For "red" will be definable in terms of one set of ostensible instances, "green" in terms of another, and in that case what will ensure that the sets of instances have nothing in common? It seems as if it is a factual matter that the sets of instances are different; how then can it be a matter of necessity? *That* is the problem for the empiricist. If one rejects the theory of meaning involved, however, the problem will be more amenable. If the considerations that I adduced on this point in Chapter 3 are correct, an understanding of terms like "red" and "green" will involve far more than the knowledge of what sets of instances they are applicable to. The understanding in question presupposes a prior understanding of what color is, and this implies in turn something about the kinds of relations that exist between or among colors. (Certain of the logical relationships between or among colors are displayed in the so-called color circle, in which chromatic colors pass by gradations into the next, and so on until one comes back to where one started from.) A child could not be said to understand what "red" means if all he could do was to apply the term in more or less the right cases, and he had no understanding of cases in which it is not right to apply the term but rather to apply others. Thus it is not a simple matter of fact that red things exclude green things. To understand the concept of color that we in fact have is to understand that this sort of thing must be so.

It is necessary to speak of the concept of color that we in fact have, because our understanding of color is not independent of the kind of sensibility that we have. It is possible, in a way, to conceive of the possibility of forms of perception quite different from any that exist at present. *Our* color perception and a fortiori our understanding of color are functions both of how the world is and of how our senses are structured and delimited. Thus in speaking of our understanding of color we must presuppose our form of sensibility.[18] We can conceive the possibility that our form of sensibility might have been otherwise than it is, but we can have no real conception of what it would then have been like, and it is foolish to pretend that we can. It remains true that our understandings of color and color relationships are ones that must be set against, and ones that presuppose, the kind of creatures we are in our relationships to the kind of world in which we exist. There is thus a sense in which the necessity of the proposition that something cannot be red and green all over in the same respect is not an absolute one; not that something that we now call red could also be green, but that the necessity in question is dependent on our having the sort of concepts that we have because we are the sort of creatures that we are. It is this that goes to make the necessity in question a nonanalytic one. But if we say in consequence that the proposition with which we have been concerned is synthetic a priori, it is important to add that there is in this no claim to produce a necessary truth about the world in any ordinary sense. The necessity still turns on the concepts involved; the synthetic character of the proposition is because of the fact that it has at its back those curious and fundamental facts about the form of sensibility that we have or, more generally, the form of life that we share.[19] These, as we have seen, are no ordinary facts, but they are facts all the same.

[18] Cf. what I said earlier about Kant's use of this notion and what I said in Ch. 3 and elsewhere about Wittgenstein's notion of a form of life.

[19] Cf. Wittgenstein's remark at *Philosophical Investigations* (New York and Oxford, 1953), p. 226 about forms of life constituting the given.

(d) Conceptual truths

What the argument in the previous section implies is that there is a class of truths that might be called "conceptual truths." If all necessary truth depends on the concepts that we have in one way or another, then conceptual truths are all the necessary truths that there are. Analytic truths will constitute a subclass of conceptual truths, and they will be in a sense a degenerate subclass at that. This will be true in two ways. First, analytic truths will constitute degenerate cases of conceptual truths in that they are uninformative and their assertion lacks point for the reasons given earlier in this chapter. Second, they will be degenerate for the reasons given in section (b) about the theory of meaning that is presupposed in classical expositions of the notion of analyticity. That is to say that it will be appropriate to identify a statement as analytic only where the meaning relation between the terms involved approximates that implied in the idea of the meaning of one term being contained in that of the other. At its limit this implies that there are atomic concepts into which others can be analyzed. To the extent that it is not possible to accept the idea of certain concepts being understood without reference to other concepts, without prior understanding of other kinds, the notion of an analytic truth must remain a limiting case only. Indeed, the supposition that all necessary truths are analytic presupposes an atomicity of concepts, a notion that is an essential part of traditional empiricism but one that must be abandoned for a wider and more adequate account of the understanding.

The understanding of a concept in its relations to other concepts in the way indicated is an understanding of what Wittgenstein calls the "grammar" of the concept. Wittgenstein used the expression "grammar" in this context because, since concepts have their expression in words, the misuse of a concept reveals itself in a misuse of words, in a failure to conform to the rules for the use of words. Such a failure is in a sense a failure to conform to grammatical rules. To what extent this constitutes an extension in the sense of the term "grammar" and to what extent considerations of grammar are independent of considerations about meaning are questions that raise large issues into which it is impossible to go here. (Is, for example, the sentence "Saturday is in bed" ungrammatical or meaningless in some narrower sense, or is it neither of these things? Is it, for example, just false?) Nevertheless, Wittgenstein's assimilation of rules of use to grammatical rules, if that is what it is, makes it possible to call what I have termed conceptual truths "grammatical truths." They are statements that depend for their truth on the grammar of the expressions involved. An understanding of that "grammar" may well presuppose an understanding of things well outside anything that is explicitly mentioned in the statement in question, just as an understanding of the grammar of an expression in the more ordinary sense of "grammar" may presuppose an understanding of the kinds of relationship that the expression may have to quite other kinds of expression, and perhaps to language as a whole. The phrase "grammatical truth" emphasizes the part that language and linguistic considerations play in our understanding; beyond this, what is conveyed by its use is the same as that of the phrase "conceptual truth." The complexity of the possible relationships between concepts and of the ways in which concepts are involved with each other may be considerable; to sort out these matters is one of philosophy's major tasks. Thus a philosophical investigation of the concepts within any particular domain or sphere should result, if successful, in the acceptance of certain conceptual truths, certain statements that have a claim to being necessarily true. To make assertions of this kind is not to lay claim to the ability to arrive at necessary truths about the world by the exercise of thought alone; it is, however, to lay claim to the ability to arrive at an understanding of how certain things must be understood.

In section (a) I made a distinction between the relative and the absolute a priori. It does not follow from the fact that a truth is a conceptual truth that it may be known a priori in the absolute sense. In the case of analytic truths there is no further problem as regards our knowledge of the truth once we understand the meaning relation that exists between the terms involved. The fact that the terms are related in this way implies that the denial of the truth would involve a contradiction, as Kant maintained; and whether or not the denial of a proposition leads to a contradiction can thus be taken as a way of determining whether it is analytic. Thus, given that the denial of a proposition does lead to a contradiction, the only course for one who wishes to cast doubt on the truth of that proposition is to dispute the principle of contradiction itself. This would not be a very profitable tactic to adopt, since it seems that the truth of the principle of contradiction is necessary to the possibility of all intelligible thought. It is not possible, as Aristotle saw, to deny the truth of the principle without presupposing it.[20] It is thus in a very proper sense a necessity of thought. It can for this reason be said to be known a priori in the absolute sense. Because the truth of analytic propositions depends solely on it and on the relative meaning of the terms, the same applies to them; though if analytic truths remain a limiting case only, little enough is being claimed in saying that. With those truths, however, which depend, as indicated in section (c), ultimately on our form of life or sensibility, the same cannot be claimed. For it is possible to conceive of the possibility that there might be other forms of life or sensibility, even if we can conceive nothing of what it might be like to have them. Thus, it seems that we must say that our knowledge of truths of this kind is a priori in the relative sense only. We know of their

[20] Aristotle, *Metaphysics* IV, 4.

truth without further reference to experience when we understand them, but that understanding itself is relative to the form of life or sensibility that we have.

(e) The a priori in mathematics and science

Discussions of these subjects often presuppose that mathematics provides the paradigm cases of analytic truths and science those of synthetic a posteriori truths. This may be true in a way, but it would be a further and more substantial claim to say that all mathematical truths are analytic and all scientific truths are synthetic a posteriori. Yet this has often been maintained. Let us take each of these points in turn.

Kant maintained that mathematical truths are synthetic a priori, but few have been prepared to go along with him in this. He thought that these truths were necessary but in such a way that they presupposed our a priori intuitions of time (in the case of arithmetic) or space (in the case of geometry). Moreover, he thought that Euclidean geometry was in some sense *the* geometry of space. His views of arithmetic have had few supporters, although the general view of geometry, without the necessary claim for Euclidean geometry, has received some acceptance among Intuitionists in work on the foundations of mathematics. Even with respect to geometry, however, it is often maintained that the discovery of alternative geometries has refuted Kant. The possibility of alternative geometries emerged from the consideration that, among the axioms of Euclid's system, that which maintained that only one line could pass through a point such that it was parallel to a given line had a different status from the others. The consideration of the possibilities that there could be many lines parallel to a given line or that there could be no line parallel to a given line led to alternative geometrical systems that have been proved consistent. If this discovery is a refutation of Kant's formal position, however, it is not so clear that it is a refutation of its spirit. It is no coincidence that Euclidean geometry was the first to be developed; the system somehow fits experience more obviously than do the alternative geometries later devloped. Since Einstein, the suggestion has been current that space may not be Euclidean. This is so because a better and simpler general physical theory is capable of development on the presupposition of a non-Euclidean conception of space than on that of a Euclidean conception.

I have used the words "conception of space" advisedly, since this is what a geometry presupposes, and is what is formulated in one or other versions of the parallel line axiom. If, as I maintained earlier, Kant's own system is developed on the implicit premise "given our form of sensibility," he can be taken as saying that with respect to space *as we perceive it* Euclidean geometry is the most plausible mathematical representation. This says nothing against the possibility that alternative geometries may provide better mathematical representations of space for a conception of the universe involved in some more general physical theory. Whether or not this is an adequate defense of Kant is immaterial for present purposes; it brings out the point that a geometry is relative to a conception of space, and which concept of space is the most adequate to our view of the world is a complex question, which brings in further questions about the acceptability of the physical theory which presupposes a given concept of space. Thus, while there may be propositions within geometry that are analytic in the sense that they depend for their truth solely on the meaning relations between their terms, this will not be the case with all geometrical propositions. In the case of the latter their necessity will be relative only to the truth of other propositions within the system, while the system as a whole is relative to a certain conception of space. Given this, there seems little ground for the supposal that all geometrical propositions are analytic in the technical sense of that term. For similar reasons it cannot be maintained that we know geometrical truths absolutely a priori, since the acceptability of a geometrical representation of space depends on considerations extrinsic to it. We can, however, say that given the conception of space that the representation fits, we can know a priori that certain things must be so, since the geometrical theorems can be deduced strictly from the axioms that formally specify that representation.

Kant, as I have already indicated, thought that the same was true of arithmetic, but in relation to time rather than space. Such a view is most implausible. On the other hand, arithmetical truths depend on more than the terms immediately involved. The issues here are immensely difficult and complex, and to deal with them adequately would entail going into issues in the philosophy of mathematics, which is beyond the scope of this book. Suffice it to say, first, that the truth of propositions like "$2 + 2 = 4$" depends on more than the simple meaning of expressions like "2," "4," "$+$," and "$=$." Or rather the meanings of these expressions cannot be set out without reference to other things, such as the rules for the development of the number series, rules that can be implicitly set out in the axioms of the system involved. Second, those axioms and rules can, as with the geometrical axioms, determine only a set of elements with certain formal relationships. They cannot determine the elements themselves, or, to put the matter in other words, they cannot determine the adequacy of the system as an arithmetical representation.[21] But what is arithmetic a representation *of* in the way that geometry may be considered a representation of space? The reasons why Kant was tempted here to say "time" are obvious. But it would be wrong to say this, even though the relations between events in time have logical properties similar to those between elements in a number series. The relations of before and after that exist between events are transitive and asymmetrical, just like

[21] The technical way of putting this is to say that the set of postulates for the system of arithmetic is not "categorical," and that this is so is a consequence of the Skolem-Löwenheim theorem.

the relations of greater and less than which exist between numbers. If 7 is greater than 5 and 5 is greater than 3, 7 must be greater than 3, and if 7 is greater than 5, 5 cannot be greater than 7. But there is no dimension of reality that has exactly the same character as space, such that we can presuppose it in the case of arithmetic as we presuppose space in the case of geometry. On the other hand, it is a fact about the world that things may comprise sets and that they may be counted on this basis, just as it is a fact about the world that things occupy space and may be individuated on this basis. Hence, although there is nothing in reality that corresponds to number exactly as space does to geometrical notions, unless we like to say that plurality itself is such a dimension of reality, the fact that things form sets and can be ordered accordingly is what gives arithmetic application. The necessity of a whole class of arithmetical truths is relative to that possibility, and the situation is similar for their a priori character. Once again, there is no objection to the position that *some* arithmetical truths may be analytic in the technical sense, but, as for geometry, this cannot be so generally.

If not all mathematical truths can be analytic, not all scientific truths can be synthetic a posteriori. The vexed question of the necessity of laws of nature has already been referred to in section (a). It could be argued that their necessity, too, must be a function of the concepts involved in some way or other. What the scientist tries to do is to impose a conceptual superstructure on the facts. To conceive of the facts as of necessity of a certain kind is, as Kneale has maintained, to put a limit to the bounds of possibility. For this reason Kneale has called laws of nature "principles of natural necessitation."[22] His own account of this conception is not an easy one to follow, and I shall make no attempt to elucidate it here. It is, however, clear enough that in invoking a conception

[22] W. C. Kneale, *Probability and Induction* (Oxford, 1949), secs. 17ff.

of natural law we do presuppose some notion of what must be so. This is not incompatible with the idea that the necessity in question is a function of our way of thinking about the world, a function of our concepts. The world itself is just as it is, as a matter of fact. Nevertheless, whatever be the correct view of the necessity or otherwise of natural laws, it is evident that we cannot be said to know their truth a priori—or certainly not in any absolute sense. I make that qualification only because of the place that a scientific statement can have within a body of theory. It has been pointed out by numbers of philosophers of science that factual and contingent generalizations can change their status as a science develops. Some discoverable property of a substance, such as its melting point, can become one of the defining characteristics of the substance, such that nothing is allowed to count as that substance if it does not melt at that temperature. Another instance of this kind is provided by the status of the laws of motion within Newtonian theory. Propositions of this kind may initially be founded on observable or experimental findings, but as a body of theory is developed around them they change their status so that they could be abandoned or modified only at the cost of the whole theory. Of course, the question of the acceptability of the theory as a whole can be raised, and it may come about as a result of something like a scientific revolution that the theory is abandoned or extensively modified. The status of any given scientific proposition may be ambiguous at a given point of time.[23]

Nevertheless, it may be possible to say on this basis that certain scientific propositions are relatively a priori. Insofar as they are necessarily connected with other prop-

[23] P. Duhem, *The Aim and Structure of Physical Theory*, trans. P. P. Wiener (Princeton, 1954) even formulated a thesis about differences of national character on the basis of differences between the ways in which Newton's laws of motion have been treated in France and England; for the French, he said, they have been part of dynamics and hence part of mathematics, but for the English they have been part of physics.

ositions in a theory they can be known to be true without any direct reference to experience. Of course, the theory as a whole meets experience in some way or other (though even here what is sufficient to justify the abandonment or modification of a theory is a very complex question). But the complex relationships of individual statements to others within a theory makes it implausible to maintain without a great deal of qualification that such statements are a posteriori. Thus to claim that all scientific statements are synthetic a posteriori is at best misleading and at worst straightforwardly false.

PART THREE

Conclusions and
Further Problems

CHAPTER 10

A Complete Theory
of Knowledge?

(a) The sources of knowledge and ignorance

The title of this section is that of a lecture by Karl
Popper.[1] In that lecture Popper gives an account of a
distinction that he makes between optimistic and pessimistic epistemologies. An optimistic epistemology is one
that abides by the doctrine that truth is manifest; the truth
is not always immediately evident, but it can become
so. This, Popper claims (though more dubiously), is often
associated with the thesis that ignorance is in some way
due to a conspiracy; we are somehow being kept from
knowledge by such things as prejudice. A pessimistic
epistemology, on the other hand, takes the view that the
truth is almost inevitably hidden from us and is reserved
for the few only. Popper associates these different attitudes with liberal and authoritarian political attitudes and
attempts to trace their incidence in the history of thought.
He thinks that these epistemologies are nearly equally
mistaken and that the whole question "What are the

[1] K. R. Popper, "The sources of knowledge and ignorance,"
Proc. Brit. Acad. ILVI (1960), reprinted in his *Conjectures and
Refutations* (London, 1963), pp. 3ff. (New York, 1968).

sources of our knowledge?" is itself mistaken. Or if it is to be answered it can be answered only by saying that there are all kinds of sources of knowledge. The question of the sources of knowledge is unimportant and irrelevant; the proper epistemological question is whether what we claim to know is true, and we try to find out the truth by examining and testing such assertions as are made, by, in other words, critical inquiry. If we must speak of the sources of our ignorance it has to be said that the main source of our ignorance lies in the fact that we are human. Our knowledge can only be finite, while our ignorance must necessarily be infinite. In this respect the pessimistic epistemology is nearer the truth, since it maintains that knowledge is hard to obtain; it is wrong in saying that knowledge must therefore be reserved necessarily for the few.

Whatever may be thought of Popper's historical speculations and his attempt to pigeonhole philosophical attitudes, there is much in his general claim that if one must ask the question "What are the sources of our knowledge?" the only proper answer is "All kinds of things." In this respect his argument is, as he indeed claims, an anti-empiricist one; it is equally antirationalist, and in both respects it is in tune with much of the argument in this book. Popper will have no truck with the attempt to answer the skeptic by the traditional empiricist or rationalist methods. On the other hand, as far as this lecture is concerned he does not adopt the skeptic's own position as an alternative. (I make the qualification only because Popper has sometimes had the tendency to say that we do not have knowledge, because the truth is never settled beyond question; we make conjectures that we put to the test, but no genuine scientific proposition is absolutely beyond the possibility of falsification.) There are all sorts of reasons why we may remain ignorant; we may be insufficiently inquiring or critical, the problems may be too difficult, we may not have the requisite tools at our disposal, and so on. But there is no insurmountable obstacle of a theoretical kind to knowledge. There may be practical difficulties and perhaps impossibilities in certain areas, but there cannot be theoretical obstacles of the kind that the skeptic presents.

I have tried to indicate similar conclusions in this book. In the first part, I examined the skeptical arguments as they are presented in a general way, and later chapters in the second part have dealt with particular versions of those arguments on particular issues. In the first part I have also looked at the conditions that must be satisfied if something is to be called knowledge—the conditions of meaningfulness and truth, and the relations of knowledge to belief. The second part of the book has discussed the various kinds of knowledge (and the grounds for claims to such) that a man may have as a result of his own powers, so to speak. I entitled that part "The scope of knowledge" in order to indicate something of that range of issues and problems. Yet the title is in many ways misleading, in that the scope of human knowledge is very much wider than a man may obtain as a result of his own individual powers, even given a general background of understanding. Normally, if we speak of the scope of knowledge, we have in mind various disciplines like science, mathematics, and history. Here the attainment of knowledge depends on following certain procedures; it implies a certain methodology or methodologies. It is also in a very real sense a social matter. The standards of truth are interpersonal, and what counts as the attainment of truth is equally interpersonal. It is not that truth is what everyone, or everyone with a certain background of knowledge or expertise, agrees upon; but the pursuit of a discipline depends on a willingness to accept criticism from others and on the belief that what is true will come to be generally accepted because the criteria of truth and of its attainment are generally accepted. It is possible to say much about the scope of knowledge with respect to and within disciplines of this kind, and it may be that particular disciplines raise special problems. I shall return in brief to this question in the next section.

If the title "The scope of knowledge" is in a way mis-

leading for the second part of this book, the title "The
sources of knowledge" would be even more misleading, as
must by now be apparent. Not all the things that I have
discussed in that part are sources of knowledge in any
sense. Memory, for example, is not a source of knowledge,
and I argued explicitly to this effect. A priori knowledge
is clearly a *kind* of knowledge, and so, in a different way,
is the knowledge of ourselves and others. Perception *is*
in one sense a source of knowledge; it is indeed the only
thing explicitly mentioned in the titles of chapters of
that part that can be called so. On the other hand, much
of the discussion in that part makes reference to capacities
that we have that make possible knowledge of the world:
perception, memory, and understanding, for example.
These have sometimes been referred to as "ways of knowing," but they are not really that any more than they are
sources of knowledge. Indeed, it might be said that there
is no such thing as a way of knowing, even if there
are many ways in which we may come to know things.
I decided in the end to use the title "The scope of knowledge" not because the discussion gave any indication of
the range of possible objects of knowledge but because
the intention was to raise the traditional question of
whether knowledge is limited to those things that we can
perceive or to the knowledge to which perception is directly relevant. My answer is that it is not so limited, and
empiricism (with indeed the empiricist account of perception itself) must be rejected, without going over to the
other rationalist extreme of reserving "knowledge" for
what reason alone can furnish. We are enabled to have
knowledge of the world because of the range of capacities
that we possess.[2] Not that those capacities are necessarily
exercised when we have knowledge of the things that
are characteristically their objects. We can come to know
about physical objects that are in our presence in other
ways than by directly perceiving them; we can know of
them because we have been told of them, or because we

[2] Cf. Ch. 1, sec. (a).

have some other authority for the belief in their presence. We can know about past events otherwise than by memory. We can come to know about ourselves and others in ways other than those mentioned in Chapter 8, and we can come to know about conceptual truths on authority rather than by understanding. Nevertheless, there is *a* sense in each case in which if we did not have these capacities we would not have the knowledge of the objects in question. It is for that reason that discussion of them is important.

It is not only possible, of course, for capacities to be exercised; they can fail to be exercised. They can be exercised wrongly or inadequately. Or they can in any given individual either not exist or be defective. All these constitute reasons why ignorance may obtain rather than knowledge. But it is impossible to lay down once and for all what has to be done if knowledge is to be attained. There are no necessarily firm foundations or even footholds that can be relied upon in all circumstances. None of this, however, means that knowledge is unobtainable, and that this should be said and said again is very important.

(b) Special fields of epistemology

I spoke in the previous section of problems for epistemology that may arise within special fields of knowledge. That there are these problems must also be emphasized. The theory of knowledge does not really come to an end when one has discussed merely the general conditions of knowledge and the capacities that make it generally possible. In Chapter 9 I mentioned some of the issues that arise within mathematics and science in connection with a priori knowledge, but these are only one aspect of the problems that may arise in connection with these disciplines. In that sense the philosophy of science and the philosophy of mathematics are branches of epistemology. This is obvious enough when our concerns are with the methodology of these subjects, since methodological considerations promote questions about what knowledge is like in these areas and how, if at all, it is to be obtained. Much of the point of conceptual inquiries in the philosophy of science and mathematics is to cast light on how knowledge is possible in those spheres and what is the status of specific claims to knowledge. It is no coincidence that much of contemporary philosophy of mathematics had its origin in skeptical worries about the status of mathematics and in a consequent attempt to see what the foundations of mathematical knowledge consist in, if they exist at all. But disciplines differ in important ways. There may be differences between or among the concepts that they employ, differences that reflect on the methodology of the discipline in question, and thus on how knowledge is to be obtained and what its nature is. Questions such as those that are raised about the place that generalizations have in science and history are therefore epistemological questions. So are questions about the validity of proofs of God's existence or about the importance of natural theology.

I shall say nothing about these questions here, but it is important to recognize their existence and relevance. Inquiries into the philosophy of these specific fields presuppose special forms of knowledge and detailed understanding of their subject matter. Epistemological issues can arise wherever it is appropriate to speak of knowledge, and although there are problems about knowledge in general, these are not the only problems that exist. Some of these other problems are best dealt with under the headings of the philosophies of the particular disciplines: the philosophy of science, mathematics, history, religion, and so on. But there is a sense in which some of the problems with which these branches of philosophy are concerned make them branches of epistemology. What is to be hoped from a general epistemological discussion of the kind to be found in this book is that the lessons to be learned from it may be applied to the specific disciplines. This cannot be done without the knowledge and understanding of those disciplines of which I have already spoken. Nevertheless, the theory of knowledge does not end where I have left it.

One further set of questions may be raised in this connection. Are there skeptical approaches to all these specific subject matters, and does one equally find the same kinds of reply that one finds within the traditional approaches to knowledge in general? The answer to these questions is, I think, "Yes," and this fact makes necessary a final brief discussion of the notion of foundations of knowledge. My remarks will be sketchy and are not intended as more than this. The purpose of this part of the book is merely to throw out hints that the reader can follow up if he so wishes. I have attempted to provide a framework. Much remains for a complete theory of knowledge—if it is to take in knowledge of all forms.

(c) The impossibility of "foundations"

I indicated in the first chapter how skepticism and skeptical considerations tend to give rise to a demand for the establishment of firm foundations for knowledge. The demand for foundations in specific disciplines arises from the same source. The term "foundations" has been used most explicitly in connection with mathematics, for skepticism about that subject as a province of knowledge arose in an especially sharp form during the previous century. One can see why that was so. It is not so clear what mathematics is about, as it is clear what science, for example, is about. The attempt initiated by Frege and Russell to reduce mathematics to logic and to deduce its subject matter from a few logical axioms was a consequent attempt to put mathematics on its feet, so to speak. But the attempt has been unsuccessful, and it was inevitable that it should be so. Mathematics cannot be reduced to something else, even if its principles have something in common with the principles of logic. But, in any case, the attempt to provide foundations here, and in other branches of knowledge also, is like an attempt to provide a proof where none can be expected. Aristotle said that it is the mark of the foolish man to demand a proof for everything, and too few philosophers have paid sufficient regard to that remark. Aristotle, too, thought that there were certain principles that were in a sense ultimate—principles such as the principle of contradiction. But he did not think either that such principles had to be simply taken on trust or that they should merely be held provisionally while subject to perpetual doubt. He thought that a kind of reason could be given for their acceptance, in the sense that the ball had to be thrown into the court of the person who seeks to deny their truth. The man who casts doubt on the principle of contradiction must be gotten to assert something and so be convicted out of his own mouth, in that it will be apparent that his very assertion presupposes the principle on which he casts doubt.[3] The only way of escaping such a consequence is not to assert anything. An argument of this kind Aristotle called "dialectical"; in a way its aim is to produce conviction in an opponent rather than a demonstration of a truth. Indeed, the whole point is that such demonstration cannot be provided.

I spoke in Chapters 1 and 2 of the various moves that a skeptic might make and the different moves that might be made in return. This has application also to skepticism in particular fields of knowledge. If skeptical doubts are raised about the validity of mathematics or about any ordinarily accepted branch of knowledge, the first move in return must be to ask what it is that is being doubted and why. I do not maintain that the opponent will be so easily dealt with as Aristotle's skeptic about the principle of contradiction, but the ball must nevertheless be put firmly in the opponent's court, and there must be subsequent argument and appeal to reasons. It is true of course that some so-called disciplines have not survived

[3] See Aristotle, *Metaphysics* IV, 4, and cf. the discussion of this in Ch. 2, sec. (d).

such treatment, and others would not do so if they were put to the test, (cf., e.g., alchemy and astrology). But what cannot be achieved is the discovery of principles that will put skepticism out of question for all time. Skeptical criticism is always possible and is indeed desirable. But the search for foundations for knowledge has as its aim the provision of an immunity from such criticism. The attempt to find such foundations is thus not only hopeless, it is also undesirable. And certainly the justification of the claims to knowledge involved in a particular discipline cannot be carried out within that discipline. To seek for the foundations of mathematics within mathematics, or theology within theology, for example, is one stage worse than looking for foundations at all. It is not only to seek the impossible, it is to seek to provide it in an impossible way. What is really wanted is a philosophical criticism of all kinds of claims to knowledge and a philosophical assessment of the doubts that are raised about those claims. Whatever the special forms of knowledge presuppose, the theory of knowledge remains a philosophical preoccupation, and philosophical argument is always open-ended.

Bibliography

The following books are meant to be suggestions for further reading. Other references will be found in the notes.

General and Chapters 1 and 2

A. J. AYER. *The Problem of Knowledge* (New York and London, 1956)

R. CHISHOLM. *The Theory of Knowledge* (Englewood Cliffs, New Jersey, 1966)

A. C. DANTO. *Analytical Philosophy of Knowledge* (Cambridge, 1968)

G. E. MOORE. *Some Main Problems of Philosophy* (New York and London, 1953)

B. RUSSELL. *Problems of Philosophy* (London, 1912)

A. D. WOOZLEY. *The Theory of Knowledge* (London, 1949; New York, 1966)

For the historical background see:

F. C. COPLESTON. *History of Philosophy* (Garden City, New York, and London, 1950–66)

D. W. HAMLYN. *Sensation and Perception* (New York and London, 1961)

D. J. O'CONNOR (ed.). *A Critical History of Western Philosophy* (Glencoe, Illinois, 1964)

See also articles in

P. EDWARDS (ed.). *The Encyclopaedia of Philosophy* (New York, 1967)

Meaning and meaningfulness

W. ALSTON. *Philosophy of Language* (Englewood Cliffs, New Jersey, 1964)

J. L. AUSTIN. *How to Do Things with Words* (Cambridge, Massachusetts, and Oxford, 1962)
Philosophical Papers (Oxford, 1961)

A. J. AYER. *Language, Truth and Logic* (Gloucester, Massachusetts, and London, 2nd ed. 1946)
"Basic Propositions," *Philosophical Essays* (New York and London, 1954)

P. GEACH. *Mental Acts* (New York and London, 1957)

G. H. R. PARKINSON (ed.). *The Theory of Meaning* (London, 1968)

G. RYLE. "The Theory of Meaning" in C. A. Mace, ed., *British Philosophy in the Mid-Century* (London, 1957)

P. F. STRAWSON (ed.). *Philosophical Logic* (London, 1967)

L. WITTGENSTEIN. *Blue and Brown Books* (New York and Oxford, 1958)
Philosophical Investigations (Oxford, 1953)
    See also G. Pitcher (ed.). *Wittgenstein* (Garden City, New York, 1966; London, 1968)

Knowledge and belief

G. E. M. ANSCOMBE. *Intention* (Ithaca, New York, and Oxford, 1957)

J. L. AUSTIN. "Other Minds," *Philosophical Papers* (Oxford, 1961)

A. J. AYER. *The Problem of Knowledge* (New York and London, 1956)

R. CHISHOLM. *The Theory of Knowledge* (Englewood Cliffs, New Jersey, 1966)

A. C. DANTO. *Analytical Philosophy of Knowledge* (Cambridge, 1968)

P. GEACH. *Mental Acts* (New York and London, 1957)

A. P. GRIFFITHS (ed.). *Knowledge and Belief* (London, 1967)

S. N. HAMPSHIRE. *Thought and Action* (New York and London, 1959)

J. HINTIKKA. *Knowledge and Belief* (Ithaca, New York, 1962)

N. MALCOLM. *Knowledge and Certainty* (Englewood Cliffs, New Jersey, 1963)

PLATO. *Theaetetus*

H. H. PRICE. *Belief* (London, 1969)

B. RUSSELL. *Problems of Philosophy* (London, 1912)

G. RYLE. *The Concept of Mind* (New York and London, 1949)

I. SCHEFFLER. *Conditions of Knowledge* (Glenview, Illinois, 1965)

Truth

B. BLANSHARD. *The Nature of Thought*, Chs. 25–27 (London, 1939; New York, 1964)

H. JOACHIM. *The Nature of Truth* (Oxford, 1906; New York, 1969)

G. PITCHER (ed.). *Truth* (Englewood Cliffs, New Jersey, 1964)
    (Contains extensive bibliography)

F. P. RAMSEY. "Facts and Propositions," *Foundations of Mathematics* (London, 1931)

B. RUSSELL. *Philosophical Essays* (London, 1910; New York, 1967)

Inquiry into Meaning and Truth (New York and London, 1940)

A. TARSKI. "The Semantic Conception of Truth" in H. Feigl and W. Sellars, (eds.), *Readings in Philosophical Analysis* (New York, 1949)

Logic, Semantics and Metamathematics, ed. J. H. Woodger (Oxford, 1956)

Perception

D. M. ARMSTRONG. *Perception and the Physical World* (New York and London, 1961)

J. L. AUSTIN. *Sense and Sensibilia* (Oxford, 1962)

A. J. AYER. *Foundations of Empirical Knowledge* (London, 1940)

Philosophical Essays (New York and London, 1954)

The Problem of Knowledge (New York and London, 1956)

R. CHISHOLM. *Perceiving* (Ithaca, New York, 1957)

F. DRETSKE. *Seeing and Knowing* (Chicago, 1968; London, 1969)

D. W. HAMLYN. *The Psychology of Perception* (New York and London, 1957), 3rd impression with new appendix (New York and London, 1969)

Sensation and Perception (New York and London, 1961)

D. LOCKE. *Perception and Our Knowledge of the External World* (New York and London, 1967)

G. E. MOORE. *Some Main Problems of Philosophy* (New York and London, 1953)

H. H. PRICE. *Perception* (London, 1932; New York, 1950)

G. RYLE. *The Concept of Mind* (New York and London, 1949)

G. J. WARNOCK (ed.). *The Philosophy of Perception* (London, 1967)

L. WITTGENSTEIN. *Philosophical Investigations* (Oxford, 1953), II, xi.

Memory

A. J. AYER. *The Problem of Knowledge* (New York and London, 1956)

H. BERGSON. *Matter and Memory* (London, 1911; New York, 1962)

R. F. HOLLAND. "The Empiricist Theory of Memory" in S. N. Hampshire, (ed.), *The Philosophy of Mind* (New York, 1966)

N. MALCOLM. *Knowledge and Certainty* (Englewood Cliffs, New Jersey, 1963)

B. RUSSELL. *Analysis of Mind* (London, 1921; New York, 1954)

G. RYLE. *The Concept of Mind* (New York and London, 1949)

W. VON LEYDEN. *Remembering* (London, 1961)

A. D. WOOZLEY. *The Theory of Knowledge* (London, 1949; New York, 1966)

Knowledge of self and others

A. J. AYER. *The Problem of Knowledge* (New York and London, 1956)
The Concept of a Person (New York and London, 1963)

S. N. HAMPSHIRE. *Thought and Action* (New York and London, 1959)

D. LOCKE. *Myself and Others* (Oxford, 1968)

N. MALCOLM. *Knowledge and Certainty* (Englewood Cliffs, New Jersey, 1963)

S. SHOEMAKER. *Self-knowledge and Self-identity* (Ithaca, New York, 1963)

P. F. STRAWSON. *Individuals* (Garden City, New York, and London, 1959), esp. Ch. 3

L. WITTGENSTEIN. *Blue and Brown Books* (New York and Oxford, 1958)
Philosophical Investigations (Oxford, 1953)
See also G. Pitcher (ed.). *Wittgenstein* (Garden City, New York, 1966; London, 1968)

A priori knowledge

A. J. AYER. *Language, Truth and Logic* (Gloucester, Massachusetts, and London, 2nd ed. 1946), Ch. 4

I. KANT. *Critique of Pure Reason,* trans. N. Kemp-Smith (London, 1929 and Garden City, New York, 1966)

A. PAP. *Semantics and Necessary Truth* (New Haven, 1958)

D. F. PEARS and G. F. WARNOCK in A. G. N. Flew, (ed.) *Logic and Language* II (Garden City, New York, and Oxford, 1953)

W. V. QUINE. *From a Logical Point of View* (Cambridge, Massachusetts, 1953)

P. F. STRAWSON. *The Bounds of Sense* (New York and London, 1966)

A. QUINTON in P. F. Strawson, ed., *Philosophical Logic* (London, 1967)

F. WAISMANN. "Analytic-synthetic," *Analysis* 1off. (1949–52)

See also my articles in *The Encyclopaedia of Philosophy,* ed. P. Edwards (New York, 1967), "A priori and a posteriori," "Analytic and synthetic statements," and "Contingent and necessary statements." There is also much in Wittgenstein's *Philosophical Investigations* that is relevant to this issue.

Further topics

S. C. BROWN. *Do Religious Claims Make Sense?* (London, 1969)

A. C. DANTO. *Analytic Philosophy of History* (Cambridge, 1965)

W. H. DRAY. *Laws and Explanation in History* (Oxford, 1957)

G. FREGE. *Foundations of Arithmetic* (Evanston, Illinois, and Oxford, 1950)

P. GARDINER. *The Nature of Historical Explanation* (Oxford, 1952)

S. KÖRNER. *The Philosophy of Mathematics* (New York and London, 1960)

D. Z. PHILLIPS (ed.). *Religion and Understanding* (Oxford, 1967)

K. POPPER. *The Logic of Scientific Discovery* (New York and London, 1959)

   Conjectures and Refutations (New York and London, 1963)

I. SCHEFFLER. *Anatomy of Inquiry* (New York, 1963)

S. TOULMIN. *The Philosophy of Science* (New York and London, 1953)

F. WAISMANN. *Introduction to Mathematical Thinking* (New York, 1951; London, 1952)

H. WEYL. *Philosophy of Mathematics and Natural Science* (Princeton, 1949)

Index